NOBODY TOLD ME NADA

Latin Pop, Llama Poop & Other Unexpected Writings

an

ENRIQUE LOPETEGUI

selection

(1992-2021)

All stories © Enrique Lopetegui, after original publication by the *LA Weekly*, *Los Angeles Times*, Voice Media Group (*New Times* and *Dallas Observer*) and Euclid Media Group (*San Antonio Current*).

The name of this book is taken from a line in the song "Nadie me dijo nada" by Jaime Roos, who granted permission for its use.

Editorial assistance by Catherine Barnes.

Cover illustration by Alejandro O'Kif (IG @aleokif).

Gloria Guerrero's Foreword translated from Spanish by Enrique Lopetegui.

First edition © 2022 by Enrique Lopetegui, © Yulelé Media, LLC.

All rights reserved. No part of this publication may be reproduced or transmitted in any form or by any means without permission in writing from the publisher, except brief quotations to be used in book reviews by the press.

Nobody Told Me Nada: Latin Pop, Llama Poop & Other Unexpected Writings. An Enrique Lopetegui selection (1992-2021).

ISBN 978-1-7353457-2-7

Author contact: candombe108@yahoo.com

This one's for me.

Contents

A Little Help From My Friends 6
Foreword 8
Nobody told me there'd be days like these… 10
La Lupita at Spice 15
Gloria Estefan's *Mi Tierra* 17
Juan Gabriel: "Watch Your Butt." 20
Rock in a Hard Place: How Argentina Won the War 24
Rubén Blades: The Thinking Man's Salsa 26
Cachao's Rebirth 32
Celia Cruz: Ageless 34
Miguel Bosé: Alive and Well 36
Tito Puente: Man on the Moon 38
Luis Miguel: The Man in Charge 41
Enrique Iglesias: Latin Pop's First Son 44
La Banda Elástica: *Rocanrol's* Voice 46
Maná: *Rocanrol*'s Punching Bag 48
The Phenomenauts: Plan 9 From Outer SF 52
Arjona 56
Molotov 57
Jaime Roos: Murga Pop 58
Freddy Fender: El Primero 62
B.B. King on Pappo 67
Manu Chao: Raining in Paradise 75
Moons Over my Grammys 77
Café Tacvba: Where It's At 79
Maria Rita: Brazil's First Daughter 81
Assassination Tango 90
Cachao, the Mambo Father 92
Spanish Harlem Orchestra: 94
Salsa for Post-graduates 94
Why We Still Love Che 96
El Moz 99
Die, reggaetón, die 102
The Incredible Shrinking Grammy 104
Ask a Mexican! 106
Mercedes Sosa (1935-2009) 108
Linda Ronstadt: Live From The Arizona Gulag 110
Rumbo: The Remains of the Daily 117
Richie Havens: Still Using His Thumb at 69 125
Gordon Raphael in SA: The Loser and the Lame 128
Slash on Lemmy, GNR and SA 132
Chaplin vs Keaton 135

Emerson, Lake & Palmer: Punk's Illegitimate Dads	137
Exene Cervenka on the new rebellion	142
Fuck, the Movie	144
Shawn on Doug	146
Mötley Crüe's Tommy Lee: "I'm definitely not a Nazi. No fucking way."	150
Julio Iglesias:	155
To All the Songs I've Screwed Up Before	155
Elvis Costello's *Spectacle*	157
Apollo 18 Actors Wish They Could Remain Anonymous	159
Lost in City Limits:	
Could San Antonio become a live-music capital again?	161
Santana: In Metraton We Trust	169
Eddie Palmieri: The Sun of Latin Music	172
Debating Vikki Carr	177
Girl in a Coma's Return	186
Public Enemy's Chuck-D: Fight the Power	195
Movies and Booze	202
John Swenson: The Music Writer	204
The Making of Los Lobos' *Kiko*:	
A ~~Chicano~~ Rock Masterpiece	209
John Lydon and Judge Judy's Eyes	218
La Presy: Rediscovering San Antonio's gift to flamenco	220
Livin' La Vida Rosa	233
How Draco Beat Cancer and Topped the Latin Charts	233
Metric's Emily Haines: What You See Is What You Get	238
Nina Díaz's Spiritual Makeover	241
Jeremy Scahill's *Dirty Wars*	246
Hilburn on Cash	252
Cumbia: How Colombia Made Selena a Star	260
Steve Vai: Strat Abuse	263
Augie Meyers: Kissing Death Goodbye and the Eternal Hustle	268
Las Marthas: The Weirdest Fiesta Ever	273
Phil Anselmo: Music, Horror and KOs	276
Belinda Sallin, director of *H.R. Giger's World*	282
Rob Trujillo on Jaco and *Jaco*	285
Sandra Cisneros: My Apology	296
Nina Díaz's latest incarnation	299
How the Last Bandoleros Reinvented Tex-Mex and Blew Sting Away	303
Barbershop singing in San Antonio:	307
Loudest Shade of White	307
Manumanía	314
Nina 2020	318
Rock is dead. Long live *rocanrol*	322
About the Author	325

A Little Help From My Friends

"I enjoyed working with Enrique Lopetegui tremendously. He was a great addition to the *Los Angeles Times* pop department. Enrique is filled with the passion and dedication that you always want to see in a critic. He doesn't just write about music but thinks and cares about it in ways that help him explain the role that music plays in our lives and culture." — **Robert Hilburn (*Los Angeles Times* critic/music editor 1970-2005, and the author of *Corn Flakes with John Lennon and Other Tales From a Rock 'n' Roll Life*, *Johnny Cash: The Life*, and *Paul Simon: The Life*)**

"I've admired Enrique's work since his days as music writer for the *LA Weekly* and *Los Angeles Times*. He's always stood out as a singular, unique voice — the rare journalist who artfully tackles just about anything you put in front of him, and does so in Spanish *and* English. No wonder I was excited when I learned about this compilation of his work! Enrique thrives in the busy intersections between pop music, sports, politics and film. His passion for cross-cultural criticism is palpable ... and contagious. Happy reading." — **Lorraine Ali (*Los Angeles Times*)**

"There are people who can write in a very scholarly and substantiated manner, but they lack that punch, that edge I love so much both in music and the written word. His personal moment [at the *Los Angeles Times*] and the era itself [in the '90s] achieved a phenomenon that hit me hard and was a great influence on my own professional development." — **Gustavo Santaolalla (Two-time Academy Award winner producer and composer)**

"The first thing you notice about Enrique Lopetegui is his passion. He doesn't think of music as a trendy lifestyle accessory or treat it like decorative aural wallpaper. For him, it's as essential as oxygen and as deep as an ocean. You always get the sense that he resents music that fails to live up to its spiritual potential.

I first asked Enrique to contribute music pieces for the *San Antonio Current* because I was impressed by his knowledge of rock *en español*. His command of the music's nuances were/are formidable, and I always found myself understanding the form better after reading his work. But it didn't take long before I realized how eclectic and unpredictable his tastes were and how adept he was at writing about a wide range of musical genres.

When he loves something, he fully immerses himself in it. He showed that with *Juanito's Lab*, the 15-year, labor-of-love documentary he and his wife, Guillermina Zabala, created about San Antonio virtuoso musician Juanito Castillo.

Enrique's passion for the music — and his need to share that passion with others — permeates all of his writing. And he has a way of making you care just as much as he does." — **Gilbert García (*San Antonio Express-News* writer and the author of *Reagan's Comeback: Four Weeks in Texas That Changed American Politics Forever*)**

"In the 1990s — a time of searing upheaval, of riots and reaction and a pandemic, sound familiar? — Enrique Lopetegui shows up at the doors of the *Los Angeles Times* armed with a critic's pen and a rocker's heart. From impossibly distant Uruguay, he was able to listen to the sounds of L.A. as an outsider's outsider and reveal us to ourselves, without pieties but with honesty and the ruthless passion of the young writer. There is no art without the critic — that lonely soul who doesn't play in the band but who pushes it along its journey into culture and history — or sometimes, oblivion. Lopetegui makes his own kind of music on the page — celebrating and commiserating, pleading and needling, wrestling and protesting a scene he was an indelible part of. ¡*Que viva el crítico*! And long live *rocanrol*! — **Rubén Martínez (author of *Desert America: A Journey Across Our Most Divided Landscape*)**

"Lopetegui is the absolute first journalist outside of East Los and indeed the USA, with the insight and temerity to coin the now extensively used phrase 'A Triple Identity' in defining how to look at, separate, perceive and understand what it is to be Chicano in a monolithic Latinx universe." — **Jesús Velo (bassist for Los Illegals)**

Foreword
by Gloria Guerrero (*)

Against the popular "hoarding is easy" belief, to compile one's historic articles in a sole paperback volume is a very, very complicated task. The scribe will have to come up with a crazy yet intelligible arrangement out of hundreds of loose yellowish pages (or open windows on a screen), and the work will be damn hard. First, the author needs to know how to choose and balance; then comes the bitterness — the chronological order of the stories ("it *has* to be chronological," he told me) will not necessarily reflect what the original intention was (History is a bitch). Then, the author will resist the temptation to manipulate the text, and this is a key point: that question, that comma, that follow-up question... "Would I have asked it differently today, after so many years?" Since those texts were published in their time, in their days and hours, nothing can be touched. Nothing.

And what happens to the author of all this *mambo*? Nobody is the same person of yesteryear; it's possible that the journalist thinks differently now, even better than before. Suddenly, thousands of little loose pieces, related by dates but not identical in their intensity, take the shape of a book and end up being another story, original and new. No, it's no easy task.

Those interviewed in this book are not the same, either. Some may have evolved (or regressed) or even disappeared. That's the strange nature of the telling of History. God bless the guiding thread of this story: the feathers of the person who is writing.

There are many feathers in Enrique Lopetegui's cap. There is the Feather of Thoroughness in terms of vivisecting geographies, societies, and cultures (his articles include the original accents of Hispanic last names, a welcome detail); there's also the Feather of Sports, because he really knows what he's talking about, and he enjoys it; the Feather of Clever Humor, sometimes tiny and unexpected, sometimes even grotesque, with which he crowns interviews or chronicles; and let us not forget his Feather of Music: his delirious review of the Grammy Awards ("The Incredible Shrinking Grammy," 2009) is superb.

Among the kaleidoscope of interviews and their diverse circumstances, there are gems that, fortunately, have been rescued in this volume: some are unsettling ("...many of Morrissey's lyrics could — and have been — compared to the poetry of Mexican *ranchera* classics, but the fact that Morrissey is an Englishman, not an American, makes him even more appealing to rebel Mexicans," from "El Moz," 2009), or even prophetic ("All Arjona needs now is to say goodbye to Eurovision-like hymns and his other catchy festival throwaways and dedicate a year to reading the sublime lyrics of others. Then there's hope — maybe," from his review of Arjona's *Santo Pecado*, 2002). And when interviewing, of all people, the elusive Luis Miguel, Lopetegui flapped his feathers: "'They've killed me several times,' says the singer, a master in the art of talking about delicate issues without revealing anything." Even then, the article was well worth it. And the questions must also be worth asking, like he did when he had his illustrious former editor Robert Hilburn in front of him: "Reading the book, it's obvious that you really loved and admired [Johnny] Cash but, as usual in your work, you had no problem being critical of him, and it is clear that Cash *did* make some awful albums..." Serenity, cleverness, spontaneous irreverence... I welcome this book, a sign of the change of millennium.

Becoming a journalist is relatively simple, but being a Witness of Your Time requires other things, more enlightening and interesting.

Lopetegui knows how.

(*) Gloria Guerrero (64) is widely considered the first female rock writer from Argentina (and, arguably, Latin America) and one of the most influential. Her legendary columns in *Humor®* magazine ("Las Páginas de Gloria") inspired the author of this book to become a music journalist. Her credits include *Expreso Imaginario* (when she was still a teenager), *Clarín*, *Página/12*, and the Argentina edition of *Rolling Stone* magazine, where she was editor in chief for seven years. She is the author of *La Historia del Palo: Diario del Rock Argentino 1981-1994* (1995, Ediciones de la Urraca), *Indio Solari: El hombre ilustrado* (2005, Debolsillo/Editorial Sudamericana, a biography of the former singer of Patricio Rey y sus Redonditos de Ricota), and *Estadio Obras, El Templo del Rock: Elogio de la Sed* (Sudamericana, 2012). She has also worked in a myriad of radio shows as host, curator, writer, and producer.

Nobody told me there'd be days like these...

"I hate writing, but I love having written," said Dorothy Parker. I wish I could be as clever as she was. All I can do is love the fact that I wrote for so many years and hate this sense of not coming close to the quality of those writers I admire.

That's been the story of my life: a million thoughts going through my mind and an uncontrollable urge to sit down and type like a madman for hours, naively thinking that "everything will fall into place," no matter how erratic and undisciplined I was. I just kept my ass in the chair and stayed until finished. Time taught me that non-stop writing was not enough, but I had to continue publishing if I wanted to calm my nerves — often at the expense of my editor's.

Of course, nobody told me about that thing called the internet. I found out about it in 1996, and immediately I thought, "I better get another job." Suddenly, I understood that, eventually, I couldn't just go to a show, take notes, type an article, and move on to the next thing — in the future, I would have to do that *plus* take video and photos, tweet about it, Facebook it, Instagram it, and on and on and on. I was right: the internet turned us into instant photo and social media "experts." Professional photographers got laid off, workdays became endless, newsrooms got smaller, and salaries stayed the same or shrank — that is, if you were lucky enough to have a full-time job. Otherwise, you had to freelance for peanuts. It could've been worse. I can't complain too much — I was one of the lucky ones, until I ran out of karma.

But I'm getting ahead of myself.

It all started in 1979, when I was 15. I was reading a community newspaper in my hometown of Montevideo, Uruguay. There was a bullshit story about a particular karate style I hated, and the author was praising the sensei of that style for his ability to kill bulls with a single punch (you know who you are, fuckers). That had nothing to do with the real essence of martial arts, so I got pissed and wrote a letter to the editor, explaining why that style sucked. To my surprise, they published it in article form, and that was my first byline.

But that was only one of the reasons I started writing. The other was my low opinion of most of the music critics in Uruguay at that time; as far as I was concerned, they were all bitter old farts who didn't like anything — like South American versions of Robert Christgau, minus the writing ability. So I took it upon myself to start writing, especially after someone told me there was something called a *carné de prensa*, which would allow me to enter shows and get records for free. Like John Lennon said after watching girls screaming for Elvis, I thought, "That's a nice job." To my parents' horror, I quit high school, started typing, and moved to the United States in 1984. I started working in an ice cream shop in East Texas, became a Hare Krishna, and moved to the temple in Los Angeles. (You can hear about my journey from Krishna devotee to the newsroom of the *Los Angeles Times* on Catherine Barnes' podcast at queenmab-music.com.)

Every day between 1992 and 1999, I would receive a check from somewhere for my writing. I would take care of three weeks' worth of deadlines in one night — in English *and* Spanish — followed by a 24-hour collapse. Then the cycle would start again: two or three weeks of interviews, planning, transcribing, and one long night of writing. I eventually ended up in India to recover from physical and spiritual exhaustion only to return and spend six months at a Hare Krishna temple/llama farm in Utah, where I preached to confused Mormons while cleaning up the endless coffee bean-like mountains of llama poop.

Things got a little simpler for me when a now-defunct daily newspaper called *Rumbo* in Texas — that Hell I swore I'd never return to — hired me to become the music editor. *Rumbo* was big and good enough to earn a chapter in this book, but it only lasted four years (2004-2008). I immediately landed at the *San Antonio Current* (2008-2014), where I wrote what I consider to be my best work and the bulk of this book.

I kept going until 2014, when I finally burned out in the middle of a rare vacation in Uruguay. A third-rate editor sent a carefully wrapped package to my inbox, beautifully arranged with multicolor bows and containing a large amount of pure vomit. I replied in style and, once and for all, decided to quit writing for a living. Instead, I engaged myself fully in the art of enjoying Montevideo's Rambla surrounded by *candombe* drums and ample opportunities to take advantage of the newly legalized magic herbs.

I started when I was 15. I'm 57 now (58 by the time this book comes out), old enough to realize it's time to step aside and let the young kids take over. Don't get me wrong; I wish I could continue, and all power to those dinosaurs who do. I just can't. I enjoy the absence of deadlines and the abundance of time to read, watch films, and *really* listen to music too much. I also know that I would have to write about that atrocity known as *reggaetón* if I wanted to continue working as a journalist. Forget it. I ain't gonna do that. You can go ahead and talk all you want about the "cultural significance" of a bunch of Puerto Ricans (and their imitators) who turned their backs on the island's marvelous rhythms and settled for the most idiotic sounds and lyrics they could come up with, but keep me out of it. (I don't mind Voltio, Tego Calderón, and sometimes Bad Bunny, and Calle 13's Residente and Visitante are true artists who transcend the R-word). Simply put, there are only two groups of people nowadays who can make a living as a journalist: the very best (usually people my age) or the very cheap (usually young kids into the R-word... some of them *very* talented, I must admit). I consider myself to be somewhere in between.

"Journalism is a priesthood," right? I was a sort of poor man's Pope for as long as I could handle it, but I reached the point at which I had to make a decision; having failed as a husband, priest, son, brother, and nephew as I published constantly and neglected family (and spiritual) duties, I embraced my new role as a father in 2009, and that's the one I don't want to screw up. Today, I can say being my beautiful Shanti's dad is my main role, besides a couple of odd jobs I must do to keep body and soul together (don't ask).

This is my last desperate attempt to make sense of the least embarrassing parts of my 42 years as a writer — an unexpected journey that took me from aspiring to earn a little weekly space in some Spanish-language newspaper to writing for some of the world's most important English-language publications

Some of my stories are good, I think/hope; others are only historically important, at least to me. But you can see the evolution from my clumsy attempts to adapt to the Times' rigid "journalistic" style to the free-form, alternative articles I wrote in San Antonio. Those *Current* pieces are the ones I'm most proud of, but at the Times I learned values I've never abandoned from my main editor Robert Hilburn: don't accept any trips or favors from record labels, and don't befriend or take photos with the people you write about (the friendship part is sometimes impossible to adhere to; chemistry is chemistry, literally or figuratively, but I tried my best to avoid it). At the Times, I also learned what real editing is about: editor and writer sitting side by side, going through each line to make sure the most potent copy was obtained.

Time revealed to me that everything good here was simply dictated by Paramatma, a.k.a. the Supersoul ("from Me comes knowledge, remembrance and forgetfulness," Krishna says in the *Bhagavad-gita*) and, as Malcolm X once said, "only the mistakes have been mine." For those, I apologize. I stand by the rest of it, and that's why I chose these stories, which represent about 30-40 percent of my total output. (I wanted to include the one good story I wrote for *Billboard* in 1994 but, to my surprise, they wanted to charge me "between $500-$1,000" for permission to use it. My laughter is still heard in all corners of Vaikuntha.)

I had a lot of fun, probably too much, and by age 29 I had already realized even more of the things I had dreamed about. I have no professional regrets, but two major personal ones that follow me wherever I go. I'm in Babadook-mode now, learning how to coexist peacefully with my demons. Peacefully, yes, but the monster is locked down in the basement.

All I can do now is paraphrase what Jerry Lee Lewis supposedly said after opening for Chuck Berry while setting his piano on fire:

Let *any* sonofabitch follow *this*.

Enrique Lopetegui
San Antonio, December 2021

PS, I Love You:

I want to sincerely thank the generosity of the editors who never questioned the nationality and background of this Uruguayan kid who somehow ended up writing (in English!) for the big leagues. A nice gesture, especially considering us Latinos are often very quick to judge somebody's ability to tackle a task based on that person's geographical origins. Those editors are (in order of appearance):

Rubén Martínez and **Sue Cummings** (*LA Weekly*), **Robert Hilburn** and his Calendar team (*Los Angeles Times*), **Dave Konjoyan** (Grammy.com), **Dan Reines** and **Andy Van De Voorde** (*Phoenix New Times* and Voice Media Group, respectively), and **Gilbert García**, **Elaine Wolff**, **Greg Harman** and **Sanford Nowlin** (*San Antonio Current*). Special mention to the great **Lorraine Ali**, who never edited me but who always offered me her support and good vibes during the time we shared at both the *LA Weekly* and the *Los Angeles Times*. And, of course, La Jefa, The Boss, the legendary **Gloria Guerrero**, my main inspiration and the reason I wanted to become a music journalist. She replied to the letter I wrote to her when I was 17 and, years later, offered me her friendship and even a glowing Foreword to the book you're reading. I always wanted to live up to her standard, and I'm relieved that, apparently, I didn't disappoint her. Just promise me you won't blame her for anything.

La Lupita at Spice
November 24, 1992
(because you never forget the first one)

(*LA Weekly*, December 4, 1992)

It was probably the L.A. Mexican *rocanrol* gig of the year. At times sounding like the Chili Peppers at their best, at others recalling Nirvana, but never straining from the Mexican spirit that they couldn't shrug off even if they wanted to, Mexico City's La Lupita sped through a soaring set at Spice. Showing off songs from their brand-new Culebra Records (a subsidiary of BMG-Ariola) debut release *Pa' servir a usted* (To Serve You), La Lupita offered proof positive that there is life beyond current big acts like Maldita Vecindad, Caifanes and Café Tacuba, and that the Mexican underground continues to be fertile underground territory.

Anchored by Poncho Toledo's solid bass lines and Bola Domene's dominating presence on the skins, La Lupita experimented with the hybrid model that characterizes Mexican rock — reggae, rap, metal, funk, punk and traditional *corrido* riffs. Lead singer Héctor Quijada's throaty vocals were perfectly matched with Rosa Adame's considerable back-up (and occasional solo) talents. The highlight of the evening was one particularly effective duet, featuring Héctor and Rosa bouncing anti-love lines off each other. "You lost tramp, I got someone else who'll love me/you drunk party animal, I didn't come back to beg forgiveness/If you didn't come back for that, why the fuck did you come back then/I only came for my things, practically everything in this house."

Toledo shone on the satirical "Paquita Disco," a send-up of the insufferable '70s Disco scene, with a rhythm line pulled straight off Side 4 of *Saturday Night Fever*; the rest of the band joined in on a hilarious falsetto chorus (in English) of "dance all night, baby." Guitarist Lino Nava rounded out La Lupita's sound with limited but capable work, a bit of psychedelic distortion here, simple but tasty staccato there. He combined both on a cover of "Qué rico mambo," a Pérez Prado standard that confirmed advanced publicity that the band was in the Caifanes-Maldita-Tacuba camp that is famous for rockified/punkified covers of Latin pop classics. On this count, La Lupita appeared to suffer some for the derivative disease, with its punk version of "Contrabando y traición" ("Black Market and Betrayal"), a *norteña* made famous by Los Tigres del Norte, and on "Jalando imecas," a short and furious thrasher that sounds a bit too much like Café Tacuba's "Pinche Juan."

But La Lupita doesn't need to justify its Mexicanness by picking up Los Tigres' instruments. There are no *sombreros* here, no accordions, no taco giveaway at the door. Just another Mexican rock band with an amazing sound.

Gloria Estefan's *Mi Tierra*
(*Los Angeles Times*, June 22, 1993)

Like all Cubans, Gloria Estefan will always remember the date: Dec. 31, 1958 — the day Cuba changed.

Her father — José Manuel Fajardo — was a guard for the wife of Cuban President [and dictator] Gen. Fulgencio Batista and he began making plans on that day — the day of the communist revolution — to send the family to Miami. While the family escaped, he was imprisoned by the Castro regime.

Gloria, who was 2 years old at the time, grew up in the United States, but the music of Cuba remained a part of her life. Her grandmother taught her old songs from the native land.

In 1975, she began her musical career when she met (and later married) Emilio Estefan, another Cuban exile who was leading a new band, then called the Miami Latin Voice. After enormous success with the group, which became the Miami Sound Machine, she embarked on her solo career in 1987.

Her new album, Mi Tierra, is her first worldwide all-Spanish album — a tribute to the '30s and '40s music of Cuba. On the eve of the album's release, Estefan talked about the album and her love of Cuban music.

Was there a lot of music in your family?

Yes, definitely. My mother sang and danced, and got a contract in Hollywood to dub Shirley Temple movies into Spanish. My father's mother was a poet and both of my uncles write songs and sing. One of my uncles, a classical violinist and salsa flute player, had a famous band in Cuba, José Fajardo and his Stars. So music was everywhere.

How did you get together with Emilio?

Some friends invited Emilio and his band to play at a party that I was attending, and he asked me if I'd ever like to sing with them . . . as a hobby. I immediately said yes. We never dreamed we'd have the success we had. All we wanted to do was have some fun, but everything eventually fell into place.

The new album must have been a longtime dream. When did you start thinking about it?

Almost five years ago. I was anxious to record an all-Spanish album that reflected my Hispanic and Cuban roots. *Mi Tierra* ("My Homeland") includes unknown songs and even new songs that are made to reflect the spirit of that era. We were even very careful when choosing the instruments we wanted to play with, because it had to be as close as possible to that old style. It's a work of love.

How do you think your English audience will receive it?

I think they'll like it because they love it in my live shows when I sing to them in Spanish. They always ask me for more.

Why wasn't [Cuban salsa great] Celia Cruz part of the superstar lineup on the album?

Oh, I love Celia . . . Emilio produced an album for her and I sing on it. But she was busy on tour while we were recording.

Is this the first time you worked with [Nicaraguan salsa star] Luis Enrique?

Yes. He's a great percussionist. The most incredible thing about him is that he's not Cuban, but plays all types of Cuban styles in a very legitimate way. He did a tremendous job, really.

Six of the tracks were co-written by you. How would you rate yourself as a songwriter?

Me? I can't rate myself as a songwriter! (Laughs) I know I touch some people and get wonderful responses from them, but I don't know. I mean, what would you rate it against? That's impossible.

***Mi Tierra* is your tribute to the Cuban music of the first half of the century. But the Cuban music since the revolution has had a great influence on the rest of Latin American popular music, especially the music of people like Silvio Rodríguez and Pablo Milanés and the rest of the Nueva Trova movement. Do you value this music — despite your political differences?**

I value whatever an artist does. That's the freedom of any human being. Personally, I haven't heard Silvio Rodríguez nor Pablo Milanés, simply because I don't generally buy music. I listen to many different styles, but I don't go record-shopping. But I know there's a lot of people everywhere who like Cuba's Nueva Trova movement, and they have all the right to do that. The only thing that saddens me about those musicians — and they also have the right to express themselves — is that sometimes they don't have the freedom to say everything they want. I don't know if [the messages in their music] is their real ideology or something they had to adopt in order to survive in a country where the government practices are totally terrorist.

Isn't it possible that that *is* their ideology? They also had enough chances of deserting but decided to remain in Cuba instead.

Maybe. There may be many reasons, and that's a possible one, of course. Look, I respect anybody's ideology, but don't forget [trumpet player] Arturo Sandoval and so many other artists who apparently were part of the regime are now leaving Cuba. That makes me doubt if they really sympathize with the revolution. Only God knows. I can't judge them because I don't know.

When [Dominican tropical star] Juan Luis Guerra received his *Billboard/Lo Nuestro* award for Song of the Year recently in Miami, many of your fellow Cubans booed because they consider him to be too left-wing. What did you think of that?

That was inappropriate because one owes respect to any human being, no matter what his ideas are. But that's also part of democracy. Sometimes I see things I don't like, like Ku Klux Klan members or skinheads, but I have no right to destroy their rights to expose their ideas.

You already have your star in the Hollywood Walk of Fame, you sing in Whoopi Goldberg's latest movie, you're rich, famous, and now this record. What's next?

I have to rest and enjoy a lot, but that also includes making more music. All I really want is to be able to see my son grow up to be an honest, healthy, and good man. I want to be with him and enjoy music throughout the years. I'm happy to work in something that I love so much. For me, there's nothing better than that.

Juan Gabriel: "Watch Your Butt."
(Los Angeles Times, July 25, 1993)

Juan Gabriel has reason to be happy. He is Mexico's biggest pop star — an icon who enjoys a kingly status among people of all ages and social classes.

Not only have his records sold 15 million copies worldwide, but he has also written more than 600 songs — some of which artists such as Pandora and Lucha Villa used to launch or revive their own careers.

But the most interesting thing about Juan Gabriel, 41, is that he has helped shatter the longstanding notion that you have to be ultra-macho to be a success in the mainstream world of Latin romantic pop. There's a delicate, sensitive quality about him.

He was raised from age 2 in a youth facility in Ciudad Juarez in the state of Chihuahua, developed an interest in music at a young age and began his recording career during his late teens.

Juan Gabriel became successful almost overnight, winning fans with his singing, songs and dancing and his refreshingly individual attitude and persona. Among his most popular albums are the most recent, the double set Juan Gabriel en el Palacio de Bellas Artes, *as well as* Juan Gabriel Con el Mariachi Vargas de Tecalitlán *and* Debo Hacerlo. *(All are available in the United States.)*

In his most prominent U.S. performance ever, Juan Gabriel will sing some of his own songs Saturday at the Rose Bowl and be joined by other singers who have had hits with his music. Proceeds from the show will go to the orphanage he started in 1987 in Chihuahua.

As he prepared for the concert, the relaxed, articulate performer spoke in Spanish about his music, his childhood, and his break from the Latin macho image.

Tell me about your childhood. How did you end up at a school for underprivileged children?

I was born in Michoacán, which is in the south of México. When my father died, my mother moved to Ciudad Juárez. She had to go to work as a housekeeper and couldn't take care of me at home. She sent me to an institution, where I spent most of my childhood.

I didn't go anywhere, except church, and would see my mother maybe twice or three times a year. That's why I think I have the authority to tell parents not to do that to their children. Give them all your love and think very thoroughly before you bring a child to the world.

So, it must have been very special when you helped finance an orphanage for other young people.

Yes... It was a great experience and it's one reason I can say I'm proud and am at peace with myself. The most wonderful thing in life is to do something for a child because they're children for such a short time. We can't allow ourselves to let them live a miserable childhood.

Do you have bitterness about the way you were raised?

I have no bitterness. Everything I went through had to happen that way, and the most important thing is that I'm here now helping so that others don't have to suffer like me.

Was music always part of your life?

Yes, music was always there. My biggest idol was (rock *en español* pioneer) Enrique Guzmán, all the way back to his years [in the early '60s] with Los Teen Tops, but especially afterward when he sang on his own.

Did you ever dream in those days of being a star yourself?

When I was 15, all I knew was that I *had* to be somebody and that I *could* be somebody. So, I exploited the only thing I knew, which was singing and songwriting. Even if my childhood had been different, I would've still sung. But the [hardships] gave me strength and made me realize that I must do something if I wanted to get out of that situation. I'm glad it paid off.

Because they used your songs, many other singers owe you a good part of their careers...

(Interrupting, laughing) You said that, not me.

How does it make you feel?

It gives me *mucho, mucho, mucho* pleasure and pride that people like my songs, whether they are sung by me or my friends.

Among the English-speaking audience, Julio Iglesias is undoubtedly the most popular Latino singer. What do you think of his success?

I have a lot of respect for all artists, especially singers. Mr. Iglesias is a very hard worker and a very thoughtful person who dedicated every single day of his life to his career, even to the point of not spending time with his family. Whatever he has, he deserves. But I'm not particularly concerned with becoming as famous as he is. I think that in life you have what you deserve, and if I'm not as famous as he is, it's because maybe I don't deserve it.

You are well-respected among the new Mexican rock movement that includes bands such as Caifanes, Café Tacuba and Maldita Vecindad. What did you think of the hardcore version Maldita Vecindad did of your hit "Querida"?

I loved it. They invited me to one of their shows, and after I met them I saw they were beautiful people, full of energy. It was a phenomenal show, and I wasn't expecting that dance . . . what is it?

Slam-dancing?

Yes! Everybody hitting each other! I'm not that old, but nevertheless I don't think I'm ready for that... Thank God I was on the second floor. I feel very close to the new generations because I'm one of their influences. They grew up or were born with my music, a fact they have admitted several times. I'm proud they invited me and let me share their art, despite the slam-dancing, which is nothing but the way they release that immense energy.

How are you able to keep such a generous attitude in the highly competitive world of Mexican show business?

Maybe the fact that I don't consider myself anything extraordinary. And I don't believe in competing because there's room for everyone. You have to compete with yourself, because your duty to grow as a human being and keeping your humility is much more important than your music career. You can get money, women, travels, but all that's an illusion.

Are you very religious?

I don't believe in anything, only in myself, but I respect all people who believe in something. I'm not a philosopher, a mystic, or a charismatic guy. But I am someone who has lived through everything.

Despite all the love of your fans, the media have often portrayed you in your private life as somewhat distant and temperamental. What do you say about that?

(Laughs) I've heard that before. There are different Juan Gabriels in people's heads, and I can't answer for all of them. But let's set the record straight: I'm not a monster, but I'm also not as good as some people say I am. I'm human and I make mistakes. Within my own family, there were different opinions about me when I was growing up — in all respects. One sister told me I was her favorite. Another one said that... well, that I was not what I was supposed to be. You know what I'm talking about, don't you?

Your sexual orientation? I was about to get into that...

I wouldn't like it.

Why not? I couldn't care less about your private lifestyle, but I find the Juan Gabriel phenomenon fascinating, considering the still rampant homophobia in Latin America and, especially, México. You're loved by everyone, even the big "machos." But you've never talked about your sexuality.

I have four sons. That's No. 1. Second, in show business, if you're male and cute and gracious, people assume you are blah, blah, blah. But people don't understand that art itself is female — it is full of graciousness, cadence, color, rhythm. It's full of love and grace.

No. 3: Nowadays, the important thing is to be careful. That's what people have to worry about, not whether one is or isn't. Watch your "bird" and watch your butt. Especially in the U.S., where there is, or there is supposed to be, so much respect for all peoples.

Rock in a Hard Place: How Argentina Won the War
(*LA Weekly*, August 5, 1993; abridged and updated in 2022)

Besides isolated cases like Freddy Fender's 1957 "No seas cruel" (a cover of Elvis' "Don't Be Cruel") and Ritchie Valens' "La Bamba" (1958), it was in Mexico that rock in Spanish was first recorded in 1956 (Gloria Ríos' "El Relojito," a cover of Bill Haley's "Rock Around the Clock"). Bands like Los Teen Tops, Los Rebeldes del Rock and Los Locos del Ritmo continued the Mexican pioneering with mostly Spanish-language covers in the late 50s through early 60s, and Perú has a strong claim, if you ask me, on the fatherhood of punk (Los Saicos' "Demolición," 1965).

But Argentina undoubtedly saw the first movement, the original blossoming of talent, fanzines, concerts and clubs since the mid-60s. Today, the smaller Mexican rock contingent offers the freshest, most original youth culture but, ironically, an Argentine, Gustavo Santaolalla, was a key factor in the turnaround.

In the '70s, Santaolalla led Argentina's Arco Iris, whose daring experiments predicted the World Beat movement. Santaolalla went on to produce Mexican groups like Maldita Vecindad, Café Tacvba and Caifanes, as well as Chile's Los Prisioneros, collaborating often with engineer Aníbal Kerpel, formerly of Argentina's prog band Crucis. Today, both Santaolalla and Kerpel — bandmates at late '70s L.A. New Wave band Wet Picnic — live in Los Angeles, and it's getting hard to write about rock *en español* without mentioning their names.

Walking up to his ample house in Echo Park, I see Santaolalla through the front window. He's sitting in his living room, strumming on an old Spanish guitar while blasting a Van Morrison record. I knock on the window, but he can't hear me. I wait while praying for the song to be short, then knock again, he turns around, smiles, and gets up to open the door.

"*¡Qué hacés, broder...!*" he says, and embraces me. His long, wavy hair is gathered in a ponytail. Santaolalla usually dresses all in black with a silver chain on his chest and pointy shoes, but today he greets me in shorts, a T-shirt, wool socks and sandals.

It's probably the fifth or sixth time I've interviewed him. He's produced the solo debut by Los Prisioneros singer Jorge González, and Café Tacvba's debut, the first Mexican rock debut to sell more than 100,000 copies in their home. Without a doubt, Santaolalla is rock *en español*'s most wanted producer, the man responsible for changing forever the way rock records are made in Mexico. Judging by his latest work with Argentina's Divididos, one of the two groups to come from the dissolution of legendary band Sumo, one thing is clear: if rock *en español* is ever going to make it into the American mainstream, Santaolalla will have something to do with it.

As a boy in the Buenos Aires' suburb of Palomar, he took in equal doses of Anglo rock 'n' roll, Argentine *folclore*, tango, Uruguayan *candombe*, reggae, plus all sorts of Caribbean and African sounds. As a musician, he experimented with these forms long before Santana's blend was widely known. Yet, there is no thing such a thing as a "Santaolalla sound."

"I didn't invent the bands," Santaolalla says. "Mexico is an incredible place, and all I did was to help them polish what I thought was already great." As a producer, he lets the artists take over, patiently complementing the musicians' strength and weaknesses. The results are street, urban meanness in Maldita Vecindad, upbeat abandon with Café Tacvba and commercial but edgy dance-oriented pop that illustrates Jorge González's biting, witty lyrics. Santaolalla's records are always clean, colorful and spontaneous.

As usual, CDs cover the coffee table at Santaolalla's living room. He picks up a recording of MC5's *Kick Out the Jams*, the latest find from his weekly shopping ritual. Santaolalla buys rare imports, new stuff, classics, African greats, Top 10. His huge collection also includes Argentine and Mexican pop and rock classics, and tons of other CDs, tapes and vinyl he'll probably never listen to.

"Can you believe these guys' aggression?" he asks as the MC5 plays. He closes his eyes and moves his head sideways back and forth. "This is a-lu-ci-nan-te (hallucinating)!" As he talks, he moves his arms eloquently while keeping a broad smile.

Santaolalla takes me to his newly remodeled basement studio, complete with state-of-the-art equipment, and plays his latest material, two parallel projects of his own. Tentatively due in 1991, they will be his first solo work in 12 years. "I've been a producer lately, and I'm happy with that. I think Aníbal [Kerpel] and I have done some important things. The Santaolalla musician was always there, but if you don't play... I guess it's just a matter of letting it out and getting back into training. Now is the time to do it." "Rock *en español* is actually happening, it's no fluke," he says. "If MTV established a 24-hour rock channel in Spanish, you can bet your butt this is growing. It's a musical reality that will prevail on a mainstream level." (*Rock en las Américas*' José Mercado contributed with information about Los Saicos)

Rubén Blades: The Thinking Man's Salsa
(*Los Angeles Times*, September 12, 1993)

Ruben Blades' concert Tuesday at the Hollywood Bowl with Tito Puente and Eddie Palmieri is part of the acclaimed singer-songwriter's farewell — at least for now — to pop music.

He hopes to record a long-awaited reunion album with Willie Colón. Then Blades — one of the most innovative and influential Latino musicians ever — will return to his native Panama, where he tops the opinion polls for next year's presidential election.

Blades, whose music has been filled with messages of freedom and social justice, hasn't declared his candidacy for the office, but he says he would accept the nomination of Papa Egoró ("Mother Earth"), the political party he launched in 1992 and was officially recognized last January, if he is drafted at the November convention and can develop a program that reflects a national consensus.

His main goal isn't to become president, he says, but to help bring to the country the social values that he has long advocated in his lyrics — values that have cut across traditional left wing-right wing boundaries by, for instance, condemning the U.S. embargo of Cuba and then attacking Cuba's own human rights violations.

"To fix Panama, you need more than charisma and records, you need a program of action," Blades said recently during his first extended interview in more than two years.

This isn't Blades' first break from pop music. He took two years off in the early '80s to obtain a law degree from Harvard University.

In fact, he obtained a law degree in Panama before moving to Miami in 1974 to join his exiled family (his father was accused of being a CIA agent by then-Col. Manuel A. Noriega, who was in charge of military intelligence). Instead of practicing law, however, Blades moved to New York, the salsa capital of the world, to pursue a singing and songwriting career.

After a stint with Ray Barreto's orchestra, Blades recorded three landmark albums in the late '70s with Colón. Their impact in salsa was comparable to that of Lennon & McCartney in rock.

They revamped salsa music with ambitious arrangements and socially conscious lyrics that helped bring substance and international respect to what was formerly viewed as simply dance music. Their brilliant album Siembra (1978) was prohibited by Anastasio Somoza Debayle's right-wing government *in Nicaragua because Blades yelled "Nicaragua without Somoza!" at the end of the hit "Plástico."*

Since going solo in 1981, Blades hasn't regained the commercial status he achieved with Colón, but he has continued to work in creative and imaginative ways. In addition to his music, the two-time Grammy winner has acted in several movies (including the upcoming Color of Night with Bruce Willis) and television productions, for which he was twice nominated for Emmys.

On the eve of his Bowl concert, Blades, who lives in Santa Monica, spoke in Spanish about his music, his politics, and his decision to return home.

Why are you so reluctant to give interviews?

For several reasons, I haven't spoken to anybody for about 2 1/2 years. I got tired of going to talk shows and being treated as a celebrity. Most of the entertainment press deals with the immediate news status of an artist, without seriously considering the work of that artist. They come to me to ask me things like, "Is Bruce Willis a nice guy?" Why don't they ask him? My patience ended when someone unqualified asked me political questions. You know, politics is a very complex issue, and the result of that was the biggest lie: "*Salsero* wants to be president." I never said that. In general, both in Spanish and English, the quality of the entertainment media is horrible. If they want me for an AIDS campaign or a literacy program, I'm all for it. But not for myself.

What made you agree to this one?

I don't know, I felt this was going to be a little better than other interviews. C'mon, I've lived in Los Angeles for seven years, and the *Times* never called me for anything. *(Note: Blades was last interviewed by Calendar in 1986).* But I'm not complaining. Actually, you should be doing this with Tito Puente, not with me. He's been around for 40 years. Him, Celia [Cruz], [Eddie] Palmieri. Give it to them, I don't need it. Besides, the Anglo press doesn't give a damn about the Latino stuff. They come now because there's a salsa show at the Hollywood Bowl. After that, for years and years they don't care.

Regarding your immediate plans, it's hard to believe that you'll be able to stop making music just like that.

My wife doesn't believe me either. I might come back in the future with a smaller group in a different format, something more theatrical, more Bertolt

Brecht-oriented, with more humor. But my passion now is concentrated in Papa Egoró, the political alternative I founded for Panama. I want to close this beautiful chapter in my life during which I said a lot of things. Now it's the time to do things.

Before we get into that, talk about your and Willie Colón's musical chemistry.

Willie is one of the first musicians who traveled from New York to Latin America and received a lot of information from other places. He developed a Pan American message of social awareness and, when he met me, he found someone with more fluency in Spanish capable of articulating many ideas. He contributed with his New York street culture, his talent as a producer and an incredible, truly Latino, pure tropical energy. A mixture of prankishness and sense of humor, of virility and feeling. He's extremely sensitive, and one of the most intelligent persons I know.

I'm grateful to him because he's the one who gave me the chance to show my music. He was like my artistic godfather, and no record label could say no to my music, because he was behind it at a time when he was the No. 1 salsa star in the world. This new record with him will be good to destroy rumors about bad feelings between us. But the most difficult thing for people to understand is that I already had a talent. Songs like "Pedro Navaja" and "Plástico" would've been hits anyway. Maybe not in 1976, but in 1979.

After you split with him, he said that it was very painful for him to listen to your music, and that he thinks you didn't listen to his work either.

I did listen to his work, because I always want to learn from him. But although I continued having success on my own, my star status also decreased. Especially when I wanted my first album without any trombones. Everybody said I was a dead man without trombones, but we went on with *Buscando América* ("Searching for America," 1984), and later won a Grammy with *Escenas* ("Scenes," 1985).

We had a lot of opposition, not only because I was being very critical of Ronald Reagan and his foreign policies, but because many thought I was going crazy for not including trombones on a salsa album. The truth is, I felt it was immoral for me to leave Willie's trombone group and compete with his sound. I wanted something completely different.

You have a reputation for arousing strong feelings in people who know you — it seems either they love you or they can't stand you.

It has always been like that — when I graduated from high school, when I became a lawyer, when I wanted to be a musician, when I moved to Los Angeles... Some people, out of their own complexes, demons and insecurities, expect you to do things according to their vision. When you do it your way, you become a problem to them. They never wish you well and say goodbye waving their handkerchiefs. Come on, they even said I shaved my mustache because I wanted to look more gringo! Or that argument that I married my American wife because I cannot handle a Latino woman in bed, nonsense like that.

What made you launch Papa Egoró?

At a certain point, people in Panama thought that everything was going to be solved as soon as Noriega was gone. Of course, the disappointment was huge. Thirty-five percent of the country's population is under 14 and has tremendous problems of drug consumption and civic apathy. I asked myself: "Am I going to keep criticizing or should I do something about it?" It's very comfortable to remain in California and talk. That's something my critics carefully avoid to mention: That I leave my comforts to go to Panama and work in politics. I'm descending to politics, not ascending.

Well, what about the fact itself of being president, the power...

What power? I saw five different presidents while my mother was playing piano. The job as a piano teacher is safer than that of a president of Panama. I don't need fame or money — I have both. If I go to Panama it's to help, to have the power, yes, but the power *to do* things. I don't want the government, I want the power. What good will it be to get the presidency if the Legislature and the Assembly don't support you? The same people who voted for you will get you out of there in five months.

I studied law because I wanted to do politics later on, but the situation is so desperate that we must do something quick, before it's too late. If my party chooses me as presidential candidate, I have no choice but to accept — it's a duty. But we need a program. Unemployment, hunger, drugs cannot be eliminated with charisma or records.

How are you going to find that program?

We're working on that. But we don't think or act as a traditional party, and that alternative alone is unprecedented in Latin America. Those parties go to the corner and say, "Listen, *imbéciles*, this is what you have to do to solve your problems!" That's the problem of all the groups, especially communism: They're movements of intelligentsias, intellectuals, not "the people."

I don't accept ideologies that are not a product of consensus. I don't have an ideology, but I do have a sense of what's right and what's wrong. And the worst mistake would be to elaborate a program without having the input of *all* sectors of society. So far, by decree, our party reserved 50 percent of the seats to women. That's an example of our attitude. Just like it's a mistake not to ask pregnant women before signing a maternity law, we want to make sure we ask everybody for opinions on how to solve the country's problems, including children. Consensus is the key.

For some, your criticism of Cuba helps obscure the achievements there in the areas of health, education and housing, something unparalleled in Latin America.

Nobody is arguing with that. I'm against the embargo and against U.S. intervention in our domestic problems, but I'm also against the Marxist-Leninist government in Cuba. I'm against the beating and jailing of María Elena Cruz Varela, who won their National Prize of Poetry, because she signed a paper demanding reforms in Cuba. She wasn't even holding a grenade or something like that.

And I think it's a big mistake of most of the Latin American intellectuals to put under the rug the obvious human rights violations in Cuba in order to "protect" their achievements in medicine, housing or education. Let me rephrase that: An education without different opinions. That's indoctrination, not education. As an artist, I can't remain silent about that.

Considering that opinion, it's ironic that you're very unpopular with the Cuban exile community in the United States. Latin radio in Miami won't even play your music.

I understand the Cubans in Miami, although some of them represent an extremist position just a bad as that of the Communists they condemn. I've said many things against the U.S. government, and I wrote anti-imperialist songs like "Tiburón" ("Shark"). They took it as a pro-Communist hymn when actually it was against fascism in either form, right or left. But I've never called them *gusanos* [a pejorative term for Cuban exiles, meaning *worms*, used by some on the left instead of *cubanos*]. That's very disrespectful. Although I share some visions with the left, especially on education, human rights, health care, I was never a Communist. I share some of their views, but I have a problem when they present Marxism as an answer to all the problems.

Your social agenda is very clear. But is it possible to install a capitalist system without having much of the population struggling to survive?

It's not necessary for that to happen. That happens only when the government doesn't allow the proper distribution of opportunities and becomes part of the corrupt system by allowing the same old hands to deal with the money. We can't say, "Let's have a country for the poor only," because that has never worked anywhere in the world.

We must accept the fact that there's a sector that invests, and a sector that works. Not a single group has the solution, and the only way to have it is to sit down with *all* the groups and come to an agreement. That will guarantee social justice and peace, without which you just can't have fair investments. And in our vital search for justice, we must make sure that the country and its institutions don't explode. Only something like a national therapy will resolve the mess Panama is in.

Cachao's Rebirth

(*Los Angeles Times*, September 13, 1993)

It was an unlikely scene, made possible only perhaps by Cuban-born actor Andy García's love of Cuban music: a crowd of 5,000 gathering last year at Miami's James L. Knight Center to celebrate the music of Israel López "Cachao."

As spontaneous as the show itself, García's filmed account of the rehearsals and the concert will help bring overdue recognition to the man who is Cuban music personified. García's film, *Cachao: Como su ritmo no hay dos* ("Cachao: Like His Rhythm, There Is No Equal"), will open Wednesday at the Nuart Theatre in West Los Angeles as part of the L.A. Festival.

Although Dámaso Pérez Prado popularized the mambo dance craze on an international level in the late '40s, Cachao has long been known among Cuban musicians as the father of the mambo. One of the reasons Cachao isn't better known outside of Cuban music circles is his low profile.

"I'm a very quiet man," Cachao, 74, said recently (in Spanish) by phone from his home in Miami. "It's never bothered me that I'm not better known . . . but I am happy for all the help this boy Andy García has given me. I love him as if he was my own son."

Until García crossed his path, Cachao mostly survived by playing birthday parties and obscure Miami restaurants. Cachao, along with his brother Orestes, composed more than 3,000 *danzones* (a danceable blend of Afro rhythms with Spanish- and French-derived music) in the 1920s, before giving birth to the mambo in 1938 by adding further spice to the *danzón*. It was a move that would change — or expand — Cuban music forever, setting the scenario for the whole salsa movement.

As significant for Latin pop music as the mambo, but even more ambitious, was Cachao's 1957 *descargas* — actual jazz-style jam sessions with some of Cuba's best folkloric musicians. With plenty of room to improvise, the *descargas* produced some of the best Afro-Cuban records ever, collectors' items that were ahead of their time and became points of reference for much of the music of future years, not only in the traditional tropical field but in Latin jazz as well.

Despite his significance, Cachao has been virtually ignored by the Cuban exile community in the United States (particularly in Miami, because his African-rooted style was never appreciated by the predominantly white, well-to-do first generation of exiles).

"They said it presented a false image of the Cuban population," Cachao said. The absence of an Afro-Cuban presence in Miami is eloquent.

In a *Wall Street Journal* article in August on García's documentary, Florida International University sociologist Lisandro Pérez said that "in Cuban history, that which is African — music, religion, even ways of speaking — is associated with the lowest economic origin. Immigration here has been very heavily influenced by the Cuban elite, people who are not traditionally supporters of Cuba's African art forms."

But not all Cuban exiles turn their backs on their former homeland's Afro-Cuban musical roots.

Guillermo Céspedes, the Cuban-born leader of the San Francisco-based Conjunto Céspedes band, praises both post-revolutionary Nueva Trova and traditional Afro-Cuban music, of which Cachao is the ultimate exponent.

"When I hear Cachao's bass, I hear African drums," said Céspedes. "Maybe he doesn't know the difference between Congo, Cameroon and Tanzania rhythms, but his true genius and mastery cannot be disputed."

After listening to Cachao's music for more than 20 years, García has made a directorial debut that couldn't have had more positive effects, both for him and the mambo father.

"I've only spent five years in Cuba," said García, "but it was enough to instill in me the music, the color, the tremendous energy of being a Cuban. With his music and humanity, Cachao represents the best of my country. This is the least I could do for him."

Celia Cruz: Ageless
(*Los Angeles Times*, October 14, 1993)

By the time they enter their fifth decade of stardom, most pop performers are winding down — doing the old favorites on stage and recycling the long successful sound on record. The amount of new ideas or passion is normally minimal.

Yet Celia Cruz — the undisputed "Queen of Salsa" for as long as anyone can remember — seems, after a three-year lull, to be picking up the pace again.

The Havana native, who declines to give her age, will headline the Universal Amphitheatre on Saturday as part of a world tour that will also include shows in Japan and South America.

The focus of the tour will be music from her most daring album in years — an RMM Records collection titled *Azúcar Negra* ("Black Sugar") that features an untraditional tropical style that has caught many listeners by surprise.

"I will die singing, and I don't plan to retire, unless the people retire *me* by not going to my shows or God takes away my abilities," said Cruz, who seems invigorated by the new work.

"I would say the album is a blend of tropical music with a Miami flavor. There are *boleros, merengue*, pop. One song, 'Te Busco' ('I'm Searching for You'), has been described as a *bachata*, but for me it's a *bolero*.

"Some Puerto Rican stations won't play it because they say it's not their style. Well, I believe that if you don't change you get stuck. It's nice to sometimes do something different than what you usually do."

Cruz's Amphitheatre concert, on a bill that also includes Colombia's explosive Orquesta Guayacán and New York's talented new-generation *salsero* Marc Anthony, is one of the year's most interesting Latin showcases.

After overcoming some initial resistance when she made her debut in 1950 with Cuba's legendary Sonora Matancera orchestra, Cruz went on to become a massively popular and acclaimed artist. She has made more than 50 albums and received hundreds of musical awards, including a Grammy in 1990 for her collaboration with Ray Barreto on the album *Con ritmo en el corazón* ("With Rhythm in the Heart").

Cruz, one of 14 children born to a poor family, earned her first pair of shoes after charming a tourist with her singing. She continued to concentrate on singing as a teenager and got her big break as a professional when she replaced Puerto Rican singer Myrta Silva as the lead vocalist for the Sonora Matancera.

Celia's dream of playing with the best Cuban orchestra was spoiled by the furious phone calls to radios and letters to orchestra director Rogelio Martínez, complaining about Celia's voice and demanding Silva's return.

"I felt very bad because I really needed that job," said Cruz in a phone conversation from her home in New York. "Myrta was going back to her country anyway, and I didn't have anywhere to go. I knew that somehow I had to stick around.

"To be in an orchestra like Sonora Matancera, I had to persevere, and that's what I did. Rogelio always supported me, and I finally succeeded in a situation that would've destroyed most people."

Gradually, the fans realized that this strong contralto was a true phenomenon, and she managed to record 15 albums at the same record label that had previously rejected her because of the argument that "women don't sell."

Cruz moved to the United States in 1960, along with the orchestra, and became a citizen. In 1962, she married Pedro Knight, the orchestra's main trumpet player, who left the group to manage her. She often salutes their relationship with sweet, tender references in her music.

Her widely admired collaborations over the years with Tito Puente, Ray Barreto, Willie Colón, Johnny Pacheco and Sonora Ponceña showed that Cruz could adapt and excel in different styles. She further demonstrated her willingness to experiment by working with such other varied figures as David Byrne (on his 1989 *Rei Momo* album) and Argentina's ska-tropical rockers Los Fabulosos Cadillacs.

As is the case with most of the Cuban exiles, Cruz does not keep close tabs on post-revolutionary Cuban music. Yet, she acknowledges the value of contemporary Cuban musicians.

"Cuba has always had great musicians and athletes," she said. "The fact that I don't support their cause doesn't mean that I'm going to deny how great they are. It's them who always say that they have 25,000 singers like me.

"I've never heard Silvio Rodríguez, but I do like Pablo Milanés' voice and the group Irakere. Of course, I listen to that when somebody gives me a record. I don't buy their music, just as they don't buy mine."

Meanwhile, Cruz looks forward to touring and recording indefinitely. "As long as I have a tight schedule," she said, "that means I'm still running just fine."

Miguel Bosé: Alive and Well
(*Los Angeles Times*, April 6, 1994)

In his role as a transvestite prosecutor in director Pedro Almodóvar's movie *High Heels*, Miguel Bosé says, "I can be the man you want me to be."

In real life, the Spanish singer-actor has struggled to establish whom *he* wants to be.

After 12 albums and 35 film appearances over a 21-year career, the teen sex-symbol image of his early fame lingers, while he works to be taken seriously as an artist expressing deeper emotions.

"The sex-symbol part never bothered me, but believe me, the 17-year-old Miguel Bosé is long gone," said Bosé, now 37, during a recent phone interview from Mexico City.

Bosé will make his Los Angeles concert debut on Thursday at the Universal Amphitheatre, then perform at the San Diego Sports Arena on Friday.

Maturity is clear in his latest album, the ambitious *Bajo el signo de Caín* ("Under the Sign of Cain"). The collection, produced by Ross Collum (Enya, Howard Jones) includes songs with direct lyrics dealing with the environment, spirituality, exile and unfulfilled love.

There is also a tongue-in-cheek song commenting on the wild stories about his personal life that have circulated in the Spanish press in recent years, including three reports that he had died — one claiming his demise was the result of a motorcycle accident, a second saying he'd gone over a cliff in his car and a third that he'd succumbed to AIDS.

"It was a demented, cheap, gratuitous attack from a small sector" of the press, said Bosé, the son of renowned actress Lucía Bosé and legendary bullfighter Luis Miguel Dominguín.

The rumors spread quickly in Spain, and ultimately spurred him to address his image through his music, with the new album ranking as his most confessional and personal.

"This is the most accurate self-portrait I've ever done," said Bosé, whose first musical influences were the records his father would bring home from bullfighting seasons in Latin America.

"It was dozens of vinyl records of salsa, *vallenatos*, *cumbias* and boleros," Bosé said. "Just the ritual of looking at the suitcase was enough for me to get goosebumps."

After spending two years as a student in England in the mid-1970s, he added the Beatles, Roxy Music, Genesis and David Bowie to his favorites. Today, Bosé's music is an uncommercial blend of American pop, Latin rhythms and flamenco grooves stressing mood more than melody, with a rich instrumentation that includes Indian violin, Irish bagpipe, mandolin and flamenco guitar and percussion — not exactly what you'd expect from a former teen idol.

"I want to do what I want to do, not what people expect me to do," said Bosé, who in July will make his debut as a playwright and stage director at a theater festival in Mérida, Spain, where his *La espera* ("The Wait") — a dramatic play based on discourses by Spanish theater heroines in times of war — will be presented.

After *High Heels*, Bosé starred in *La Nuit Sacree* [dir. Nicolas Klotz]. In *Mazeppa* [dir. Bartabas] he played a young 19th-Century artist obsessed with horses. Although he plans to continue acting in films, his main interests remain music and writing.

"After each movie I always end up desperate to write and record new material right away," he said. "I'm in a perfect age for things to come, and I proved to be very good at survival."

Tito Puente: Man on the Moon
(*Los Angeles Times*, October 14, 1994)

Few stars in the world of Latin music are better known and loved than Tito Puente.

The 71-year-old New York-born percussionist, bandleader and composer has recorded 104 albums since the late 1940s, ranging from simple salsa to complex Latin jazz and covering virtually all the many Afro-Cuban rhythms.

Although the two-time Grammy winner is best-known for his hits "Para Los Rumberos" and "Oye Como Va" (popularized worldwide by Santana in the early '70s), he is much more than the "Mambo King." Puente's challenging spirit and energetic versatility have been an inspiration to those who know the dance part is only a fraction of the magic of Latin music.

On Saturday, Puente and 17 other artists will appear at Hollywood Bowl in "La Combinación Perfecta" ("The Perfect Combination"), an all-star concert based on the 1993 RMM Records release of that name featuring salsa duets by some of today's best soneros, *singers known for their improvisational skills.*

In a recent interview during breakfast in Los Angeles, Puente talked about his career, the state of Latin dance music and his plans for the future.

Were you ever uncomfortable with the title of "Mambo King"?

It doesn't bother me to be associated with mambo, but I'm not the king of anything (smiles). I've played all kinds of styles with all types of musicians, and all I ever wanted to do was to become a good musician and create good music. That's all.

What's your impression of today's tropical music?

Colombia is producing very good salsa orchestras like [Grupo] Niche and [Orquesta] Guayacán. Puerto Rico has advanced greatly in arrangers and recording quality. But the New York orchestras are different, more exciting, and I don't know why. Puerto Ricans are good but lack what Americans call the *d-r-r-r-r-ive*, when the mambo picks up and everybody feels it. Puerto Ricans are lighter, more subtle. In New York it's different, maybe because of the presence and influence of jazz. Now, the Cubans... what else can I say about them? Orchestras like NG La Banda, Los Van Van...

Those Cuba-based orchestras seem to be miles ahead of everyone else.

Way up! They sound like Weather Report! When things get solved in Cuba, the Cuban musicians will scare a lot of musicians from here. I always tell everybody: As soon as the Cubans come, a lot of people are going to have to go back to school all over again. In Cuba it's different — there they really *study* music. If you are a musician in Cuba, that's all you do. Brazilians also play a lot of jazz, but I think Cubans [are] more advanced in both jazz technique and rhythm.

In the last few years you've concentrated on Latin jazz instead of dance music, and now you're playing with the Golden Latin Jazz All Stars, a sort of Dream Team.

You can't get much better than that. Every time we play with any major Anglo jazzmen, as Americans say, "We put 'em away." It's because we are playing *Latin* jazz, and it gets very interesting for the congas and all that. We beat everybody because we have the *clave* [the distinct rhythmic pattern essential for Afro-Cuban rhythms]. That's why I say Americans can't and will never be able to play Latin jazz properly.

That'll be hard for many American players to digest...

But it's the truth! I have never heard any good American Latin jazz orchestra, *never*. You can know lots of music, but the *clave* is something you can't learn anywhere. I go to universities all over the place for Latin jazz workshops and I see that. They don't even know what a drum is.

What about the idea that music is a universal thing, that you can feel it no matter where you come from?

I only talk about what I see. Of course, there must be exceptions but, in America, I still haven't seen it.

Who is your favorite *sonero* [salsa singer, expert at improvisation] today?

I think [Venezuela's] Oscar D'León is the best of them all. He is much superior to all others.

After 104 albums, what's left for you to do?

I have a crazy dream — to stay alive in the year 2000 and have the first Latin orchestra to play on the moon (laughs). I'll put my timbales instead of the flag. My chops are still good, but performing is the most difficult part — it gets harder every time. You go around the world and find more and more people who can play better than yourself. But I still have enough for a couple of more years. After that, I'll give my timbales to the younger generation and concentrate on producing.

Puente, Celia Cruz, Oscar D'León, Marc Anthony, India, Cheo Feliciano, Ray Sepúlveda, Ray De La Paz, Domingo Quiñones, Van Lester and others appear on Saturday at the Hollywood Bowl, 2301 N. Highland Ave., 7 p.m. $11.50-$66.50. Puente plays tonight at the Orange County Performing Arts Center, 600 Town Center Drive, Costa Mesa, 8 p.m. $9-$32.

Luis Miguel: The Man in Charge
(*Los Angeles Times*, September 20, 1995)

For more than a decade, Julio Iglesias has been the most famous Latin pop singer in the world, but he's been overtaken in the Spanish-speaking realm by a man who may someday replace him everywhere: Luis Miguel.

If so, it would mark the culmination of a daring series of moves that began when he fired his father as his manager in 1986, risking his stardom for new challenges.

"It came to a point when I hated my old career," says Luis Miguel, 25, of his teen idol days. "At first it was fun, but after a while I felt a horrible pressure. I didn't like what I was doing, and I'm not proud of any of that. I'm proud of what I am now."

What he is now is Latin America's most important singer of romantic material, both commercially and critically.

But what about the rest of the world? In the age of the "crossover dream," few in Latin pop appear in better position to reach the English-speaking audience that embraced Iglesias in the '80s.

Two of Luis Miguel's last three albums — the memorable jewels *Romance* (1991) and *Segundo Romance* (1994) — together sold more than 5 million copies worldwide. The recordings created a revival for the *bolero* — the old-fashioned, string-based romantic messages of unrequited love were embraced even by young listeners.

Overall, his 21 albums have sold more than 45 million copies (his next release will be a live album, due next month). He's won three Grammys, and was the first Latin artist to sell a million copies of a non-English recording in the U.S.

So when is he making his crossover move? The ever-calculating singer isn't losing any sleep over it.

"Not in the near future," he says during a recent break in rehearsals for his shows tonight through Saturday at the Universal Amphitheatre. "It does interest me, but sometimes you have to pay too big of a price. My language and my world [are] Spanish, and I'm very comfortable with that. If I'm going to do something else it has to be at the right moment, when I feel very confident it's going to be good for me and my music. That time is not coming yet."

In a rare interview, Luis Miguel speaks in both English and Spanish as he sits on a couch facing the stage in a Hollywood rehearsal studio.

The singer is deeply tanned and his fingernails are finely manicured. He wears a black silk shirt, tight jeans and Italian black leather shoes, and he munches on raw celery stalks as members of his staff take turns walking by to make sure that the interview doesn't last too long.

"I'm used to singing for two, three hours nonstop, four nights in a row," he says. "But for everything to come out right, we must run a very strict, disciplined system."

Luis Miguel Gallego, born in Puerto Rico to a Spanish father and an Italian mother, grew up in Mexico and considers himself a "Mexican born in Puerto Rico." He began singing on stage at age 9 and was a Latin American superstar at 12. After the 1986 split with his father, the late singer Luisito Rey, Luis Miguel's new career went on to dwarf his first one. He's become one of the few Latin stars to control virtually every aspect of his career, from business decisions to musical production.

"At this point of my life, I don't feel the need to have someone telling me what to do," says Luis Miguel, who works closely with his record producer Kiko Cibrián. "I listen, but I know exactly who I am and what I want. If it's wrong or right it is my problem, and that's the way I want it to be.

"I mean, it's you out there, your name is everywhere. As they say in English, 'Follow your heart.' I never take too much guidance from other people because people confuse me a lot. Otherwise, I would be very unhappy and embarrassed. You have to do what you desire, otherwise you are faking it and people sooner or later are going to notice that. I've done it this way since I turned 18 or 19 and, so far, it's been pretty good."

Miguel still seems relaxed and talkative after 45 minutes — a surprise, since he's often described as arrogant and narcissistic. Far from the intimidating image, he seems simple, down-to-earth, and vulnerable. But he admits to being difficult.

"I'm a very volatile person," he says. "When I'm working, I want to be aware of everything and make sure everything is as perfect as possible. And always, whether I'm alone or working, I hate routine and I'm always trying to make new plans.

"Maybe that's why I'm a little afraid of marriage, because I've seen the way some relationships function. Many times, those types of relationships kill the passion. I don't want that, I want to have options."

If the price of crossover is, in fact, too high, at least Luis Miguel knows what to expect. He's one of the favorite targets of the Spanish-language tabloid press, which reports on both his old family problems (besides firing his father, he hasn't spoken to his mother, Marcella, since his parents divorced in 1986) and his "romance of the week."

"They've killed me several times," says the singer, a master at the art of talking about delicate issues without revealing anything. "I never answered any of that and refuse to give too many details about my private life. I like to entertain myself by seeing how things grow out of proportion. It's like a balloon that grows and grows, and as soon as it explodes a new one is created."

Luis Miguel performs tonight through Saturday at the Universal Amphitheatre, 100 Universal City Plaza, Universal City, 8:15 pm. Sold out tonight and Thursday. Friday and Saturday, $50-$55.

Enrique Iglesias: Latin Pop's First Son
(*Los Angeles Times*, November 29, 1995)

Guess what question the hottest newcomer in Latin pop is invariably asked?

Hint: His name is Enrique Iglesias.

"Yeah, all right, I'm Julio's son," said Iglesias, 20, during a recent visit to Los Angeles. "But, hey, this is me right here, OK? He is 52, and my world and my music are completely different."

An easily distracted, hyperactive, talkative heartthrob, the 6-foot-tall singer doodles on a piece of paper during an interview at the Van Nuys office of his record label, Fonovisa, which released his debut album, *Enrique Iglesias*, in September.

Iglesias wants to hear the questions, but is also diligent about not missing the other conversations taking place in a nearby conference room. In the middle of a question about his formative years, he suddenly explodes into laughter about a joke someone told half an hour ago, then proceeds with the answer.

"I was never spoiled as a child," he says, speaking in Spanish. "I never had a Ferrari and I never traveled in first class. I was a simple boy."

According to Iglesias, not even his father knew about his intentions to start a singing career.

"I didn't want any pressure and I didn't want an uproar, creating false expectations," he said. "I wanted to do this for myself and by myself, not because I wanted to be famous."

Iglesias began writing songs on his own at home in Miami, eventually collaborating with a friend and recording some demos. Several labels expressed interest, he says, and last December he flew to Los Angeles to sign with Fonovisa. The next morning he was back home. Julio found out four months later, through a third party.

"He was a little shocked, but all he told me was to do it right or not even try it at all," the younger Iglesias said. "Besides that, so far I haven't asked him for advice, not a single time.

"Just by observing him I've learned all I needed to learn — that as soon as you get famous, the human leeches come to suck your blood, so you better be ready. You don't have time to know them all well, so you must be able to make an instant conclusion. Beyond that, I want to learn from my own mistakes."

Even though many sons of Latin pop stars have enjoyed considerable success, none have been able to surpass their parents' achievements.

Argentina's Emmanuel Ortega (son of '60s hero "Palito" Ortega, now a politician), Mexico's up-and-coming Alejandro Fernández (son of mariachi legend Vicente Fernández), Cristian Castro (son of actress-singer Verónica Castro) and Spain's Marcos Llunas (son of Dyango) are only a few of the youngsters who are trying to follow in their parents' footsteps —with varying degrees of credibility.

While he doesn't establish himself as an outstanding singer on his debut album, Iglesias shows that he can at least hold his own with a microphone — enough to make it a hit anyway. The album is currently at No. 1 on the Latin charts.

"He will be a superstar in no time," predicts Seth Briggs, his vocal trainer. One asset: Aside from some trademark Julio inflections and phrasings, his voice does have its own character.

"If my name were Pepe Grillo, you'd never think of Julio Iglesias after hearing my voice," Iglesias says. "Of course, there are things here and there, because I think my father is the greatest. But my thing is completely different."

Mostly written by the singer and friend Roberto Morales, *Enrique Iglesias* was coordinated by the successful Spanish producer-composer Rafael Pérez-Botija, who also wrote three of the songs.

"He came up with 20 songs, but I insisted on having at least five songs of mine," Iglesias said. The album was rounded out by a song written by Chein García-Alonso and another by Marco Antonio Solís of Los Bukis fame.

Although bilingual, Iglesias is not planning an English-language career right away.

"I sing English rockers even better than my Spanish ballads," he said. "If I'm going to succeed, I'll succeed in any language at any time. But now I was inspired to do this record in Spanish. Then we'll see."

As the son of one of the most successful singers ever, Enrique Iglesias is Latin pop's first son. He knows that helps — but that it isn't enough.

"You can be the son of the King of the World, but if you are not good, you won't get anywhere.

"Even my dad — if he makes a bad record, people won't buy it. I must work as hard as anybody else. But it's also fair that if I'm successful I get due credit for what I do, not for who I am. The name gives you the opportunity, not the success."

ENRIQUE LOPETEGUI

La Banda Elástica: *Rocanrol'*s Voice
(*Los Angeles Times*, December 19, 1996)

Emilio Morales began producing his magazine, *La Banda Elástica*, in his Long Beach bedroom in 1992 as a photocopied, four-page newsletter with a circulation of 500.

Four years later, it reaches 20,000 readers throughout the United States and in several Latin American countries, and is widely regarded as the leading publication in the U.S.-based world of rock *en español*, the Spanish-language rock movement that has become an increasingly strong force in contemporary pop. The magazine also paved the way for the outpouring of fanzines that has become one of the most fascinating byproducts of rock *en español*.

La Banda Elástica celebrates its fourth anniversary on Friday as the honoree at the "Revolución '96" concert, a massive gathering of rock *en español* acts at the Universal Amphitheatre.

"All I wanted to do was provide a source of information for die-hard fans, but it ended up bigger than I thought," says Morales, who distributed the first issue at a rock *en español* contest in Huntington Park.

Thanks to a few advertisers and a steadily increasing list of subscribers, *La Banda Elástica* (a wordplay between "the rubber band" and *banda*, or rock *en español* fans) gradually improved its look and added more pages. The turning point came two years ago when then-BMG Records executive Jorge Erinwald, impressed by Morales' striking graphic designs, offered to buy some space to assure the magazine's stability and the regularity of its publication.

Despite concerns expressed by some critics that this alliance compromises his editorial independence, Morales, 32, says he has maintained the magazine's credibility and influence.

"We have nothing to do with either journalism or entertainment," Morales says. "All we're doing is exposing something that's happening, not pontificating. It is the task of future generations to deal with any journalistic considerations. Rock *en español* can't afford not to take advantage of [every] opportunity."

Morales cites the success of his magazine and the presence of the only radio station in the country to air a considerable amount of rock *en español* 24 hours a day — KRTO-FM (98.3) — as two indicators of Southern California's importance in the world of Spanish-language rock.

"Our own growth is proof that something is going on with the Latino youth here," Morales says. "We're not as fully developed as the Mexico or Argentina scenes, but our growth rate is much faster."

Friday's "Revolución" concert, the third staging of the annual event, is a rock *en español* rarity in that most of the bands come from countries other than Mexico and Argentina, the music's two leading centers.

Besides major forces such as Maldita Vecindad, Fobia and La Lupita, all of Mexico, the festival marks the long-awaited Los Angeles debut of Colombia's Aterciopelados, one of the movement's hottest acts. Aterciopelados' singer, Andrea Echeverri, who grew up listening to Mexican rancheras, and the punk-influenced bassist Hector Buitrago rank among the best songwriters of rock *en español*. Other acts playing L.A. for the first time include Puerto Rico's Puya and Sol D' Menta and Panama's Rabanes.

"Rock *en español* is no longer the property of Mexico, Argentina or Spain," Morales says. "It is a global movement, and Los Angeles is one of its main centers. And this is just the beginning."

"Revolución '96," featuring Maldita Vecindad, Fobia, La Lupita, Sol D' Menta, Aterciopelados and others, Friday at the Universal Amphitheatre, 100 Universal City Plaza, Universal City, 4:30 p.m. $15-$75.

Maná: *Rocanrol*'s Punching Bag
(*Dallas Observer*, October 10, 2002)

In the end, it may have taken Carlos Freaking Santana himself to put an end to rock *en español*'s favorite sport: Maná bashing. For 11 years, the Guadalajara-based band has been among the genre's biggest punching bags, derided as *fresas* ("strawberries" — softies) who make crappy music for preppy kids who don't know any better. The reason? For starters, Maná outsold everyone (16 million copies and counting) and became the most successful Spanish-language rock group of all time, and it did so with a pop-heavy sound that drew comparisons to the Police — sans Sting. They were sitting ducks for sharp-shooting purists (including this writer) who never did quite understand what all the hoopla was about.

But that was all before Santana donated his golden guitar to the cause.

The rock legend toured with the band, then put his seal of approval on *Revolución de amor*, Maná's first studio album in five years and, to no one's surprise, a commercial success already. The album made its August debut at the top spot on *Billboard*'s Latin charts, and the band's concerts this month at Los Angeles' Universal Amphitheatre sold out in all of 20 minutes. What may be surprising is that *Revolución...* is also Maná's strongest album yet musically. Featuring Rubén Blades on the tropical "Sábanas frías" ("Cold Sheets," arguably the best song on the album) and Ozomatli's Asdrúbal Sierra singing the chorus on the powerful "No quiero ser tu esclavo" ("I Don't Want to Be Your Slave"), it's a balanced offering of mild and hot, highlighted by guitarist Sergio Vallín's all-out style and with songs written by three of the members of the quartet. But it's "Justicia, tierra y libertad" ("Justice, Land and Freedom"), the track that opens the album with guest guitar from Santana, that has critics finally taking a second look at Maná.

Truth is, despite the *rockeros*' gripes (and the band's own limitations in the studio), Maná *always* rocked onstage and could *always* play alongside anyone. It was the music itself — syrupy pop offered up at a time when the best in Mexican rock (Maldita Vecindad, Caifanes, Café Tacvba) were busy making "proper" rock — that drew the barbs. Fher Olvera, the band's singer and main songwriter, says Maná always got a bad rap.

"C'mon, man," says Olvera (Vallín, bassist Juan Calleros and drummer Alex González round out the group). "The Beatles started out [with] 'I Wanna Hold Your Hand'! '*Te quiero agarrar la manoooo...*' — gimme a break! OK, great song, but in today's context it's a very corny thing. But that was Lennon as a kid, man —was the way he expressed himself. [And] that's the process of a band. You start somewhere, ascend to a certain point and then you fall. It happened to everyone, and it'll happen to us."

Maybe, but not just yet. *Revolución de amor* features plenty of the usual Maná, the catchy, leechy kind that rockeros hate — but this time it's done intelligently, with good taste and with a vengeance. It's a guitar-oriented album, for which the band tried more than 100 guitars and dozens of amps, and the result is an earthy, analog feel, one of Maná's main goals.

"We want to sound studio when we're live, and live when we're at the studio," Olvera says. "We want to continue making artisan music, organic, natural…We don't mind little mistakes here and there; you just can't dehumanize music. You wouldn't buy a painting from a guy who did the thing on a computer."

Maná is a band of contradictions: The pop world loves them as much as the rock world scorns them, but in that pop world, Maná is *all* rock, from its lyrics about women, alcohol and pot to its political commitment, something that the Latin music industry as a rule considers *passé* (proudly *zapatistas*, pro-labor and pro-environment, the band members have never been shy with their opinions). Fresas or not, Maná is more genuinely aware of the world's social and economic environment than many of the so-called "serious" bands out there refusing to take a stand and alienate some fans.

And while they've broken sales record after sales record, they've done it on their own terms — literally. "We're not actors," Olvera says, dismissing suggestions that the band sings in English to boost its crossover appeal. Not that it matters — with *Revolución de amor*, Maná is closer to a *real* crossover than anyone else in the business: Sung entirely in Spanish, the disc debuted at No. 22 on *Billboard*'s Top 200 chart.

Olvera and Co. are a contradiction musically as well. They bounce from sugary ballads and Latin fusion to reggae, pop and rock, never fully embracing any one style; that fickleness is only mitigated by the rare talent of two guys (Olvera and the Cuban-born González) who still don't quite understand they might be the best songwriting team in all of Latin pop music.

"We had so many songs [for *Revolución*…], we almost released a double album," says Olvera, drinking red wine under a full moon next to the Mondrian Hotel's swimming pool. "That would have been a mistake. We decided to take it easy and save the songs for later. But we've never been so fired up."

What happened in the five years since the band's last trip to the studio? No more and no less than one successful album that they recorded in their sleep (1999's *MTV Unplugged,* which earned the band their fourth Grammy);

meetings with heroes Gabriel García Márquez, Mario Benedetti, Sting, Paco de Lucía and others; and a few intense musical experiences around the globe, most notably in Spain and Turkey.

"We spent three months in the caves of Granada listening to the *cantaores*," Olvera says. "But not at the tourist sites — the real fucking thing! We were right there with the fucking gypsy sons of bitches...You go in and smoke a puff of hash, because that's your admission ticket, and [when] you enter the cave they're playing raw *flamenco, cabrón* — not the Gipsy Kings' stuff." The memory clearly excites Olvera; he's practically yelling. "And then we went to Istanbul and got some *more* hash, and nourished ourselves on Arab music, and brought a huge pile of records... I mean, *five years* like that, at our speed ... it was like being on a bullet train. It all became like a huge musical diarrhea."

"Musical diarrhea." Having spent time with García Marquez and Benedetti, the best description Olvera can muster for the experience is a scatological one, and that laziness reflects in Maná's lyrics. As he sings in "Ay Doctor," "...nothing consoles me/ Not pasta, not ganja, not alcohol." Yes, *pasta,* even though, to be fair, he didn't mean vermicelli.

Fortunately, Vallín's guitar and the harmonies of the chorus save a song only Maná could have pulled off. But if its lyrics remain Maná's weakest link, its intentions are unfailingly noble. Despite the group's success, Maná knows the earth is not a pretty place: "Give me faith, give me wings," sings González on "Faith," which he wrote. "Give me strength to survive in this world." Not exactly Octavio Paz — but nonetheless an oddly optimistic reminder that the world still sucks.

Maná's roots reach back to Guadalajara in the early '80s, where Olvera, Gustavo Orozco and brothers Juan, Abraham and Ulises Calleros formed Sombrero Verde (Green Hat), a pop band so lightweight it made Maná sound like Judas Priest. After a series of personnel changes (Abraham and Ulises Calleros [he's Maná's manager] dropped out, as did Orozco; drummer Alex González, guitarist César "Vampiro" López and keyboardist Iván González joined), the band found success as Maná, touring extensively — hundreds of shows a year, whether its albums had been released in the local markets or not. When a cassette they'd given someone in Ecuador — where the albums weren't yet available — turned up on the radio and reached No. 1, a lightbulb switched on: The more they toured, the better they'd do.

"We thought, 'If we made it to number one and the album wasn't even *released*,'" Olvera says, "'then we can release the album everywhere and *play* everywhere.'" The plan worked. *¿Dónde jugarán los niños?* (1992) sold more than a million copies and established Maná as a Latin rock superpower. But César "Vampiro" López and Iván González were not happy, and they left in '93. Enter Vallín, an *hidrocálido* (a native of the state of Aguascalientes, even though he lived in Guadalajara) who got the job after the band reportedly auditioned 5,000 guitarists throughout the Americas. The new lineup worked even better.

It's the lineup that remains to this day. And its members couldn't be more different.

Calleros is courteous and affable but shy; he doesn't talk — period. Olvera, the voice and symbol of Maná, is neither a rocker nor a pop idol, but a gypsy. Give him a guitar, a woman and a few shots of tequila (Herradura or Patrón, not Cuervo), and he's a happy guy. González, meanwhile, is Olvera's perfect opposite: the aggressive and business-savvy band member; he's a Keith Moon with work ethics, a PR publicist's dream.

And after nine years, Vallín is still "the new guy" (Vampiro, now with Jaguares, is a tough act to follow). Nonetheless, Vallín's arrival gave Maná the electric power it needed; he's Steve Vai-meets-Santana-meets-George Harrison. He also gave the band its finest ballad, "¿Por qué te vas?" ("Why Are You Leaving?").

Heartfelt and heartbreaking, "¿Por qué te vas?" was born of a series of recent tragedies within the band. First, several years ago, after nearly 30 years of marriage, Vallín's parents passed away less than a year apart, his father in a car accident, and his mother "from love." Adding to the pain, Olvera's girlfriend recently lost what would have been his first child in a miscarriage ("It was going to be my first *chavito*," Olvera says). In the song, Vallín's mother stares at a photograph of her dead husband, asking him why he left.

"We were recording the *MTV Unplugged*," Vallín says of the day he received the phone call informing him of his father's crash. "There was no time to say goodbye." He starts playing with his fingers and is about to choke, then snaps out of it. "Anyway, 11 months after that, I saw my mom at the hospital. She had gotten sick soon after my father died. I realized the only thing that kept her in this world was her love for us. She was struggling. So I told her, 'You know what? Go. We're fine, you go, rest in peace. We have the basics, what you gave us. Now go.' So she left. And the song talks about a person saying, 'Why do you go, when I love you too much?'"

It's a simple but moving jewel, and it proves that, by the way, Maná now has not two, but *three* singers.

"It doesn't matter who scores," Olvera says. "The important thing is to win."

The Phenomenauts: Plan 9 From Outer SF
(*Phoenix New Times*, November 28, 2002)

It wasn't quite Captain Kirk vs. Ricardo Montalbán in tights, but Commander Angel Nova considered it a successful intergalactic mission.

"[We] had planned to commando the 2002 Vans Warped Tour [i.e., perform in the parking lot] in San Francisco, but when we started setting up in front of the show, the security told us, 'No way,'" says science freak Nova, 27, the singer and guitarist for extreme novelty band the Phenomenauts. True to his persona, he communicates via e-mail as well as phone. Nova calls his band's performances "missions," his bandmates "my men," and the group's road crew the "cadets." But before getting deeper into what the award-winning, toilet-paper-throwing, theremin-helmet-wearing Phenomenauts are all about, allow the commander to describe the sci-fi psychobilly band's greatest triumph.

"On our way back to the Phenomabomber [an '83 Dodge van — and spaceship] to retreat, we noticed that there were musicians with instruments going in the back gate, so we just followed them in. Once we were in, the security saw us from across the park, so we ducked behind a dumpster and plotted our attack. After about a half an hour, we set up across from a stage where a band just finished playing. We blasted off and about two songs in I got a tap on the shoulder. I thought we were caught. But it was the sound man. He told us that the band that was supposed to be on next was late and if we wanted to jump on the stage we could. I told the crowd, 'We have just been upgraded to the stage!' Some helpful cadets helped us move our gear and we played for about 20 minutes. When we got off the stage, we sold all the merchandise we had, $250 worth, and we walked out the front door, right past the security. Mission accomplished."

Thus ended a typical working day for the Phenomenauts, recently chosen as California's Best Live Band by the *East Bay Express* and Best Lifestyle Music artist by the *SF Weekly* (both papers are sister publications to *New Times*). "The Phenomenauts are the world's bravest rocket roll band," says Commander Nova. "If you go to a recital, you will see, in person, the Streamerator [a leaf blower turned into a device that shoots a whole roll of toilet paper into the audience in a matter of seconds], the Smokearator and Fogarator [which blasts off smoke and fog, duh], the Phenomabomber [the band's equivalent to the Batmobile], etc., etc., etc." The etceteras could be summed up as a fun, fast-driving blend of rockabilly, punk, pop and surf guitars and above-average songwriting that usually gets overshadowed by the band's visuals — except for Commander

Nova, the Phenomenauts are bald-headed, and they all wear spacesuits and thin, wrap-around sunglasses, much like Cyclops from the X-Men.

Rockets and Robots, the band's self-released debut album, is full of cosmic references. In fact, that's all the band talks about. "Earth Is the Best," a favorite among Oakland's Phenome-heads, is a planet-by-planet neo-imperialist explanation of why we're in just the right place: "Uranus is the 7th planet from the Sun/With a stupid name that is just plain dumb/Neptune is cold and it smells real bad/Like sick ammonia and methane gas/Earth has its faults/And to that we confess/But you can't blast Earth/Because Earth is the best." "Tiny Robots," however, suggests a break from the best planet: "I can't wait for NASA/I want to go into outer space/Before I get too old." (Perhaps we can rename it "My Rocket-Bound Generation"?)

Real female beauty is described in "Phenomenator," but this ain't no earthly chick: The Phenomenator is a smaller scout ship that travels hand-in-hand with the Phenomabomber. "She's got dual quad thrusters with thrust reverse/Makes the plasma so hot/You're going to need a nurse." And "Galactic Pioneers" adds a new perspective to the theory of evolution. "We were here before/Before four score/Before four thousand years/We interbred, which changed your head/At least you kept your ears."

Make no mistake: The Phenomenauts are dead serious. When this Hare Krishna-turned-devil's advocate writer reminds Commander Nova that science is always changing, that the scientist's imperfect senses suggested 50 years ago, for example, that smoking was good for you, the Commander comes back in full force.

"Science is always correcting itself," he clarifies. "While religion, you just have to trust, without ever questioning it. Science means there is a bunch of people all over the place making sure it's accurate." Oh, okay. Still, science is supposed to be cold and calculating. To some ears, there might be more science in the pipes of Eddie Vedder than in the funbot Phenomenauts.

"Oh, please," says Commander Nova, at the mere mention of angst-shriveled Vedder. "There's a lot of people always whining about stuff. But really, life is not so bad, at least [in the U.S.]. There are people in the world who are making a dollar a day. Just be yourself and have a good time. And yes, we're fun, because science is fun, just like rock 'n' roll. Have you seen Bill Nye, the science guy, on TV?"

That's a salient point, commander.

After playing '80s covers as the Space Patrol in the mid-'90s, the Phenomenauts as we know them began as a guerrilla-type street performance act. They would set up battery-powered equipment in front of key venues and shows (the latest came last April 27 at Oakland's California Music Awards) that allowed them to play a few songs before clueless security guards found a way to force them to "retreat."

"They try to unplug us, but they can't figure out how," the Commander says. "It's because there is nothing to unplug!" Word of mouth spread, and the Phenomenauts became a full-fledged rock 'n' roll band with a growing cult in California.

"I'm the guy with the hair," says Commander Nova, the lead singer/guitarist in charge of "maintenance of equipment and Phenomabomber sub-systems." He's also the Elvis answer to the higher-pitched Corporal Joe Bot, who also sings, plays guitar and is the "thermaratorhelitron operator," or the guy who plays the Therimatic Helmerator (you know, a skateboard helmet with a wireless theremin attached to it). Major Jimmy Boom, the drummer, is the "helmsman and syncopation officer," and Captain Chreehos is the "low-end spectral output officer" (he takes care of the standup bass). Offstage you have Professor Greg Arious ("effects and ladies' man") and the intriguing Colonel Reehotch ("Top Secret").

"There's definitely a romance between sci-fi and rock 'n' roll," says the Commander. "Sci-fi got really big at the same time [rock 'n' roll] got really big." But, needless to say, a vital part of the band's mission is to keep that romance in a proudly independent basis. Or something like that.

"The Phenomenauts are on our own label," continues Commander Nova. "We play all our own instruments, write all our own songs, and build our own effects. We recorded the album ourselves and did all the graphics ourselves because that is what the Phenomenauts are all about and that will never change. Unless, of course, we get a big fat paycheck from a major label."

But before that happens, the Phenomenauts face one more tough challenge. Phoenix is the home of Killbot, a self-proclaimed "robot programmed to kill," a ferocious nonstop instrumental metal machine. No time for clapping — once the 40-minute set is over, Killbot is offline, no encore. Killbot is equal parts power trio, lights, smoke, wires, tubes, junk from a nearby alley, masks, a projected video backdrop of robots, a video game footage, and a lunatic selection of special sound effects like the Alien Fart, Martian Mind Ray, and Plasma Cannon.

"When you go see Killbot, it's like going to the movies, except there's beer," says guitarist Bob Bot, who has a message for the West Coast invaders. "The Phenomenauts? Ha! More like the Phenome-NOTS! We're not afraid of anyone whose diet consists mostly of government moon cheese."

Commander Nova's official reply suggests the Phenomenauts prefer to let the Streamerator speak for itself.

"Alien Fart, huh? I'd love to hear that."

Arjona
Santo pecado
(Sony/BMG Latin)
(*Phoenix New Times*, December 19, 2002)

I'm into poetry. I wrote a few lines. Don't worry, I offer just a few. This one details the passing of time: "The past is thirsty, and the present is an athlete with no feet." Do you like it? How about this one? "In the branch of hell there are no windows." It's about a kidnapped girl in a dark room — her "hell," which has no windows, because it's all dark. Get it? And "the girl doesn't know that God also makes mistakes," because the kidnapped girl doesn't know that God, well, He's only human.

You don't think my lines are all that original? Well, don't blame me. I didn't write them. I lied. It comes from Guatemala's Ricardo Arjona, an excellent guitarist and singer, and potentially a great songwriter. He gained notoriety in 1990 with a song that started with the narration, "Jesus tuned up my guitar." The song and album were named *Jesús Verbo No Sustantivo* (That's "Jesus Verb, Not Noun" in English). Arjona's ballads are predictable, his rockers Jurassic, filled with corny '80s guitars and synthesizers. Yet the state of Latin pop is so troubling, someone like Arjona can sell millions and be embraced by the masses and a sizable portion of the music elite.

Arjona has even drawn comparisons to Silvio Rodríguez and Pablo Milanés, the symbols of Cuba's post-revolution *Nueva Trova* movement. Now they're beginning to call him "the Latin-American Dylan." Poor Bob. Milanés even invited him to sing a duet with him on one of his records. But Arjona definitely ain't no Silvio. *Santo Pecado* is nothing more than the latest in the Arjona "good intentions" series. Ironically, the best moments take place when Arjona doesn't try to say anything. When he gives up the pretentious "let me say something deep here" bullshit, he's a fine artist. "No sirve de nada" ("It's Useless"), a *ranchera*-rock with strings, is a plain love song. The result is almost as good as the groundbreaking "El último adiós" ("The Last Goodbye"), Paulina Rubio's only worthwhile song.

All Arjona needs now is to say goodbye to Eurovision-like hymns and his other catchy festival throwaways and dedicate a year to reading the sublime lyrics of others. Then there's hope — maybe.

Molotov
Dance and Dense Denso
(Surco/Universal)
(*Miami New Times*, February 13, 2003)

Contrary to popular belief, the Spanish word *puto* doesn't mean "fag." Only a homosexual who also happens to be an asshole is a *puto*. But *puto* is anything that's bad, or wrong. For example, if you accused Molotov of homophobia for its 1997 hit "Puto" (which repeated a "Puuuuuto-Puuuuuto" chorus dozens of times), well, that automatically qualifies you as a *puto* — the song was a favorite in gay discos in Mexico City. See, according to Molotov — the Mexican bilingual hardcore rap and metal quartet that sold over a million copies of its debut album, *Dónde jugarán las niñas?* — Bush and Saddam are *putos*, the Border Patrol *gringos* are a bunch of *putos,* and those who hold suspected terrorists with no charges and no lawyers are *putos* as well. But the biggest *putos* of them all are those who can't see that, beyond the shock value and the curses and the musical differences, Molotov is Mexico's answer to Divididos, the Argentine *aplanadora*, the most powerful machine in all of Spanish-language rock (Divididos is not known in the U.S. because here in America we're still in the pre-lactancy/idiocy state of that hungry beast named "rock *en español*").

Dance and Dense Denso, Molotov's third album, marks the return of ace producer Gustavo Santaolalla (also Divididos' producer), who did the first one but only produced a few of the songs for the second, *Apocalypshit*. Santaolalla is an expert at balancing fierce metal with organic Latin fusion, without dropping the ball in either case. Musically and lyrically, the band members seem to be saying "Let's fuck" and "Don't you touch me fucking immigration police bastard," but ultimately ask their American friends, "What would you do if you were in our shoes?" One rule, though: Listen to the album nonstop, from beginning to end. Treat it as a scientific marvel. You may not understand all of what it's saying, but Molotov will ultimately knock your socks off.

Jaime Roos: Murga Pop
(*Miami New Times*, March 13, 2003)

"I don't like to rush it when I'm cooking," says the 49-year-old Jaime Roos, a hugely influential Uruguayan musician who hasn't released an album of originals since 1996. His most recent album, *Contraseña* (*Password*), is a collection of covers of Uruguayan classics by Alfredo Zitarrosa, Eduardo Mateo (Roos's aesthetic role model), Leo Maslíah, Jorge Galemire, Jorge Drexler, and others. Only three of the songs were written or co-written by Roos.

In comparison to new Uruguayan names like Drexler (the most important solo artist since Roos) and popular rock bands like La Vela Puerca, it may seem as if Roos is beginning to slow down after a long and successful career. But relax: The covers album is just a stopgap release during a well-deserved break. After paying tribute to his influences, Roos is warming up for a new chapter in his own career. "I'm always looking forward, I'm still in the fight," says Roos in a phone conversation from Montevideo. "I always write songs that I'll record one day, but I'll record them when they have to be recorded."

The singer, songwriter, and composer can make everyone wait. His blend of candombe (an Afro-Uruguayan beat that's arguably the fiercest rhythm you'll ever hear), murga (a Uruguayan vocal and percussive Carnival style with roots in Spain), Piazzolla-esque tango, Beatles-esque pop, rock, jazzy solos, and Latin American folk has turned him into one of the most popular artists in Uruguay and Argentina for the last three decades.

But things weren't always easy for him. To begin with, he left Uruguay in 1975 during the military dictatorship's decade-long rule when "the thing" to do was "to stay and resist" them. For the next several years, he floated around Europe, surviving by making salads on ships and playing on subways, nightclubs (anything from salsa, rock, and jazz to cumbia and Andean music), and as a session musician. After an adventurous four-month hitchhiking trip from Mexico to Uruguay, he released his debut, *Candombe del 31* (1977).

Roos' time spent away from Uruguay didn't negatively impact his career, but it did keep him from achieving massive success. He had good compositions, but he didn't perform them in his native country until 1980, when he played a show marred by bad sound and a censorious government that kept him from performing some of his most popular songs, including "Los Olímpicos," a murga song about exiles.

On top of that, Roos didn't seem to care for the *Canto Popular* movement, a trend he once described as "a bag of great and horrible things." "After

I released my first album, they questioned the fact that I didn't stay, but I never cared," says Roos. "My answers have always been albums." When he presented *Aquello* in 1980 (his third album, chosen by Uruguayan critics as best album of the year), he would sarcastically announce, "I'm a rocker," when the press tried to forcibly lump him into the folk-oriented and nationalistic *Canto Popular*.

He wasn't completely lying. From an early age, Roos has been a proud Beatlemaniac. Their influence affects his music in three ways: simple but imaginative song structures; a poetic balance among the mundane, the unpredictable, and the sublime; and long, hypnotic, trancelike choruses à la "Hey Jude."

After five increasingly popular and critically acclaimed albums (now recorded in Uruguay, where he has lived since 1984), Roos finally achieved widespread commercial success. In 1985 *Brindis por Pierrot* (*A Toast for Pierrot*, pierrot being the symbol of a Carnival bohemian character) became the best-selling album in Uruguayan history and earned more than 75 gold and platinum records (gold certifications representing 3000 copies sold), an unprecedented figure for a country with a population of little more than three million. It is a masterpiece of murga that turned Roos into his country's number one popular artist.

The title song, sung by guest vocalist Washington "Canario" ("The Canary") Luna — then considered one of the best murga singers in Uruguay — is a heart-wrenching farewell song to Carnival. His life is like a soccer stadium: "They throw you in the field/Without asking you whether you want to play or not/In case this wasn't enough, you're the goalkeeper/You spend your whole life covering holes/And if by accident you become good at it/They take a dive/And the referee calls 'penalty'!" "It's a song about strength, despite its tremendous skepticism," says Roos. "My career is before and after *Brindis*. It brought my previous semi-hits to the attention of a massive public."

"Brindis por Pierrot" would also change the course of a good portion of Argentine rock. "I turned to murga and candombe when I heard "Brindis por Pierrot," says Juan Subirá, keyboardist for Argentina's platinum act Bersuit Vergarabat and co-author of "Negra Murguera" and other Bersuit hits inspired by Roos's *murga-canción* (murga-song) style. "It blew me away. I had no idea of who he was. I immediately went to Uruguay and soaked myself in Roos, murga and candombe."

Even Rubén Blades used Roos' candombe ballad "Amándote" on his Grammy-winning *La Rosa de los Vientos*. "What a beautiful song," Blades said when this writer played him "Amándote" for the first time. "Wow! What a great song. How can I get a hold of this guy? I want to use it in my next record."

Blades wasn't bluffing: He included "Amándote" as the last track on that 1996 album, even though it was a collection of songs by other Panamanian composers.

"I'm a big fan since 'Cometa de la Farola,'" says top Latin rock producer and two-time Latin Grammy Award winner Gustavo Santaolalla, referring to a song on Roos's *Candombe del 31*. "He's one of the key pillars of Latin American music."

However, in *El sonido de la calle* (*The Sound of the Street*), a book by Uruguayan author Milita Alfaro, Roos humbly described himself as a "consolidator" of different streams of Uruguayan popular music rather than an "innovator." But after 12 critically and commercially successful albums (not counting rarities, compilations, and his productions for other artists), there's just too much water under the bridge. "True, I've always considered myself more important as a consolidator than as a creator," says Roos, "but after so much music I must raise a little flag and say, 'Hey, I've also done something, haven't I?'"

Yet despite recording, touring, and becoming increasingly popular in Buenos Aires, for some reason his music is virtually unknown beyond the Río de la Plata, which has prompted some to say that Roos is too comfortable with his status as a Uruguayan icon. "I was always interested in playing everywhere," protests Roos. "But I was never offered a serious proposal [to come to the U.S.]. Some people suggested I come by myself and form a band here. I wasn't interested in *that*." In 1989 he was invited by RCA to spend a month recording in Nashville for what he derisively terms "a so-called Hispanic project," but nothing happened. "It wasn't about money, it was about the musical angle," says Roos dismissively. "They wanted me to make commercial music and be their puppet."

Finally, a New York-based Uruguayan promoter named Emilio Baglini got in contact with Roos through the latter's production company and sought to bring him to the States, a serious risk considering that the legendary musician is mostly known here among a handful of music experts. He's bringing an 11-man band (ranging in age from 24-38) that includes some of Uruguay's top musicians: brothers Andrés, Martín, and Nicolás Ibarburu (bass, drums, and electric guitar, respectively); Gustavo Montemurro (keyboards); legendary Walter "Nego" Haedo on percussion; Roos on acoustic guitar and vocals; plus singers Freddy Bessio, Emiliano Muñoz, Pedro Takorián, Ney Peraza (who also plays guitar), and Alvaro Montes. Since 2001, Roos's backing group has been able to endure his famously obsessive rehearsals. What they produce together onstage as a result is truly eloquent, a nonstop candombe and murga tour de force with jazzlike virtuoso playing, chilling percussion and vocals, and a rock and roll attitude.

Gustavo Santaolalla, who is not known for giving away praise, attests to the power of Roos' music. "I saw them recently in Uruguay, and they cracked my head open."

Jaime Roos performs at Billboardlive, 1500 Ocean Dr., Miami. 8:00 p.m. Saturday, March 15, $20-$25.

Freddy Fender: El Primero
(*San Antonio Current*. November 14, 2006; updated in 2022)

When I read in *Rolling Stone* that "Thee Midniters were the original *rock en español*," I wanted to puke. Don't get me wrong: I lived in Los Angeles for 23 years, and my worship of Los Lobos inevitably turned me into a lifetime member of the Willy G church.

But Thee Midniters didn't start rock en español — Freddy Fender had already taken care of it. He was *el primero*, the first one. And while he enjoyed fame, considerable record sales, and even his visage on the water tower of his native San Benito, he hasn't been granted what he most sought during the last years of his life: proper credit.

"My first two recordings, 'No seas cruel' ('Don't be cruel')/'Ay amor' ('Holy One') I [recorded] in 1955 and came out in 1957," Fender wrote in an unpublished paper "seven or eight years ago," according to his widow Vangie Huerta. "They initiated a wonderful cultural change in music. Ritchie Valens in California and from South of the border, the Latin artists soon followed the initiation of Hispanic rock 'n' roll, including Spain."

Fender's timeline is accurate: "No seas cruel" (a cover of "Don't Be Cruel," an early Elvis hit) is from 1957, a year before Valens was signed by Del-Fi Records. In the early 1960s, Mexico's Los Teen Tops and Los Locos del Ritmo followed suit (mostly with covers), and in 1965, Argentina's Los Beatniks started the all-original "rock nacional" movement, considered by most experts to be the strongest Spanish-language rock movement to date. (And don't get me started about Los Saicos, Perú's "fathers of punk," who released the ferocious "Demolición" in… 1965!

"[Fender] was just tired of people passing him up," Vangie said on the phone from her house in Corpus Christi. "I told him 'Why don't you write something and tell people how you feel?' He wrote it, but it wasn't published anywhere. It always bothered him because all the credit was always given to Richie Valens."

In 2000 the Latin Academy approached me to write and edit the official program book of the first three Latin Grammy ceremonies. I decided to include a timeline and historical commentary about the rock *en español* movement. My research led me back to Freddy Fender and, after six years of digging, I still haven't found an earlier Spanish-language rock song than "No seas cruel." The more I look, the bigger Freddy gets. *[2021 update: Soon after I wrote this story, I "discovered" Texan Gloria Ríos, who released "El relojito"/"Hotel de los corazones rotos,"* covers of *"Rock Around the Clock"* and *"Heartbreak Hotel,"* respectively, in 1956 in Mexico.]

Finally, three months ago, Vangie Huerta called me as I was about to board a plane at the Houston airport.

"Freddy is having a good day and wants to talk," she said. She gave the phone to an energetic and alert Freddy, who went on a fact-based rampage that could be summarized as "I never get no credit, man." It was either "miss the plane" or "call him back when you're back in SA." I chose the latter. Bad move.

We were supposed to talk the following Sunday, but it never happened. And I never heard from Vangie, either. I instinctively knew something was wrong, left her a message, and never called again.

Freddy died at noon on Saturday, October 14, and around 1 p.m. I called Vangie and some of Freddy's closest collaborators.

"He opened the doors for bilingual music," said Flaco Jiménez, who recorded *Dos Amigos* with Freddy in 2005 and was a fellow Texas Tornado.

"I've known him since 1957, and I never heard a voice like that," said a particularly somber Augie Meyers. "He was the Mexican Elvis."

"He was the Chicano Roy Orbison," said Max Baca. "He sang like a bird."

The national press remembered Fender in the predictable ways: the Texas Tornados, "Before the Next Teardrop Falls," "Wasted Days and Wasted Nights," his star on the Hollywood Walk of Fame, and passing mentions to his life as Baldemar Huerta/The Bebop Kid (1957), Eddie Medina (1961), and Scott Wayne (1962). But nobody bothered to mention the fact that he invented *rocanrol*.

"I never heard anyone credit that to him," said Ron Morales, who co-produced Freddy's last three albums, including a yet-unreleased bolero collection in the vein of the Grammy-winning *The Music of Baldemar Huerta* (2002). "I guess it's because he had the rock career before his country career, and when people think of Freddy, they think of the country hits. The stuff he did before, no one remembers. And that's a shame."

Even after Fender's passing, Vangie continues her struggle to honor the memory of her husband. Six days after Freddy's death, she called me to ask me to follow up on a letter she had received on September 18 from WGBH in Boston, a PBS affiliate working on a Latin music special in conjunction with the BBC. The producers told her they "couldn't tell the story without Freddy." At least someone cares, I thought. It was then that Vangie told me about Freddy's difficult last days.

Around September 20, Fender was supposed to have a chemotherapy treatment and CAT scan in San Antonio. Instead, he found out the cancer had spread from his lungs to his whole body.

"He was sad, because the doctors took his only hope away by telling him that," said Vangie. "I was not mad at the doctors. I was just like... hurt. I couldn't believe it. We didn't know what to do. We were very discouraged."

Fender refused to undergo another chemo session, so they went back to Corpus. On September 27, Vangie and her daughter drove him to Tulsa for more evaluation.

"He was already feeling a little bad. He wasn't himself anymore, he was so quiet." Due to complications, Vangie spent $10,000 airlifting him back to San Antonio, where he received more medication. On Friday, September 29, "he went into a ... not even a depression. A sleep. And he stayed there and he didn't come out." According to Vangie, the doctors wanted to send him home with no medication.

"And I said, 'No! I can't do that! No! You need to put a feeding tube in him because I will not bring him home like that. I'm not gonna finish killing him off. If the Lord wants him the Lord will take him, but I'm not gonna have anything to do with this.'"

They put a feeding tube in him, but no medication, and he was home by Friday, October 13.

"They brought him in an ambulance that night, so the people around here wouldn't see, because it seems every time we do something the newspaper knows about it," said Vangie. "We had to come in like thieves in the night to slip Freddy inside."

On Saturday just before noon, minutes after the family greeted him, Freddy's blood pressure went down drastically.

"I got all shook up and called everybody," said Vangie. "We were praying for him when he gave three breaths. He breathed in, held it there for a couple of seconds, and let it out. He breathed in again for more seconds and let it out, and then he breathed in and held it for a couple of seconds and let it out, and then he didn't breathe anymore. And we all started screaming and yelling because, you know, this was not supposed to happen. Not to Freddy Fender."

When I mention to her my talks with Flaco, Augie, and Baca, she interrupts me.

"So how come they didn't come to the funeral? How come they didn't go if they were in such pain for him? 'Cause these guys were close. Do you need an invitation to go to a funeral? Flaco called several times, and my daughter asked him 'Are you coming to the funeral?' and he said he had this and that to do, and I said, 'Well, maybe he did, OK?' But there were two days, the memorial and the funeral. It was so beautiful. We even had Governor Rick Perry."

"I was in San Francisco in the studio," said Meyers. "When Doug Sahm died, Freddy didn't go to his funeral, either. And we've all known each other since way back, 1957. And Freddy didn't cancel his gig. These things happen. We still love him, no doubt about that. His passing bothers me to this day."

Jiménez said he couldn't make it to Fender's funeral due to a scheduled gig in Austin.

***

On September 9, Freddy had a vision. Vangie went to the Catholic bookstore in Corpus Christi while Freddy stayed in the car listening to the religious station. When Vangie came back, Freddy was crying uncontrollably.

"'Vangie, don't tell anybody, but something just happened to me,'" said Freddy, according to Vangie. "Freddy told me that, when the program finished, the programmer said in Spanish, '*En el nombre de Cristo, en el nombre de Cristo …* ' ["in the name of Christ… In the name of Christ…"] So Freddy said that he closed his eyes and leaned back on his seat, and he said, 'In the name of Jesus, in the name of Jesus … ' His eyes were closed, but in the distance he still saw this coming closer and closer.

"This man dressed like in the Middle East, and the man had a beard, but he couldn't see his face. This apparition puts his arm around him, embraces him. It was like an electrifying embrace, and he could feel his beard on his cheek. Ever so tender. 'It just felt so good,' said Freddy. And then, all of a sudden, the apparition became really small … and disappeared into his chest. We both started crying and praying. And I told Freddy 'The Lord appeared before you.' He was in a lot of pain before that, but after that we went home and it was a very joyful time for the rest of the day. Now that I think about it, the Lord appeared to Freddy to tell him he was going to take him to end his suffering."

A Posthumous Triple Treat

Freddy's body gave in, but his body of work goes on. In 2007, there will be three new albums featuring Freddy and/or his music:

THE BOLERO ALBUM: Produced by the Morales brothers (who were behind *La Música de Baldemar Huerta* and *Dos amigos*), it was recorded with Joe Reyes and Chepe Solís on guitars, Gabriel Zavala on percussion, Bobby Flores on strings and a *guitarrón* player from México. "It was the music he played in the cantinas on the border when he was a kid," said Ron Morales. "He had a wealth of knowledge when it came to the history of music. He would say 'This was written about two lesbians who used to live here, and one tried to kill the other…' Stuff like that."

THE TEXAS TORNADOS: Augie Meyers, Flaco Jiménez, Freddy and Shawn Sahm (Doug's son), and the original TT back-up band (Max Baca on bajo sexto, Louie Ortega on guitar, Speedy Sparks on bass, and Ernie Durawa on drums) recorded 14 new songs early this year. "Freddy recorded his three songs and then he got real sick and we put it on the shelf," said Augie Meyers. "Now that Freddy is gone, we'll try to put it out in the U.S. and Europe." Flaco, Augie and Shawn plan to do some shows early next year.

THE TEXMANIACS: The second TexManiacs album will include Freddy's "You'll lose a good thing." "Speedy Villanueva did a great job singing it," said Baca. "It'll be our special tribute to him. This CD sounds like the new generation of the Texas Tornados. It's going to be great."

B.B. King on Pappo
(2004 and 2005 conversations, personal blog; abridged Spanish version first published by *Rolling Stone Argentina*)

The following is our first phone conversation, which took place on September 16, 2004, ahead of his September 29 show at the Majestic Theatre in San Antonio. (And, for those living in a jar, Pappo was Argentina's top bluesman, who passed away on February 25, 2005.)

Remember Pappo?

Yes, I know Pappo. He came to my hotel when I first got to Argentina. He showed up with a bottle of wine and a big cheese.

A big cheese??

Yeah, a big cheese. A huge round cheese. Ever since, I remembered him as The Cheeseman. Pappo is The Cheeseman.

Was the cheese any good?

Are you kidding? Excellent! Both the cheese and the wine.

I don't know if you're aware of this, but you revived his career.

I didn't know that. But I know we're friends and we've been friends since I was [in Argentina in 1994].

Years go by, and still there's people who say unless you're black — or, at least Anglo— you can't play the blues. Once and for all: Can white Latinos play the blues?

Pappo is a good guitarist, a good friend and a great musician. I don't know where that stuff comes from, but I think in this world anybody can learn anything. Are you Hispanic?

Yeah, whatever that means...

And here you are, speaking in English! If you can speak English... I can't speak Spanish fluently; I only know just a few words. But that's the proof: if you can speak in English and I can know a few words in Spanish, that means any person can learn whatever he or she wants. That contradicts what those people say, right? I don't believe [Whites or Latinos can't play the blues]. Music is for everybody.

You debunked another myth: speed equals greatness... You always stressed precision and good taste over speed.

I'm not very fast. Simply, I do what I do. I don't try to do what you do or what they do or what anybody else does. I just do what I do and try to do it as good as I possibly can. Stevie Ray Vaughan was very fast, and there are many today — I could mention a lot [of names] — that are extremely fast and do their thing very well. Many times I wish I could do what they do. But I must accept the fact that I am me and I can only do what I do. There comes a time when you realize you are you. It doesn't matter who your idol is. You realize you are at your best when you do what you do best, which is being yourself. That's my advice to all young musicians.

Without a doubt, you're the greatest living legend of the blues...

[interrupting] I would say "with doubts," because I don't see it that way. [laughs]

Who, then?

There are so many... I'm not a critic. I couldn't tell you who it is. Except for this: I believe Eric Clapton is the number one rock and roll guitarist, and he plays the blues better than many of us.

Even yourself?

Yes. But there are so many guitarists... And so many styles, like flamenco. Most Spaniards and Hispanics are leaders of flamenco and other guitar styles. I have a friend in Spain, I can't remember his name right now...

Raimundo Amador?

Yes! Yes! He's fantastic. What I mean to say is: besides the blues, there are a lot of people in other styles that are exceptional. There was a Spaniard called Andrés Segovia [1893-1987]. To me, he's the father of guitar. Nobody is better than him. And within the blues tradition, in my opinion nobody is better than Muddy Waters and others on that level. A lot of people think Robert Johnson was the best. I don't argue with them, but I don't agree. I think [Alfonzo] "Lonnie" Johnson [1899-1970] was the best blues guitarist in history. That's my opinion. But when people say Whites, Hispanics or people from other countries can't play the blues, that's a myth. It's not true.

Can you tell and identify the love showered upon you by different cultures? Can you tell the differences? Or is it always the same?

Of course it's different: they speak in different languages. Every person who speaks that language understands that language better than others. That's understandable. The international crowds are all different because the people are different. However, as I said before, music is for everyone. I can sit and listen to Hispanics or the Japanese play, and whoever plays good will satisfy my ear. Maybe I won't understand the language, but music speaks for itself. Do you know what I was told? "Music itself is a universal language everyone understands, because it speaks to each one of us individually." I believe that.

At Ray Charles' funeral, you were one of the most emotional...

Ray, to me, was one of the greatest musicians I met. And he was a great friend. We recorded together and I think we both started around the same time. I started in '49, playing and as a deejay at a radio station. And Ray started around that time. He was younger, I think he was 73 when he died [he would've been 74 the day before this interview]. By the way, today's my birthday, 79...

Happy Birthday!!

Thanks...

I knew it was in September, but I didn't know the exact date...

[laughs] Today! September 16. Seventy-nine...

Seventy-nine young years...

I don't care about the "young" part. [laughs] You know something? When you have a life as mine, you know it took time to get here and you know that you've survived. You reach a point in which you don't care about age too much and you thank God for allowing you to be here for so long.

Let's get back to Ray Charles. Did you ever forgive Elvis Costello?

I never knew what he said.

OK, then let's move on.

No! I want you to tell me!

Many years ago, after a few drinks, in order to upset someone that was arguing with him he said Ray Charles was "an ignorant nigger." It was a big scandal...

Ignorant nigger?? [big laugh]

He later apologized... and you didn't hear it from me! It surprises me that you didn't know.

You know... When people are high they can say many things [he looks at me like he somehow knows I can understand the concept], because in those moments one doesn't know and he doesn't even care what the devil he's talking about. But I don't think [Costello] had really said that. Ray was a college graduate. He wasn't stupid.

Anything else you want to add?

Muchas gracias. And it's an honor to be in Texas, a musically self-sufficient state that doesn't need anyone to come and teach anything.

The following year, on May 10, 2005, we spoke in person inside his tour bus, minutes before his show at Sunset Station in San Antonio.

"Enrique? Let's go. Mr. King is waiting for you," said his son and manager Willie. B.B. King is sitting in front of a laptop, fully focused on a web page about "Noisy Reptiles," or something like that. He looked up, smiled, greeted my wife and exclaimed, "Nooo... Don't worry about it!" when I told him, "I'll be brief, we don't have much time."

It was almost two months after Pappo's passing.

When did you find out about Pappo's death?

Much later, maybe a week later after it happened. Some friends told me. They later sent me the papers and described to me in English what the papers said.

You can get all romantic and say, "he died on his own terms," or you can get practical and say, "it was a terrible accident," or you can say that he blew it because you don't drink and drive. Who knows...?

You just said it: Who knows? You answered your own question: Who knows? I don't. I wasn't there. All I know is what friends tell me.

How did you react when you found out?

I'm not gonna talk too much about it because he was a friend. Just like my son, who is dying from cancer. I can say, "Yes, he's dying from cancer. He's got less than two years to live," but I won't talk about it. Pappo was a good friend, that's... A good friend, you miss. But I'm a believer in God. I believe that God takes us away when He's ready. And regardless of what man is trying to do, when God is ready, I believe, He takes us away. Who am I to be critical of Pappo or anybody else? I'm just a person. And I think that whatever Pappo was doing I'm sure he must have enjoyed it. And if he was happy, I'm happy for him. Even though sometimes we may or may not do things that others think we should or shouldn't do. But if one does something for oneself, without trying to hurt anybody else, I'm with him. One hundred percent. Because every man has to live his own life. And each woman has to live her own life. What are we? Who are we? We're not God. We can't tell what they should do. People are critics, I'm not.

In musical terms, how can you describe Pappo's skills as a guitarist?

I couldn't, he's just himself. Like I am. I'm myself. You describe it, she describes it, they describe it, but I'm B.B. King and I play B.B. King. That's the way Pappo was. To me, at least. Yeah, I miss him, he was a friend, he was *amigo*. He was a good friend.

You recently turned 80...

Yes!

(my photographer, Jaime Carrero, asks him, "What is the formula?")

For what? This is the only time I've been 80 (laughs hard). Well, for one thing, I don't drink. Only this (picks up a can of Diet Coke) and water. I don't smoke and I'm a diabetic, so I try to keep it under control. The doctor gave me my medicine and I'm trying to follow. I rest. Like I'm playing a concert tonight and then I go home and I rest. That's all.

You're doing a lot more talking in your concerts, these days...

I don't think of it. I don't try to measure it. I do what I feel. If I feel like talking, I talk. Sometimes I don't feel like talking and I don't. You understand? Excuse me, may I offer you something?

I'm fine, thanks.

At least, take this. (He hands me a guitar pick with his printed signature on it)

Thanks...! Now, with this [Hurricane] Katrina thing, I can't help but ask you about your many shows there...

I was there maaaaaany times... But it didn't only happen in Louisiana. It also happened in Mississippi, where I'm born.

And nobody talks about it.

I know, but I do.

Why is that?

I don't know, you'll have to ask. (Points to the sky, either God or Bush) I don't know why everything was destroyed. The Supreme Spirit? Simply, nobody talks about [Mississippi] just like nobody talks about New Orleans.

I don't want to get you talking about politics, but...

I'm not a politician. If you ask me politics, I won't answer because I don't know politics. I'm a guitar player. At least, I'm trying to play.

How's [his guitar] Lucille?

Fine, very good. I got a new one. They made a new one for me for my 80th birthday. And tonight I'm going to play her. You have to look at it closely, because it's just a little bit different from the other one. I say that Lucille got a facelift.

What's that on your screen (he's online, reading about "Noisy reptiles")?

I like life. And anything I don't know much about I try to find out. I didn't finish high school, only finished 10th grade. So, there's a lot I don't know. But the years have been wonderful for me, because it has given me a chance to learn a lot of things I wouldn't have known. Things like the computer and software. For example, an elephant: I learned that an elephant has 100 gallons of blood. One hundred gallons! I learned that they have passed through many, many things, even from the Ice Age and way back. I learned that they walk like a professional dancer, on their toes. Then the foot goes out like that (makes gestures with his hand). Now I learned something else and I'm gonna ask you a quiz on it. Do you know the difference between an alligator and a crocodile? [laughs at my ignorance and starts describing the similarities between the pulmonary systems of both animals] But there is one distinctive feature.

I'm clueless...

The length of the head and the teeth. [He demonstrates this by opening and closing his hands, as if the fingers were teeth, and laughs like a child] I learned that today! I learned that today! I try to learn one new thing every day. That way I feel it wasn't a day lost.

Despite of everything, this is a great time to enjoy art, everything is so accessible now...

It's great to be alive. My mother died when I was nine. I had a very hard time. I had no aunts, no parents to take care of me. And growing up I learned that there are a lot of good things that happen. I learned to think of the good things and not the bad things. So today I have to really go back and think of bad things. Even today, it hasn't been all so sugar and honey. But the good things overcome the bad things. And makes me feel very happy to be here and talking to you. I'm 80 years old and it is a fact that wisdom does come with age, as you grow old. You know that, you're married now.

Manu Chao: Raining in Paradise
(*San Antonio Current*, June 27, 2007)

Manu Chao is a soccer fan. He's insane about it, to the point of rooting for Brazil, not his native France, in the final of the 1998 World Cup.

"I want Brazil to win, but if France wins it's OK, because it'll be a slap in the face to all those racist fuckers in power," he told me days before that final. "On the other hand, look at the French team: Zidane, Henry, Vieira... All immigrants, from all races. If they win the World Cup, it'll be a symbol that, with immigrants, we can benefit as a country... and we can kick the soccer world's ass, too."

France won in 1998, but Brazil and Italy won the two subsequent World Cups. If that didn't suck enough, today France has a new president who, well, let's just say he ain't no Zidane.

Not that this matters too much to Manu, who's warming up for the big tour that will happen alter he releases *La Radiolina*, his first solo album since 2001's *Próxima Estación: Esperanza*. And perhaps it was that soccer-fan spirit that kept hands up, bodies shaking, and joints burning at Austin's Stubb's a couple of weeks ago. But Manu's world is not a stoner's world. It's more like a joint on the right, a Red Bull on the left, and a T-shirt with Che on one side and Marley on the other.

It was such a fast and hard-driving party that, even though he performed two encores, he didn't get around to playing two of his biggest Mano Negra-era hits ("Sr. Matanzas" and "Santa Maradona"). And no one noticed.

He talked little and played a lot. But when he did speak, he was clear and wasted no time.

He dedicated "Me gustas tú" and "Welcome to Tijuana" to "those who are dangerous for the future of our kids, those who fight violence with more violence, those who fight violence with Guantánamo."

The September release of *La Radiolina* is the musical equivalent of a rubber match. *Clandestino* (1998) was his immaculately groovy entrance, but while the follow-up kept the groove going, it didn't go beyond. And the rash talk started.

Fito Páez, one of Argentina's top rockers, denied ever saying "I don't like the fact that a Frenchman carrying 16 credit cards comes and tells us what it means to be a Latin American."

"It was all an invention by a Chilean journalist," Fito once told me, before adding "Manu is OK. For the beach he's OK" (a backhanded compliment that makes me suspect he may not have made the infamous insult, but nonetheless has Manu up his ass).

When I tell Manu this, he ignores Fito and looks at the big picture.

"Look," he said to me in Spanish on the phone from Los Angeles, days before coming to Austin and sounding just like Barack Obama (the "*mira*/look" part). "When you're a public person you're exposed to exaggerated adulations and also criticisms. It's always positive to listen to everything and then do your own internal analysis of what you're doing. And I have people around me to tell me if I fucked up. I do my balance not every year, but every night when I go to bed. And I sleep well knowing that my day was honest."

All that matters for Manu is that his music reflects what he calls "Malegría" (roughly translated as "sadppiness"). Things look bleak, but we gotta keep on dancing and bitching. His new single, "Rainin' In Paradize," a fierce rocker that can be downloaded for free at manuchao.net, is the soundtrack of a world in pain. And this time, even the rich white guys are trembling.

"That song travels around some of the suffering points, but there's a lot more," he said. "For a long time, the First World thought it was saved from the problems affecting the Third World. But now, even in the First World, paradises are falling, it also rains there. Problems are global and the tragedies caused by the First World in the Third World are sending their feedback."

And in the middle of all that, art keeps the flame alive.

"We have to remain optimistic. What other choice do we have? But it's very clear: if we look at the world with a little bit of lucidity, for the next 10 or 15 years there's going to be a storm."

Moons Over my Grammys
(*San Antonio Current*, September 19, 2007)

Lady Binx is not the first artist to raise the issue. But, speaking in general terms, to accuse the Latin Grammy of being a "discriminatory" award (you know, if Latino artists are good enough, we should sweep the "Grammy-Grammys" instead of having a separate ceremony) is so passé.

Ever since the Latin Grammys debuted in 2000, the fact that Emilio Estefan was the main motor was enough to piss off a loud minority for a while. Some dismissed the event as "The Emilio Estefan Awards," while others — especially heavyweights Pepe Aguilar, Vicente Fernández, and Los Tigres del Norte — justly complained that Mexican regional music (70 percent of the market) was represented in less than 10 percent of the event's TV time.

Gradually, however, everyone cooled off.

"Things changed for the better," Latin Grammy and three-time Grammy winner Aguilar told *Rumbo* last year in San Antonio. "There's still a lot to do, but I think they're getting there."

Tigres del Norte won and appeared in the awards show, and Fernández seemingly contracted amnesia as soon as LARAS (the Latin Academy of Recording Arts & Sciences) honored him as Person of the Year in 2002 with a star-filled tribute dinner and a live appearance on the telecast.

Fact # 1: The "Grammy-Grammy" already gives "Grammy-Grammys" to Latin artists in eight categories, but to expect that La Raza will or should take over the Grammy is just plain bullshit. It ain't gonna happen and it shouldn't happen. Period. We might get a Shakira or a Ricky Martin here and there, but that's it. As far as I'm concerned, I'm happy seeing people like Aterciopelados from time to time on *Saturday Night Live* or Juanes on *The Tonight Show*. But those categories are useful and Latinos are being heard, as when Eddie Palmieri said "Fuck this shit!" and the "new" Latin jazz category was created.

Fact # 2: The amount of deserving artistry (and, yes, garbage too) in Latin music is jaw-dropping, and a separate awards show was needed. And thanks to the Latin Grammy, the careers of out-of-the-loop serious artists such as Mercedes Sosa, Jorge Drexler, Juanes (now a mainstream superstar), Bebe, Aterciopelados, Julieta Venegas, Fito Páez and many others have been recognized and the quality of mainstream pop has vastly improved, even though there's still plenty of crap around.

And historically, those best served by the mere existence of the Latin Grammy have been the *alternativos* and *rockeros*, who find in the Latin Grammy the outlet still denied them by mainstream TV and radio. This year, a band like El Cuarteto de Nos, from my native Uruguay (Latin America's smallest Spanish-language market) earned a deserved nomination for Song of the Year ("Yendo a la casa de Damián"). Before the Latin Grammy era, Cuarteto de Nos was a talented group doomed to obscurity, except locally.

The *alternativos* are not the only artists who enjoy the special attention, as was demonstrated by the recent announcement of the nominees for the 8th annual Latin Grammys (November 8 in Las Vegas).

Critically acclaimed *merenguero* Juan Luis Guerra returned to secular dance fusion after a surprisingly tolerable Christian album and scored five nominations, leading the pack. Ricky Martin (!) followed with four, as did post-reggaetón sensation Calle 13.

That trio of top nominees says a lot about the state of the Latin music industry (and I don't mean what's featured on the radio or Univisión): Guerra is a Berklee graduate who feels the Beatles as much as tropical music and who is a motherfucking monster of a songwriter. And Ricky is not what you think: His *MTV Unplugged* was a carefully planned work of art because, instead of looking for, say, Emilio Estefan, he called Spain's alternative flamenco pop Chambao to record a jewel called "Tu recuerdo," which deserves to be Song of the Year. And Calle 13 is the hottest and smartest Puerto Rican act, a duo that gets closer and closer to Café Tacuba and further away from Daddy Yankee (thank God). Of course, Guerra will win, but who cares?

My point is this: It's bad enough that many of the best Latin albums of the year (in any genre) are not released in the U.S. The internet improved the situation a little bit, but I want to be able to go to the store and get the damn CD, I want to touch it. And a Latin Grammy nomination is a powerful tool that enables the music to be more easily available everywhere.

After all, it's all about the music, isn't it?

PS: Don't get me wrong: I don't know Lady Binx but I'm dying to hear her upcoming album. And if she raps as well as she speaks and thinks, I think I'm gonna like her. Not that she cares, but … who knows? One day she could be nominated for a "Grammy-Grammy."

If not, we'll always Miami.

Café Tacvba: Where It's At
(*San Antonio Current*, October 17, 2007)

When Café Tacvba came out of nowhere (Mexico City, to be exact) in 1992, few realized that we were witnessing the arrival of the New Messiahs of Spanish-language rock.

"I think they're ridiculous," a then-prominent L.A. deejay from Argentina told me. This same person refused to play Mexican music at his club because "we don't want the club full of those people" (I'm paraphrasing).

OK, the guy was kind of deaf and a racist prick, but in a way you can't blame him: Café Tacvba had a singer with a raunchy voice, charro hat, campesino sandals, and a different moniker for each new album (Ruben Albarrán); a bassist, Joselo Rangel, playing a *tololoche* (acoustic stand-up bass); a guitarist (Quique Rangel) who had a simple Spanish acoustic guitar instead of a Fender Stratocaster; and a drummer that... well, there was no drummer: Emmanuel Del Real did everything with a drum machine.

It wasn't until *Cuatro caminos* (2003) that the band surprised everyone by doing the unthinkable: adding real drums and electric guitar. The change only proved that Tacvba's status as critics' darlings was intact and that the foursome could shine in whatever format they chose to play.

It was once said that Maldita Vecindad's *El circo* (1991) was Mexican rock's *Sgt. Pepper's*, and that Café Tacvba's *Re* (1994) the White Album (though it was red, actually). But the new Tacvba album, *Sino* (released on October 9), is Café Tacvba outdoing itself. It sounds as if The Who, The Beatles, Depeche Mode, the Beach Boys, Pink Floyd and the Sex Pistols fell into a huge blender at a mom-and-pop bakery in Mexico City.

"Well, I like it more than *Cuatro caminos*, that's for sure," Albarrán (named "Ixxi xoo" for this album) says in Spanish, laughing as if there was something embarrassing about the Grammy-winning *Cuatro...* When pressed, he backtracks: "I like the album, but in this one we... we..."

We kicked ass, he should've said. With Victor Indrizzo (Beck) on drums, the Tacvbos recorded an epic album that not only dwarfs the competition, but annihilates it. Maná may sell more records, Soda Stereo's influence may be more easily acknowledged, but when it comes down strictly to music, no one can touch Tacvba.

"It's one of the 10 best bands in the world in any genre or language, period," according to two-time Oscar winner Gustavo Santaolalla, who "discovered" and produced most of Tacvba's albums.

And, who knows? They may even go back to the early days.

"It's hard to go back to the drum machine, isn't it?" Albarrán says. "The power of a real drum is unparalleled, incredible. But that doesn't mean we'll never use a drum machine again."

Even though they've never been overtly political, on every Tacvba album their biting humor has debunked left and right alike, but this time the targets are more specific. In "Gracias," the band uses sarcasm to thank who-knows-who for "the democracy and freedoms" that we enjoy. Is it Bush, is it Mexico's government? Probably both.

"If the glove fits, put it on," Albarrán says. "Unfortunately, Mexico has been divided in a terrible way. Obviously, that's the game politicians play: to divide us. And we put on T-shirts that don't have anything to do with us. How can we be divided for any stupid thing instead of finding a point of encounter?"

More than any other album, *Sino* (a ying-yang-ish wordplay between "if not," "but" and "yes/no," among other combinations) is an album about real freedom, not the one that the "free world" wants us to believe in.

"In terms of countries, I don't believe there is such a thing as 'freedom,'" he says. "There are too many circumstances that don't allow us to have freedom, and they're always cheating us with that so-called 'freedom.' The only freedom we can aspire to is inner freedom. And the United States, supposedly the great nation of freedom, has one of the most abused and slave-like peoples in the world."

Santaolalla once told me that out of all the artists he's ever recorded, only Café Tacvba would spend breaks in the studio reading books. Maybe that's why Café Tacuba sounds so good: they make fun music, but they don't eat shit.

Maria Rita: Brazil's First Daughter
(personal blog, New York, November 2, 2007; original conversation in Spanish, English, and Portuguese)

(I really don't remember what the hell I was doing in NY on that day, but this happened in the lobby of some hotel in Manhattan)

To many (including myself), your mother [Elis Regina] was Brazil's greatest female singer, but she died when you were very little. Do you have any memories of her?

I don't have too many. Almost no memories of my mother. Something here and there, but not many.

Do you listen to her albums?

A little. In my teenage years I listened to them a little bit because I felt the necessity of understanding my roots, my history. So, I sought to read her interviews and to listen a little bit of her music in order to understand how my mother thought. The fact that my mother sang and *believed* so much, both politically and personally, was a present, a gift.

Yesterday, [LARAS, The Latin Recording Academy] gave an award to your father, César Camargo Mariano. How was it?

(laughs) Unexpected. (laughs again) The members of the Academy didn't know I was there in the ceremony, so they called me to the stage to... (she can't find the words)

English, Portuguese, Spanish... Anything you want. We can go back and forth.

English... I'm not working [sic] anymore. OK, thank you. I'm not functioning anymore. It was scary! "You have an interview in 20 minutes!" "What???!!!" Sorry... They didn't know I was there, so they called me on the stage and... They didn't tell my father either that I was there, so... They play this song of his, and then they played the video and then my dad went up onstage and all I did was stay onstage and cry... (laughs) It was pretty emotional. The song they picked to honor him was beautiful. It's called "Samambaia," a very beautiful song, one of his best-known songs. I just cried, that's all I did. I was very touched.

Was *Maria Rita* (2003), your debut produced by Tom Capone, a one-time thing or you were planning to make more albums together?

Without a doubt, without a doubt [we were going to make more albums].

As a producer, he was the most nominated artist at the 2004 Latin Grammy and, between the two of you, that night you won three awards. But that same night he died in a motorcycle accident in Los Angeles, after the post-Grammy party. In other words, you went from Heaven to Hell in one night. I don't even know how to ask you this, but…

Yeah, that's just that… There's no way of… It was very strange. It was all very weird, and to this day I just don't… [gets teary-eyed]

***Segundo* [2005, co-produced by Maria Rita and Lenine], is another wonder, but much more naked…**

Naked. That's the word.

It's very beautiful, musically and aesthetically but, unfortunately, some idiotic colleagues…

[laughs hard]…with all due respect… [more laughs]

…believe that it wasn't as good as the first one because it's not as "explosive" or as "flashy" as the first one…

[continues laughing] Thank you. First of all, thank you. [turning to publicist Tracy Mann: "He just had a fit right now."]

Tracy: "A fit of enthusiasm?"

MR: No, he's just mad at some people.

Yeah, those who think the second album is not as good as the first one...

Tracy: We're mad at them too.

MR: [with a "mean" voice] They're silly people. Yes. Aesthetically, as you said, everything starts with the song. As we say in Brazil, if I'm an interpreter, just give me anything and I'll sing it, but that wouldn't be real, it wouldn't be truthful to the listeners and to myself, firstly. It's funny because the sound, *la sonoridade* [of the album] is very similar to the first one, actually. They're both recorded live, and the second one is completely recorded live. I don't know what they expected. (laughs) It got to a point in which I said, "If I do something completely different, they'll claim that I don't have a personality, that I don't know what I'm doing. And if I do the same thing, they'll say that I'm working on a formula and that the album is not as good as the first one." So, to start things off, I was already losing, so I just did whatever I felt I wanted to do at that time. It had more to do with me, and with my messages and sense of aesthetics, and sounds, than... I didn't do it for them. You know what I mean? And the decision of making a DVD with "the making of" of the recording was also a decision that... The feeling I have is that people have an idea of me as an untouchable diva, do you understand? So, I decided to show them the human side of the singer.

You always include at least one song in Spanish. First it was "Dos gardenias" and then one by my countryman Jorge Drexler, "Mal intento." How did you end up with those two songs?

I always loved "Dos gardenias" very, very, very much. When I saw Buena Vista Social Club in '95, I believe, I loved it and one day, in the studio, I asked Tom Capone, "Do you like 'Dos gardenias?'" Tom became serious and told me, "I like 'Dos gardenias' very much." So, we started playing it and trying different things. With "Mal intento," I met Drexler in Brazil and we went to a restaurant for dinner. We talked a lot and, eventually, he sent me two or three songs, and "Mal intento" was there. And I identified with the song. It's *so* simple, and people take that for a bad song because it has no screaming and yelling. It just very... It doesn't have to be... There's no need for anything else in there, you know what I mean?

And it's perfect for your voice. You're not the typical singer who goes [imitating Mariah Carey or Christina Aguilera] AAAAUUUOOOOOOOAAAAA, always singing as if saying, "Look what I can do with my voice." I don't know… You just open your mouth and the voice comes out on its own, you don't have to do anything, it's an independent entity… You're the Brazilian singer who most respects the song.

Thank you, that's truly what it is. The way I see it, I have to add on to their work, to the songwriter's work. They write something, and they trust me with their creation. That's like giving your child for someone else to take care of. You know what I'm saying? To do something with them. It's a scary thought, so I usually try to… There's this one song in *Segundo*, where I sing it wrong. "Casa pre-fabricada." I changed a word while I was recording it. Instead of "sob" I said "sobre."

On what line?

Ah… (thinks) Right in the beginning. "*Abre os teus armários/eu estou a te esperar/para ver deitar o sol/sobre os teus braços castos.*"

Did you change it on purpose?

No. I changed it because I wasn't paying attention, I was recording and… I don't know. But the take was very good, I liked it a lot. So, I called the composer [Marcelo Camelo] and told him, "Look…" And he told me, "No, no, no… If it's fit to go, go." And then he listened to the song and…

…and he loved it, and you both ended up in a long embrace [as seen on the DVD]. You were so scared, but when he kept repeating, "How pretty!" you felt relieved and went to embrace him.

Yes, yes, yes… I felt the need to show it to him, so he wouldn't be mad at me… (laughs).

You said that song makes you want to fall in love again.

Yes. And that's what I mean when I [said that I] try to add on to their work. I try to respect it.

Eat a little while I ask you the questions. Then, when it's time for the photos, I'll ask the waiter to put the plate on the microwave. [she laughs and makes a gesture and noise of a microwave's revolving plate]... MPB [Brazilian Popular Music], jazz, interpreter... How do *you* feel? Your music always has a jazzy feeling.

I never had any preconceptions... Is that a word? No musical prejudice. When I lived in New York I would go to salsa clubs. I even listened to... I had a Korean roommate, and even Korean music I would listen to. So, I was always very... I just listened to everything and I think that that's... That might be something. And then, the passion. The passion explains it all. That's what I do.

I want to talk a little bit about two songs I like a lot: "Ciranda do mundo" and "Lavadeira do rio." Lenine's original version of "Lavadeira..." is completely different.

He was one of the very few Brazilian artists I would listen to while I lived in the USA. Other than Tom Jobim, Caetano [Veloso], [Gilberto] Gil, Marisa Monte, there wasn't much that was getting here. I found out about Lenine through my brothers. I was already living in Brazil when I was putting a band together to perform, and I just loved that song. And it talks about "Rita" and I went, "OK." We were rehearsing and playing along with it, to make it a little less open than Lenine's version of it, which is the original. And then I ended up performing it so many times that I included it in the first album. And "Ciranda do mundo" also is from Pedro Luís e a Parede, from Rio [de Janeiro], and they're awesome [the song was written by Edu Krieger]. It has... Again, that happens to me a lot. I listen to a song and it just hits me, "I have to sing it." Sometimes a song won't sound as good when I sing it as the original, so I just don't record it, I don't do anything to it, even though I might like singing it a lot. "Ciranda do mundo" worked out fine. We tried a whole bunch of different versions for it, and this had a little Latin feel to it, similar to "Lavadeira..." Not in the Latino feel, but it has an urban sonority to it, very down to Earth.

While we're at it, I ask for your blessings to continue playing a *candombe* version of the song...

(laughter). Yes, of course! Please continue!

Tonight, you have three more nominations. Do you think about winning? How much do you care?

I was thinking about that as I was coming here. It's so bizarre... I don't have any expectations. I don't think I'm gonna win. "Win..." That word, in and of itself, is awful. I think we don't compete against each other. There's got to be a change in the thinking of it. We're participating in the same categories. I'm not against anybody. I don't want you *not* to win. In any case, I don't think I'm gonna "get" the award. There's so much other stuff that's going on in the categories, I just don't... But...

Having said that...

(laughs) "Having said that..." I do consider myself — honest to God, I'm not trying to be cute or anything — already a winner, 'cause my father has been honored, and I'm here for the fun. This time I'm gonna try to have fun, because last year I was so in awe of everything. "Oh, that's that dude from that movie... Wow, that's that dude from the TV show..." Really in awe... So, this time around I'll try to have some fun. I do consider myself... I got the nominations from the Latin Academy. So much has been said about this album, sometimes I feel it's been misunderstood, but I'm here. I'm a survivor.

Great album. And in due time...

[interrupting] I'm not in a rush.

I know, but I meant the album will acquire more value with the passing of time. It's a classic.

You can't expect second albums to be... The first one was unanimously... Unanimous [praise]. I didn't get that. And the second time I knew that I was going to get heat. So, I just blocked it out.

You got mixed reactions also in Brazil?

Also.

What were they expecting? Sparks coming out of your head, three

tongues, your head spinning like Linda Blair in *The Exorcist*? It's a great album!

(laughs) I don't know. And I'm glad we don't know.

Are you already thinking about the third one?

No, I'm not going to record in 2007, but I'm going to participate in projects and...

Oh, shit... I almost forgot to ask you about "Soledad..."

Oh, God... Brazilian critics didn't like it.

They don't know what a *zamba* is!

[laughter] Exactly. Again, such a simple and direct song and it's such a moment where you can tell that Jorge [Drexler], or whoever wrote it, let's not give names cause it's all a little weird, that the person who wrote it was completely naked and in pain. It's absolutely unbelievable. And I recorded it... There was an awards ceremony in Rio, I was nominated as well, and I was all dressed up, the long dress, the gown, heels, and the hair, and I had like a... Hair extensions, and make up, and the ceremony ended and I had to go to the studio to send it back to Jorge in Spain, and it was such a moment. I'm all dressed up, and I go [sweetly] "*Soledaaad... aquí están mis credenciales...*" ["Solitude... Here are my credentials"] Completely in love with the song, going through all my pain, along with it, and then I opened the newspaper and "It's a bad song." I'm like, "You know what? You all don't know what you're doing." They didn't get it! That's so sad. It's sad for them. It's simple, and it's pretty. It doesn't have to be all full of *puajjj* [makes a gesture as if emptying a bucket full of stuff] for it to be a good song. It doesn't!

I'm imagining a caricature of you singing the "Soledad" with a hairdo and make up...

[laughs] You have no idea what it was like! The engineer of all my things, Alvaro Alencar (he has to be there whenever I go to the studio), at one point he goes, "I don't believe what I'm seeing... This is a chapter in and of

itself of your biography. What is this?" All dressed up, and singing, 4 o' clock in the morning.

Does Jorge know the details of how you recorded it?

No, I don't believe so. He called me on the phone after he listened to it. I recorded the whole song and he edited it later, we didn't record together. He called me, and he was screaming: "How beautiful!!!!!" He was so excited, "Blah blah blah blah!" and I go "I'm glad you liked it" and then he goes, "OK, bye." That's all we talked about that. Wonderful, wonderful, wonderful song. Can you imagine someone going through some experience and sitting at home and thinking, "Ok, solitude, here I am, it's you and me now." C'mon, now!!! How can someone say that's not beautiful?? I don't get it. I don't get it. Oh, well...

It's one of the best songs about solitude I've ever heard, and it reminds me a lot to "Esa noche," by Café Tacvba. *"No me hubieras dejado esa noche/porque esa misma noche encontré un amor"* [*"You shouldn't have left me that night/because that same night I found a love"*]. **At the end of the song, one realizes that the new love was, precisely, solitude.**

"Esa noche..." It's the same... Wow... It's the same message from "Veja bem, meu bem" [from *Maria Rita*]. "*Veja bem, meu bem/Sinto te informar/ que arranjei alguém/pra me confortar*." The guy is telling, through a letter, or whatever, to the woman... Between the lines you can read that the woman thinks he's cheating on her. And he goes, "Yes, I'm trying to tell you that I did find somebody to comfort me, in my lonely lights." And that somebody is solitude.

Solitude in music is constant, but the great ones always figure out new ways to find magic in a highly explored theme...

Damn! That's *saudade*... *Saudade* is a little different... You can only... Fuck... The story you can understand, but the very last line... "*Enquanto isso, navegando eu vou sem paz. Sem ter um porto, quase morto, sem um casi...*" And then, "*E eu nunca vou te esquecer amor/Mas a solidão deixa o coração neste leva e traz... Saiba, traições snao bem mais sutis.*" You should know that betrayal is a lot more subtle than, you know... Sort of like, if I'm betraying, you, if I'm cheating on you, you would know. "*Se eu te troquei/não foi por maldade.*". Did you get it?

***No fue por maldad*...It wasn't out of malice...**

No fue por maldad... "*Se eu te troquei/não foi por maldade... Amor, veja bem, arranjei alguém,*" I did find somebody, "*chamado saudade*" [named *saudade*]. So, it's the very last line of the song.

But *saudade* in Portuguese...

It's kind of like solitude. Kiiiiind of...

In Portuguese you don't have a word for solitude?

No, no. No other language. No other language. There's no absolute translation. There's no word that actually sums up... *Saudade*...

***Saudade* is like *nostalgia*, longing, right?**

Yes. It's *like*, sort of. A nostalgia that has a little happiness and a little sadness, and a little bit of everything a person can feel for another or for something. *Saudade*... For me, when I say the word "*saudade*" I do feel a little bit of pain, also. It's tiny. So, it has a little sense of solitude.

Assassination Tango
(*San Antonio Current*, January 8, 2008)

"Yeah, we're going to South America. You know, *Uruguayyy*…"
— Answering machine in the Coen Brothers film *Blood Simple*.

* * *

"The problem with Putumayo is that they don't like tango," a colleague told me a few months ago in Miami.
My friend was right.
The multifaceted, cool, gorgeous-looking, Starbucks-friendly, commercially successful (but artistically uneven) label had only one tango track in its extensive collection (judging by a "tango" search on putumayo.com). Weird, considering the label specializes in popular World Music, and tango has proven to be one of its most reliable genres, both in its purest and most contemporary, experimental forms.

That's why I was pleased and surprised when I received Putumayo's recently released *Tango Around the World* collection. Crissa Requate, publicity manager for Putumayo, says the label "loves tango" and "was waiting for just the right mix of songs" to represent the genre.

For starters, the album's title is a little misleading: This is not a straight-ahead tango CD. It's comprised of an interesting — and, at times, superb — selection of international nuevo-tango exponents, from Argentina to Serbia and Finland. These are the the more roots-oriented guys right behind heavyweights Bajofondo and Gotan Project (Disclosure: I wrote Bajofondo's liner notes), the main exponents of the fusion of tango with dance and electronica.

Tango Around the World's complete liner notes (in English, Spanish, and French) score a three-pointer when they correctly state that Argentina has no monopoly on the roots of tango: Cuba and, especially, Uruguay deserve a good piece of the pie. (Disclosure #2: I'm Uruguayan. Disclosure #3: I don't give a fuck about Uruguayaness, but facts are facts.)

Why is it, then, that *Tango Around The World* doesn't have a single track from Uruguay or Cuba? While Cuba's contribution to tango merely (and significantly) lies on the fact that the roots of tango are the *danzón* and the *habanera*, it was in Uruguay and, mainly, Argentina that tango developed and became what it is today. To have a tango collection of anything without a track from Uruguay is like having a rock collection without an American or British band in it.

Requate says several Uruguayan tracks were dropped "due to repertoire or licensing issues."

Call me a Uruguayan crybaby, but this is nothing personal, just the facts, ma'am: Why do Argentinians call tango "*argentino*" when *candombe* (the Afro-Uruguayan rhythm) and *murga* (the Spain-influenced vocal style developed in Uruguay) are considered (by them) as *música rioplatense* (music made on both sides of the De la Plata river, which unites and divides Buenos Aires and Montevideo)? And why do Argentinians love to say "*argentinos y uruguayos* are all the same" but when you go to any record store you find Carlos Gardel (tango's greatest singer) in the Argentina section? (He died with a Uruguayan passport stating he was born in Tacuarembó, Uruguay, but his nationality is disputed between France, Argentina, and Uruguay. My take: who cares? He sings better and better every time, even though he died in 1935, and he's more *rioplatense* than the *mate*, whether he was born in Toulouse of Ouagadougou.)

But those who know, know. Two-time Oscar winner and Bajofondo founder Gustavo Santaolalla once told me that "Buenos Aires is the capital of tango, and Montevideo the capital of *candombe*)." And Uruguayan Jaime Roos, one of the most influential *rioplatense* artists of the last 30 years, admits that "there was always tango in Uruguay, but most of the best tango was made in Argentina," and "there was always candombe in Argentina, but," he adds, "the best candombe is from Uruguay."

However, when it comes to tango, Uruguay (except for the bi-national Latin Grammy-winning Bajofondo project) was wiped from the map long ago.

In Robert Duvall's *Assassination Tango*, he asks Luciana Pedraza's character (I'm paraphrasing), "Do you think I'd have a chance if I were younger?" The girl replies, "Maybe you have a chance now."

Uruguayans, who come from a tiny country with a population of a little more than three million, should ask: "Do you think if we were a bigger, more influential country, our contributions to tango would be properly acknowledged?"

In light of Jorge Drexler's Best Original Song win at the Oscars in 2005 (for "Al otro lado del río," included in *The Motorcycle Diaries*) and a new generation of talented rock and electronic artists, maybe Uruguay does have a chance. But, as of today, tango's official story remains closer to Pedraza's greeting to Duvall: "Welcome to Argentina, my friend."

Cachao, the Mambo Father
(*San Antonio Current*, April 2, 2008)

The passing of Israel López "Cachao" — the great Cuban bassist, composer, and bandleader — in Miami on March 22 at age 89 from kidney complications, was well reported by the Spanish media. But his funeral, which took place Wednesday, March 26, at Little Havana's St. Michaels Church, was overshadowed (at least on Spanish-language TV) by the usual *chismes* and the repercussions of Emilio Navaira's life-threatening bus accident on Easter Sunday.

I had been told that Tejano music was dead and Emilio a mere has-been. In fact, Emilio proved, under tragic circumstances, that he's lost none of his star power, and his hospitalization eclipsed the death of one of the key figures of 20th century Latin music.

The "Mambo" *danzón* Cachao co-wrote with his brother Orestes in 1938 is believed to signify the first time the word had been used, thus setting the stage for the craze popularized worldwide by Dámaso Pérez Prado in 1943. Cachao's resurgent glory in the mid-'90s, when he was hailed as "the true father of mambo," however, didn't come without controversy.

"That's what Cachao always told me: 'Pérez Prado is the mambo king, but I'm its father,'" actor Andy García says to me over the phone from Los Angeles. García, a lifelong Cuban music buff and percussionist, was Cachao's producer and bandmember from 1994 until Cachao's death.

But Cachao should ultimately be remembered for his stirring *descargas* (jam sessions), his unparalleled skill with the stand-up bass, and the fact that he was one of the very few who would perform *danzones* live. He won two Grammys (for *Master Sessions Vol. 1* and *¡Ahora sí!*) and two Latin Grammys (for *¡Ahora sí!* and *El arte del sabor*, a collaboration with pianist Bebo Valdés and percussionist Patato Valdés), but he deserved to win most of his countless nominations.

And even though he recorded three very good albums between 1970 and 1986, his name was only known by diehard fans or the top Latin jazz musicians in Cuba and abroad.

"Those who need to know who Cachao is, know," Paquito D'Rivera, the great clarinetist and co-founder of Irakere, who worked on both *Master Sessions*, once memorably put it. At the CD-release party in 1994, D'Rivera told Cachao and those who wanted to hear that he wouldn't attend the Gonzalo Rubalcaba show that was taking place that same night in Los Angeles (Rubalcaba was still associated with the Castro regime by the Miami crowd). Most agreed, but Cachao simply smiled and looked elsewhere, without saying a word. For Cachao, it was the music, and Afro-Cuban music in particular, the only thing that really mattered.

García deserves credit for taking Cachao out of the Miami bar mitzvahs and wedding ceremonies at which he was performing in the mid-'90s. He did it first with the fascinating *Cachao: Como su ritmo no hay dos* ("Like his rhythm there is no other") documentary, then with six superb albums. But he also received a lot of flak for sitting down with Cachao's orchestra and getting as much screen time as the maestro.

"That was a completely spontaneous thing," García says. "It was Cachao who asked me to play. It's easy for people to criticize because they think you're doing something that's self-serving. That's the cynical nature of society at times. But it doesn't matter what they say, because the reality is that we were there for him. And everybody who showed up for everything, whether the records or the concerts or whatever, we did for him; they all know I never got a penny for it."

What García did for Cachao he also did for singer Rolando Laserie and almost did for pianist Bebo Valdés.

"Early on, Paquito [D'Rivera] came up to me and said, 'We have to record Bebo Valdés,' and I said, 'That would be great,'" García recalls. "Immediately, Paquito went and recorded him and he formulated a relationship between [*Calle 54* director and Oscar winner] Fernando Trueba and Nat Chediak, and look at the legacy that Bebo was able to bring forth, also in his later years. And that's great. We were also able to record Rolando Laserie's last song ["El guapachoso"] in the *Master Sessions*."

At the end of *Cachao: Como su ritmo no hay dos*, Cachao says, "I'm an old man and I won't be around forever, but what's important to me is that the youth continue the tradition."

"I gave him the opportunity of 16 years of more music, and he had a glorious life," García says. "He was able to fulfill his musical genius with the world, and that's something that makes me and everybody else who stepped up to the plate proud."

Spanish Harlem Orchestra: Salsa for Post-graduates
(*San Antonio Current*, April 30, 2008)

During the early stages of Rubén Blades' revolutionary and influential solo work (starting with *Buscando América* in 1984, the first of three unprecedented trombone-less salsa albums), Oscar Hernández played a pivotal role.

As pianist and musical director of Seis del Solar, the band Blades assembled inspired by the notable Joe Cuba Sextet (or "Sextette") of the '50s and '60s, the Bronx-born Hernández (who previously had spent some years with the great Ray Barreto) was the perfect arranger for Blades' challenging music and socially conscious lyrics. And even though Cuba didn't use trombones either, Blades was the first one in the salsa era to give up the instrument in favor of vibraphone and keyboards. All at a time when having a salsa orchestra without trombones was like having a heavy metal band without guitars. It proved to be a risk worth taking.

"It was more a risk for Rubén than for myself, to be honest," Hernández says on the phone from Amsterdam. "Thanks to his work with Willie Colón, he was the number-one salsa star of the time, and what he did was to turn his back to the sound that propelled him to that place. On the other hand, his success with Willie was possible, in great part, thanks to [Blades'] voice and songs. But he stuck to the new sound and we were able to stay together for 13 years and make music that stills sounds good today and of which I'm proud."

Founded in 2000, Hernández's current group, the Spanish Harlem Orchestra (which plays at the Empire Theatre on May 1), is arguably the best tropical orchestra in the world (if you ask me, only Cuba's Afro Cuban All Stars even come close). With a mix of solid originals and totally re-arranged covers, SHO pays tribute to the golden era of NY's *salsa dura* (the glorious hard salsa of the 1970s), the opposite to the tepid *salsa romántica* and commercial Dominican merengue and bachata that seem to control today's tropical music market.

"Sincerely, originally we were only going to record an album with the concept of recovering what *salsa romántica* had destroyed, but we weren't expecting the success that we've had," Hernández says. As it turned out, SHO released three albums, the second of which won a Grammy for Best Salsa/Merengue Album (*Across 110th Street*, with Blades as a guest).

Why is it, then, that listeners and dancers dig SHO, but musicians refuse to follow its musical path in favor of more commercial crap?

"I'm not exactly sure," Hernández says. "To be perfectly honest, when you see the band now, it's a level that's hard to match. I mean... merengue is horrible, man. The only person to me who is playing merengue the way it should be played is Juan Luis Guerra. I'm a fan of his, and I'm honored to have recorded on three of his records. The merengue I grew up with in the '60s was good, but the merengue other people do now is kind of obscene and so un-musical."

Blades' songs, though excellent, were a dancer's nightmare (full of stops, pauses, twists and turns), but SHO has a more straight-forward, dancer-friendly approach. Musically, however, it's as good as it gets.

So a message to the dancers: You'll be able to dance at the Empire Theatre show, but you better be ready to listen as well.

"The good thing about SHO is that we're not that interested to play at salsa dance events," Hernández says. "[Those places] tend to trivialize what we do. When you go see SHO in concert, you're treated to a really good show on a musical level, regardless of the fact that it's salsa. Sometimes it's a stereotype that we fight.

"When you see us live, you realize we're not just a dance orchestra, even though at the end everyone is dancing. But we're a concert band and promoters need to promote it as such. We need to raise people's consciousness about our music, not only about SHO, but in general. We're not about 'get up and dance.' Latinos also like to enjoy music from an aesthetic level."

Why We Still Love Che
(*San Antonio Current*, January 21, 2009)

Those who are weak don't fight.
Those who are stronger might fight
for an hour.
Those who are stronger still might fight
for many years.
The strongest fight
their whole life.
Those are the indispensable ones.
— **Bertolt Brecht**

[Spoiler alert for those living in a jar: this column will reveal the fate of the hero in Soderbergh's new movie.]

Rule number one when drinking *mate*: You don't stir it. If you stir it, you ruin it. And please, stop spelling it *"maté."* It's MATE [MA-tay, or something like that], for Krishna's sake.

In 1969's hilarious *Che!*, the fact that Jack Palance was Fidel Castro and Omar Sharif played Che Guevara was irresistibly absurd enough. But when Sharif appeared in a scene stirring his *mate* (the national stimulating herb infusion of Argentina and Uruguay, also consumed in Chile, Paraguay, Bolivia, Brazil and, I bet you, New Jersey), as if it were 5 o' clock tea, that was a classic moment documenting what happens when clueless people handle touchy subjects.

By his own admission, Steven Soderbergh didn't have too many clues about the Che Guevara beyond the poster (taken by Alberto Korda, it is the most reproduced photograph in history), but at least he seems to have done his homework. I haven't seen Soderbergh's two-part epic starring Benicio Del Toro (who took Best Actor at the Cannes Film Festival), which opened to limited release in December and nationwide (excluding, of course, San Antonio, where it's scheduled to open February 27). The movie revives talk about the idolized guerrilla, but also reminds us that those who hate him often hate him more than they hate Fidel. Compared to Che, some say, Fidel was Mother Teresa. And, in a way, they're probably right.

The main argument used by Che's detractors is that he himself executed several suspected informants in his ranks. He would continue ordering massive executions of alleged torturers after Fidel took power, but many Cuban Americans say too many innocents were thrown into the mix. "He was a murderer," they say. "Che was brave, well-educated, charismatic, but also a disciplined, merciless guerrilla fighter who wouldn't tolerate the smallest crack in his ranks," we Che-niacs repeat in unison.

Soderbergh chose not to include the executions part in the movie, which must've thrilled the folks in Miami.

"The section of his life where he basically became an administrator is kind of its own film," Soderbergh said in *Filmmaker* magazine, "and it's not one that interested me personally." He instead concentrated on the two extremes of Che's life — his victory in Cuba, his defeat in Bolivia.

Like most Che admirers, I think of him as an exemplary man, and I see his defects as further proof of his humanity. But I don't blame the critics who are still scared shitless of him: If you messed with Che, you were lunch.

Why do we love him so much? The fact that he didn't let asthma stop him from fighting a revolution? The fact that he chose ammunition over inhaler when the shit hit the fan in the mountains? The fact that he always fought first, showed up first at work, and was the last to leave? The fact that he cut his salary in half as soon as he was appointed Cuba's Ministry of Industry?

He was brave, and he was no rat.

"Whenever I tried to find out how many people he had with him, where he'd come from, he would smile [at] me and he would say, 'You know I cannot answer that,'" said Félix Rodríguez, the CIA operative who hunted him down in Bolivia, in the documentary *The True Story of Che Guevara* (2007).

Che didn't squeal. And, by all accounts (including the superb critical biography by Jon Lee Anderson), he was brave at the time of his execution. Bolivian soldier Mario Terán put him down with nine bullets, seconds after Che stood in front of him and, looking straight into his eyes, told him "Shoot, coward! You're only going to kill a man." Che died biting his hand to avoid crying out. But, in Latin America and many parts of the world, his ideas resonate louder and clearer than ever.

No, I didn't have to suffer under Fidel Castro. But I am the product of a Third World U.S.-sponsored right-wing military dictatorship that today, supposedly in an age of "peace" and "freedom," still suffers from the inequalities that pissed off Che in the first place. And even though he succeeded in Cuba but failed in changing the rest of the world through revolution, he did set the standard for surrendering oneself to a conviction, and never demanded anything from anybody that he didn't demand of himself. He was the best in battle, the bravest, always in the front lines, and paid the highest price without breaking down. Most important, he never gave up the struggle with himself, and is the embodiment of the kind of indispensable people Brecht wrote about. And yes, he died with a notebook full of poems by Pablo Neruda and others. Che was magic and, as Jean Paul Sartre pointed out, "the most complete human being of our age."

Perhaps if the Bolivians had helped him the way Cuban campesinos helped in Sierra Maestra, the story would have ended differently. But today, ironically, even in Bolivia, you can feel Che's presence — and his victory.

"If we had a Che Guevara [in Bolivia] we'd be easily undergoing huge transformations," said (democratically elected) Bolivian Socialist president Evo Morales. "His principles for a life of sovereignty for Latin America, for the people, are principles we share when we go forward, not only in times of war. Now is when we need a Che, not so much for the armed force, but for the defense of humanity."

It is Soderbergh himself, a relative newcomer to Che's universe, who best articulates why, despite all his imperfections, many of us still remember Che with awe and reverence.

"I realized very late that what I was drawn to in Che was not necessarily the ideology but his willingness to fully engage and his ability to sustain," said Soderbergh. "I think most of us go through periods where we feel like engaging, and then we get tired or frustrated and then we disengage. [Che] never did."

El Moz
(*San Antonio Current*, March 4, 2009; Third Prize, AAN Awards 2010)

In Mexico
I went for a walk to inhale
the tranquil, cool, lover's air
I could sense the hate
of the Lonestar State
And a small voice said, "What can we do?"
(Morrissey's "Mexico")

Thanks to her rendition of Juan Gabriel's ballads, in the world of Latin pop music no Spaniard is more Mexican than the late Rocío Dúrcal. Thanks to his ability to soothe an immigrant's heart without even trying, in the world of rock no one is more Mexican than Morrissey.

It always fascinated me how and why in the country of machos a supposedly gay man like Juan Gabriel could overcome prejudice to become a national icon.

"I have four sons," he once told me in 1995 when I asked him about his sexuality in a *Los Angeles Times* piece. "How many do you have? In show business, if you're male and cute and gracious, people assume you are blah, blah, blah," he added. "But people don't understand that art itself is female — it is full of graciousness, cadence, color, rhythm. It's full of love and grace."

If Juan Gabriel is gay, Morrissey is... Well, he's El Moz. A sexual enigma who has become an iconic underground hero not for what he is, but for what he says and how he says it. No single Anglo solo artist is more beloved in the Latin alternative world than Morrissey.

"To argue that Morrissey's contemporary audience skews Hispanic would be inaccurate," wrote Chuck Klosterman in *SPIN* magazine. "Morrissey's contemporary audience IS Hispanic."

And Morrissey, it seems, couldn't care less.

"I'm going to sing a couple more songs... then all of you can go back to Mexicali," said Morrissey years ago at a concert in Arizona, where the crowd was screaming a loud, soccer-style "Me-hee-CAW, Me-hee-CAW!"

"Only one white man in the world — and he's not the Pope — can tell a group of Mexicans in the United States to return to Mexico and not only avert death, but be loved for saying so," wrote *Ask a Mexican!*'s Gustavo Arellano in the *LoopdiLoop* fanzine.

While the study of the "Mexican Morrissey" phenomenon has endless angles, most commentators agree on one thing: Morrissey's lyrics and attitude touch a nerve among immigrants (especially Mexicans) everywhere.

"Morrissey sings to the disaffected, and God knows alienation is part of the assimilation tradition — the equal and opposite reaction of the immigrant's drive to blend in," wrote Arellano on the *OC Weekly*. "We ache; Morrissey soothes."

More specifically, many of Morrissey's lyrics could — and have been — compared to the poetry of Mexican ranchera classics, but the fact that Morrissey is an Englishman, not an American, makes him even more appealing to rebel Mexicans.

In an email, Chihuahua-born Gabriel Rodríguez-Nava (former *Rumbo* national editor, now with Univisión Online), once a die-hard Smiths and early solo Morrissey fan, remembers when he showed up to class in Monterrey wearing a Smiths T-shirt.

"The [British] teacher said, 'But how could you like them so much? — They're so, so ... English!' To which I replied: 'That, dear, is precisely why I fancy them.' I don't imagine myself replying the same way if I had been wearing a T-shirt of... of... forget it! I've never wore a T-shirt of an American band, even though I love many of them, but there isn't a single American band I can fully identify myself with."

Sensing the legion of Morrissey fans who speak Spanish as a first language, Lost Highway and Nacional Records (a leading Latin alternative label) formed an unlikely alliance: *Years of Refusal*, Morrissey's new album (released on February 17), will be heavily promoted by Nacional Records in the Latin market, while Lost Highway will promote Manu Chao's Latin Grammy-winning *La Radiolina* among its Anglo contacts.

"I have seen magazine photo spreads on the Morrissey phenomenon within the West Coast Latino world, and they hit the look right on the head," said Nacional's Tom Cookman in an email. "This devotion and attraction to Morrissey is a wonderful example of an artist really connecting with an audience through music, lyrics, fashion, and even attitude."

To my surprise, Rodríguez-Nava is not too crazy about Morrissey's new album.

"To be honest, I stopped buying his albums several years ago," he said, "and I've only heard one of the new songs. The reason? Partly, because I'm an adult well-situated in the world who has overcome my student traumas, and partly because Morrissey is an adult well-situated in the world who has overcome his student traumas... and, therefore, has become a little boring."

Too bad: *Years of Refusal* is a solid album that indicates — to me, at least — that Morrissey is the type of person who gets better with age.

But that's my luck. Now that I'm getting a little bit into Morrissey, I don't know too many barely situated adults to share El Moz with.

"Don't despair," Rodríguez-Nava says. "I still listen to my Smiths albums and tear my clothes off remembering the torment that it was growing up in [Ciudad] Juárez."

Or, as Morrissey said (to himself?) on "You Were Good in Your Time," one of the new tracks:

"You made me feel less alone/You made me feel not quite so/Deformed, uninformed, and hunchbacked/Time takes all breath away/You were good in your time/And we thank you so."

Morrissey will play Houston's Jesse H. Jones Hall on April 11, and Austin's Bass Concert Hall on April 12.

Die, reggaetón, die
(*San Antonio Current*, June 3, 2009; Third Place, AAN Awards 2010)

Daddy Yankee has two daddies.

They're also Puerto Rican, call themselves Residente (rapper, writer) and Visitante (programming, instrumentation), are known worldwide as Calle 13, and are responsible for killing *reggaetón* dead.

For that, we thank them.

Actually, to compare Daddy Yankee to Calle 13 at this point is meaningless: Calle 13 only records conventional *reggaetón* (a Panama/Puerto Rico mix of dancehall, hip-hop, and tropical rhythms) as if to prove that they can do it, too, but deep down, they couldn't care less about the genre. What they do is *music*, absorbing like sponges the local rhythms of every city, town, and village they set foot in and mixing them with rap (closer to El Gran Combo than Dr. Dre) and arguably the best lyrics in Spanish-language alternative music.

Which doesn't stop the conventional *reguetoneros* from getting pissed off whenever Calle 13 beats them at the great award shows, storming off or complaining like bitches.

"The public knows who is the real Queen," said Ivy Queen — a great vocalist trapped in a cheesy, commercial *reggaetón* concept — after Calle 13 beat her in one of those Latin Grammy shows (Calle 13 won one Grammy and four Latin Grammy awards; Daddy Yankee only has one Grammy).

The reason is that Tego Calderón, Voltio, and Calle 13 — in their lyrics and their music — keep reminding us that that the bulk of what *reguetoneros* are doing is rubbish; Calle 13 sweeps all their nominations, are the critics' darlings and, more often than not, outsells them as well. (Their first two albums sold more than one million copies.) And, if *Los de atrás vienen conmigo* ("Those behind are coming with me"), Calle 13's powerful third album, delivers the greatest beating ever suffered by the duo's critics, the single "La Perla" is the knockout punch.

Named after a San Juan neighborhood, "La Perla" is the symbol of the whole album's intention: a message of unity in diversity to every single poor neighborhood in the Americas. Its rhythm is the usually dark, thunderous Afro Uruguayan *candombe*, this time softly played Brazilian style by an Argentine percussion group (La Chilinga, headed by Daniel Buira, former drummer of Los Piojos), and it has a rap written and executed to perfection by Panamanian salsa great Rubén Blades (who also guest-raps and sings in the chorus). A match made in Caribbean heaven, but directed to all barrios in the Americas, from San Antonio's West Side to Uruguay's Barrio Borro.

The chorus (written by Residente, as was the rest of the song), paints La Perla as a humble paradise surrounded by water, where the neighbors — despite complaining about gringo tourists "hurting the view"— leave their doors open and don't lack anything because they have "the night as a bedsheet."

In his self-penned rap, Blades talks to Calle 13 from Panama and pledges his allegiance to "neighborhoods with mothers who... died without vacations./ As my grandmother used to say, 'Those are the cards: In a poor man's home, even the fetuses work.'"

Whether or not you are familiar with *salsa* or *candombe*, the song instantly grabs you by the balls. But there's more: A call-and-response salsa-style *soneo* between Blades and Calle 13 in which the author of "Pedro Navaja" (the biggest song in salsa's history) screams that "a good man is not fearful, is not fearful of the darkness."

"The song is a mix of barrio and national pride," said Residente in Spanish on the phone from Mexico. "That's something felt in any country, no matter what your political party is. And as far as the 'a pair of gringos hurting the view' line, it's real. People hate it when there's a bunch of tourists taking photos. I wrote what I saw."

Even at their most trivial X-ratedness, Calle 13 outsmarts their counterparts and invariably tops booty references with left-field lines that put the song into a whole new category. "Electro movimiento," a seemingly harmless '80s-flavored dance single on the new album, ends with Residente inviting everyone to the party ("homosexuals, lesbians, bisexuals, those into bestiality, pedophiles, and heterosexuals").

"Yeah, you can say there are two Calle 13s," says Residente. "But triviality helped us reach a broader public that perhaps isn't ready or interested in understanding our social message. But we always add the Calle 13 touch."

"La Perla" has Latin Grammy written all over it, and if Calle 13 gets nominated (a slam dunk at this point), to see Blades/Calle 13 summit on live television is worth the torture of watching Univisión for three hours.

Yes, they'd love to play the song at the Grammys. But, in another eloquent display of the aesthetic skills that took them to the top, they don't want to do it "Latino USA" style — they want to do it right. (And, by "Latino USA," I don't mean the fine NPR show by María Hinojosa)

"Yes, I agree with you: it could be Song of the Year, and I'd like to play it at the [Latin] Grammy," said Residente. "I got offers to play it at the Billboard, Juventud, and Lo Nuestro Awards. But I want to play it at the [Latin] Grammys with Blades, and I want to do it properly. I don't like the idea of a broad with fake tits presenting our performance of a song like 'La Perla.'"

The Incredible Shrinking Grammy
(*San Antonio Current*, July 8, 2009; Third Place, 2010 AAN Awards)

Starting in 2010, the Grammy Awards will merge the Rock and Hip-Hop categories into a single new slot: "Best Rock/Hip-Hop album." For example, you'll have, say, Bruce Springsteen, competing against Eminem.

Weird, huh?

Of course, I'm only kidding. Who would think of such a thing? There's no way the National Academy of Recording Arts & Sciences, which organizes the Grammys, would do that. And it didn't.

What NARAS *did* do was merge the Latin Urban category (which includes hip-hop, urban regional, and reggaetón) into the Latin Rock/Alternative category, thus reviving the "Latin Rock, Alternative, or Urban Album" category (the *urbanos* earned their own category two years ago, when the reggaetón craze was too big to ignore, but the low number of Urban entries put things back to where they began). So now we have Daddy Yankee versus Maná. God save us.

Immediately, the *rocanrol* intelligentsia went berserk.

"We must protest! We must do something!" wrote Alicia Monsalve, founder of *Al Borde!* (a Latin alternative magazine in Los Angeles), on her Facebook page. "This shows a profound ignorance of Latin culture and music," she added on an *Al Borde*'s blog entry in which she urges everyone to pressure the Academy to reinstate the two separate categories. Good luck.

"The biggest record of the last two years [Wisin & Yandel's *La Revolución*] now does not have a home at the Grammys," said Los Fabulosos Cadillacs manager Tom Cookman in *Billboard*. "The folks at NARAS seem to be acting like old-school major-label types that do not realize that things have changed," he added in an interview with the *Current*. "Doing what they have done is a display of disregard for such an important creative and commercial community."

"This is not a good thing, to put it mildly," wrote Leila Cobo, *Billboard's* Latin Bureau Chief, stressing the "ironic" fact that a week after the announcement "three of the top four albums on *Billboard's* Latin Album charts were urban. Is someone like Don Omar likely to boast that he bested Julieta Venegas in an awards competition?"

As a well-connected friend told me, "Not only did they screw the urbans, but they screwed rock and alternative as well. ... They didn't know what to do with *urbano* (mistake number one), so they sent them to the recycling bin (mistake number two). That's why there are less and less nominated artists present at the NARAS pre-Grammy telecast."

Some blame NARAS's stupidity; others (read NARAS) blame it on the *reguetoneros*' inability to submit their damn albums for consideration on time. Latinos can dance, but we're not great at organizing; I'll grant you that. (This axiom doesn't apply to occasional revolutions).

See, NARAS (and LARAS, its Latin counterpart) have a strict 25-minimum rule; if you don't have at least 25 albums for consideration in any given category, the category is out or put on probation for a year or so. And the rule sucks. I wish I could give you the names of the brilliant minds who came up with this crap, but, you know, privacy rules. At least one NARAS person is speaking, though.

"We want to create a lot more competition," said Bill Freimuth, NARAS' VP Awards, via phone from Los Angeles. "We don't feel that it's fair, for example, that one out of every five Latin urban artists would receive a Grammy nomination, whereas one out of every 50 rock artists receives a nomination. We're trying to make a little more of a leveled playing field. We don't want to make it that it's a lot easier to receive a Grammy nomination in a smaller subgenre than it is in the larger categories."

But I don't believe the way to fix a lack of entries is to "level the playing field" by just mixing apples and oranges while pissing everyone off in the process. The way to do it is by honoring the albums on their own merits, not on how many entries there are. If you do that, you'll have some peace, and nobody will be bitching about how useless or clueless NARAS is. Maybe suspend the category until the artists and managers and labels get their shit together, but don't eliminate it. Especially, if you consider that the *urbanos* submitted 24 entries for the upcoming awards — just one short of the required 25.

Lousy decisions like these only defeat the Academy's purpose, which is to encourage and recognize musical excellence (get that smirk off your face). If you don't believe me, ask Joe Treviño, who engineered a superb polka album by Max Baca and Alex Meixner days before the Academy announced that, due to low submissions, the polka category would be eliminated. "While the Polka category may have been eliminated, Polka albums are still eligible for submission and consideration in the Best Traditional Folk Album and Best Contemporary Folk Album categories," said Freimuth in a statement.

"Ay, Chihuahua ... !" said Treviño. "That's the one that's gonna kill us. It's really unfortunate. When you have Alex, one of the best accordionists in the world, and Max, one of the premier bajo sextos, lumped in with the folk category — everyone loses."

Ask a Mexican!
Special SA-only Edition
(*San Antonio Current*, September 23, 2009)

I always knew Gustavo Arellano was baaaaad.
His early LA and OC Weekly *music reviews in the '90s were the type of stuff that would scare even the most confident music critic. I and my fellow struggling rocanrol writers admired his work and liked him personally (he's the coolest cat), but silently celebrated the fact that he spent most of his time in Orange County. That meant more work for us. His humor is hilarious, his sense of sarcasm, lethal. But none of us ever thought his* Ask a Mexican! *thing would be so powerful and successful. Cheers to a good, talented guy who made it. And double cheers for the fact that Arellano is officially visiting San Antonio for the first time next week — as long as he goes back to L.A.*

Dear Mexican,
I'm a South American blue-eyed güero. Mexicanos ask me where I learned to speak Spanish, and gringos tell me they didn't know there were white Mexicans. Whenever I fill out a form, I want to check both "White" and "Hispanic" boxes, but I can only check one, and the person behind the desk (whoever s/he is) looks at me as if I lied or something. What can I do? Who am I?

You are a chingón writer whom I've admired for years, and I'm wondering what the hell are you doing in San Antonio — come back to El Lay! Don't bother with racial classifications — they're for pendejos.

What are you doing in San Antonio, anyway? Or I should say any güey? You get it? You get it? Ha-ha.

I've been invited by San Antonio College to speak to its student body [Ed. note: and the general public]. It's my first visit to the city, and I've been getting bugged by residents to visit ever since the Current began running my column. Also: I need puffy tacos!

By the way, why don't you move to SA, as many starving, formerly well-off Angelenos are doing? L.A.'s too expensive and you can't eat gorditas there, can you?

Of course I can eat gorditas — my mami makes the best ones. And how dare you accuse me of being an Angeleno — might as well call me a Guatemalan...

What's that about you writing a Tex-Mex cookbook? I hear there is no such thing as "Tex-Mex food," just like there is no such thing as real Mexican food in the U.S. Please enlighten me.

Not a cookbook, but a history of Mexican cuisine in the United States — how it's become a multibillion-dollar industry, its best manifestations, and the like. Tex-Mex, of course, plays a huge part in this story. Won't be out until 2011, so everyone: Buy my other books in the meanwhile!

¿Quién es más macho? David Beckham or Cuauhtémoc Blanco?

Blanco, totally. Beckham es una fresa!

Mercedes Sosa (1935-2009)
(*San Antonio Current*, October 7, 2009)

I don't recall a second of my life in which Mercedes Sosa was not a superstar. From an early age, in the late '60s, I knew that the Argentine with the blackest and straightest of hair and the most enigmatic eyes I had ever seen was some kind of badass singer my parents (and everyone around us) adored. Later on, I became a devotee myself as soon as I heard her voice for the first time. I don't remember what song it was; all I remember is that it was a voice that seemed to be simultaneously coming straight from the center of the earth and from beyond the earth. It was an entirely spiritual affair.

And finally, as I'm writing this, it hit me: "La Negra" is gone.

Mercedes Sosa, 74, arguably the greatest Latin American singer ever, died on October 4 in Buenos Aires from complications from kidney disease. She spent most of her last 13 days in a pharmacological coma, until her body gave in. The Argentine government declared three days of mourning, and her body was displayed in the National Congress, where thousands of fans showed up to say goodbye. Her body was cremated on October 5.

Even though Sosa's fame spread well beyond the confines of the Río de la Plata (her recording career spanned 50 years and dozens of styles, and she could sell out both Carnegie Hall and the Roman Coliseum, as she did in 2002), to everyone she was Mercedes Sosa. For Argentines and Uruguayans, however, she was La Negra, a vocal powerhouse who sang to each one of us and who single-handedly destroyed stylistic differences just by opening her mouth. She wasn't the first artist to delve into folk and rock (to name two of the many styles she recorded), but none had the reputation and respectability to tell the folkies that rock 'n' roll was cool, or to tell the rockers that you cannot be a true *rockero* unless you appreciate the best native folk has to offer. Her first big statements on this were her monumental live recordings at the Buenos Aires Opera in 1982, when she returned from forced exile and called on *rockeros* and *folcloristas* to sing with her. Later, she solidified that dialogue with *Alta fidelidad* (1997), a classic album written and produced by Charly García, Argentina's number-one rocker.

As noted in Sosa's *New York Times* obituary, Joan Baez (who illustrated the cover of Sosa's 2005 Latin Grammy-winning *Corazón libre*) once said that Sosa was "monumental in stature, a brilliant singer with tremendous charisma who is both a voice and a persona. ... I have never seen anything like her. ... As far as performers go, she is simply the best."

In total, Sosa won three Latin Grammy awards and will probably win at least one of her two new nominations for *Cantora*, her latest double CD of collaborations (winners will be announced in November). But I'll always remember her for her incredible voice and for my two encounters with her.

The first took place in Los Angeles in the mid-'90s. AIDS-stricken Juan Carlos Nagel, a writer for *La Opinión* and a friend of Sosa, had helped organize a show for her at UCLA's Wadsworth Theater. Months before his death, Nagel attended in a wheelchair, and at the end of the show Sosa dedicated the performance to him. As we were leaving the theater, a visibly moved Nagel asked me, "Did she really say that? Did Mercedes Sosa dedicate her show to me? I can die now... I can die now." Such was Sosa's stature, even among friends.

The last time I saw her was in LA in 2000, right after she won her first Latin Grammy for *Misa Criolla*. Even though I had written the official program book for the event (as I would do with the next two editions), I had mixed feelings about the whole voting process: Many major artists with superb albums were ignored, but some major artists, like Mercedes Sosa, earned deserved recognition. It was the first Latin Grammys, and her classy acceptance speech (and her mere presence) was a much-needed endorsement for an event that began on shaky ground. On a personal level, seeing her with the gramophone in hand made me a believer — yes, perhaps it *is* possible for the music industry to do both business and art.

As she was walking out, followed by her staff, press, friends, and a handful of fans backstage, I mentioned this to her, and asked her if this honor helped to somehow soothe the pain and persecution she had to endure for some time due to her social conscience and commitment to human-rights movements. She smiled, looked at the gramophone, and replied, "*Y tú qué crees?*" ("What do you think?")

"*Gracias a la vida, que me ha dado tanto*" (Thanks to life, that has given me so much) she sang in the ultimate version of Violeta Parra's "Gracias a la vida," her greatest hit. Today, the outpouring of affection and recognition for her remarkable career is nothing but life giving thanks to her.

Linda Ronstadt: Live From The Arizona Gulag
(*San Antonio Current*, November 6, 2009)

The short story: Linda Ronstadt performs her best-selling *Canciones de mi padre* with Los Angeles' Los Camperos de Nati Cano, one of the world's finest mariachis. The show is tomorrow night at the Municipal Auditorium (100 Auditorium Circle, 8:30 pm, $35+, ticketmaster.com), and it will benefit the Community Sustainability Partnership.

The long story: She couldn't care less about her "Queen of Rock" years in the '70s and is more than ever committed to singing what she always wanted to sing: *rancheras*.

But even more than that, what she wants is for people to understand what's happening in the U.S.-Mexican border and other places that make the life of border-crossers miserable.

She talks about her love of mariachi music, but also about Arizona's private prison system, Lou Dobbs, Rush Limbaugh, the Minutemen, the dormant political power of the Mexican American community, and her dreams of a border-awareness concert tour.

If this Q & A were a song, it would be called "We Need A Lot More Rancheras (And A Lot Less Rock And Roll)." And, of course, it would take up a whole album side.

You recorded *Canciones de mi padre* with Mariachi Vargas de Tecalitlán, but have been performing with Los Camperos for a while.

Right. I've been working with Los Camperos de Nati Cano for 20 years. They're just brilliant players. I think Mariachi Vargas and Los Camperos are the two best in the world. There's nobody better. Of course, it's not about "who's better," because art is not a horse race. Los Camperos and Vargas are equally and evenly matched, they're fantastic players and wonderful showmen. They really know their tradition, and they do their own section of the show. I've also got really good *folclórico* dancers with me, and I think it's the best show I've ever had on the road.

That's a bold statement!

You know, I always felt the Mexican show was the best show I ever did. The production values are great, the music is solid, there's tradition… I've played that show in Carnegie Hall and state fairs, and it's equally effective. No matter where you put it, you can't kill it with a hammer. You always get your money's worth.

You've sung everything, from rock and country to gospel, opera, you name it. But you're particularly fond of rancheras. Not anyone can really attempt it unless he/she has a huge voice.

I've been listening and singing these songs since my early childhood. We always sang in Spanish. I always thought Spanish is what you sing and English what you spoke in. But to learn it on a professional level I had to do some work. I knew the songs my whole life. I listened to Lola Beltrán, Mariachi Vargas, the Trío Calaveras, Amalia Mendoza, Miguel Aceves Mejía... My father was a good singer, and he would come with all these records under his arm every time he'd go to Mexico, and that's what we'd listen to. We sang in harmonies and, whenever there was a dinner party, or just being around the house at night, my dad would get his guitar out and sing one of those songs. That's what we did, and I always wanted to record those songs, but I was always told by the record company that I didn't have a chance of selling them, they weren't interested. It wasn't until I sold so many hits for them, that I felt I had the power to tell them, "This is what you're getting. I'm going to do this." (laughs) And they sold it. To their credit, they stepped up to the plate and they really tried to help me sell it. They were shocked as to how many [copies] they sold.

If I'm not mistaken, *Canciones de mi padre* is still the best-selling non-English album in U.S. history, with more than two million copies...

I don't know anything about those kinds of things... (laughs) I just knew I had to sing those songs, and we put them on a record, because it was the recording that made it possible for me to learn them properly. The recordings are really me trying to learn them, and the performances are me already knowing them. (laughs)

How hard did you have to fight in order to record those songs?

Oh, they did everything they could to talk me out of it. But I just wasn't going to be talked out of it. I had waited my whole life to do it, and I tried to record in the '70s in Spanish. You know, we'd written some stuff, and I recorded a Spanish translation of "Blue Bayou," which wasn't a very successful translation... I wanted to do all my stuff in Spanish, but not only that: I wanted to do *rancheras*. I love Lola Beltrán, she was the biggest influence on my singing, of any of the singers. There's an old *Rolling Stone* interview, and they asked me, "Who's your biggest influence on your singing?" I said, "Lola Beltrán." They didn't know how to spell her name, so they wrote "Laura Beltruan." (laughs). They didn't check spelling in those days, I guess.

She was your biggest influence, more than any other singer, for any of the styles you sing?

She was the biggest influence on my vocal style, without a doubt. The way that I phrase... That's why my style was a hard fit for rock and roll, because my phrasing was based more on *ranchera* than rock and roll. It incorporates a lot of the *son*, which is the staple of ranchera. It's a really fiendishly difficult rhythm to learn and to sing over. Fortunately, if it hadn't been for the fact that I was able to learn it from an early age, I don't think I would have been able to learn it. It's written in 6/8, but it's really not in 6/8, it's an indigenous rhythm. It's not even West African, which we know really well in the United States.

Correct me if I'm wrong, but I can only compare *ranchera* singing to opera, despite of the differences…

Yeah, they're operatic in style, I agree.

But besides that, what do you listen to now? What's left of the "Queen of Rock" of the '70s?

I never felt I was a rock artist. I never felt that defined me in any way, shape, or form. I never tried to sing any song that I didn't hear growing up in Tucson before I was 10 years old. And most of it was stuff that I heard before I was five. I didn't even hear rock and roll until I was about six. So the Mexican style, the standards, that was more who I was. And even the operatic Gilbert & Sullivan, my mother used to play some of that at the piano when I was growing up. Rock and roll I came to rather late in the game, and I just never felt that's how I wanted to be defined.

But did you start singing rock and roll because of labels or producers telling you, "You have to sing this," or…?

No, I always chose the songs, but I sang rock and roll because I like to eat, you know? I could've sung rancheras until the cows came home, but they wouldn't have paid me anything. I tried to, but the record company said, "We're not going to have that stuff."

Still, your very first album, *Hand Sown... Home Grown* (1969), which I love, is neither rock nor *ranchera*, but an alternative country gem. What do you think of that album?

(pause) I never heard it since the day I made it. (laughs) I never listen to my records after they're finished. I don't know what they sound like. I don't think I know how to sing them, so I don't know...

Have you seen *Capitalism: A Love Story*, the new Michael Moore film?

I loved it. I love Michael Moore. I thought it was great. I wish he'd do something on the border because it's so important. I'd love to tell him, "Look, we need to do something about the border." It's so awful and people just don't care. I've never seen such an ungenerous heart from the United States in relation to the migrant workers, the Mexican, *salvadoreños*, Guatemalans... They have such a terrifically difficult journey, they risk their lives in every possible way, and they're the smartest, and the strongest, and the best, the hardest working. They send the best ones they've got, they don't send the weak ones. We have a chance to take advantage of this wonderful pool of labor and smart minds that are trying to migrate up from the south, and we're not getting the best of it. We're making it so hard for them that they're trapped, they can't advance themselves once they get here. And they're paying taxes and doing jobs that Americans won't take. They're paying into the health-care system by paying their Social Security, so they're actually swelling the financial pool for the rest of us. They're doing us good in a lot of ways, plus they're buying goods and services once they get here. But people don't see that, they don't see what a benefit it is to have them here. They don't treat them fairly, they don't pay them fairly, they arrest them and harass them and put them into the private prisons, which are operated for profit. You saw in the Michael Moore movie about the prisons for profit. In Arizona they're going to make all prisons for profit. It's a total and complete scam to steal out tax dollars. They're taking sometimes $20 million a year in profit out of those private prisons. And the biggest customers for them are the undocumented workers.

Will those be general prisons or only for undocumented aliens?

For any criminal, but the most number of arrests... If they don't get a lot of immigrants, then their business isn't good. The want to make the laws as Draconian as they can, and what they do is arrest them and they put them in these private prisons. [Maricopa County Sheriff] Joe Arpaio has 10 city jails in Southern Arizona, and I'm telling you: There's no air conditioning, no heat in the winter and no A/C in the summer, which can be 115 degrees, and in the winter you can get 12 degrees. It's freezing or it's just unbearably hot. They brag about $0.75 cents a day they spend on food for the prisoners; they keep everybody hungry all the time. People come out of those places after three or four months and they've lost 40-50 pounds sometimes. It's like the Arizona Gulag. And if there's a bigger person that wants to take your food, you get nothing. It's a terrible, cruel thing. And, in addition to that, [Arpaio] only allows The Food Channel and The Weather Channel, so that they can see how bad the weather is going to be the next day, and he works them in chain gangs in the full hot sun for 12 hours at a stretch. So people are dropping dead from strokes, and heart attacks, and heat exhaustion. If you're an illegal immigrant, it shouldn't have a death sentence on it.

You should do an album about it, like what Johnny Cash did for Native Americans with *Bitter Tears*, or Ry Cooder with *Chavez Ravine*...

(laughs) What I'd really love to do is a series of concerts at the border, to give people awareness of what's going on, how people are being arrested, treated very badly and then thrown back across the border with no money, no identification, often no shoes and no belt, into a town like [Ciudad] Juárez, Nogales, or Tijuana. And they're just stuck. They can't wire home for money because they don't have ID to collect the money. It's very cruel. And it's happened every single day, I've been there. It's deliberate, cruel, and unnecessary.

How do you envision those shows? Would it be you and some guests?

Maybe not me at all. Maybe just get a bunch of acts to do it. We're just starting to talk about it. I just spoke to Little Joe y La Familia. Doesn't even have to be Mexican acts, but anybody who is interested in social justice. People are going off to Africa for causes of social justice. You don't have to go that far! (laughs) Go to the border, man! You'll see plenty of bad stuff going on that needs to be paid attention to and needs to be remedied.

Have you encountered any Minutemen in your visits to the border?

Oh, my God…! There's so many Minutemen! My father was a rancher and my grandfather was a rancher. We used to go to areas where we would hunt, and fish, and have picnics and *pachangas*, and it was empty. And now it's so crowded in the desert. You see groups of Minutemen, Border Patrols, border-crossers, and other groups of Samaritans like us trying to help. It's just unbelievable out there. But the Minutemen are just disgusting. They're smug, they're generally not from that area, they generally moved from the East or from the South, and they're just angry people who are looking for a cover for their anger and their cruelty. They're looking for ways to act on their anger and cruelty and make it look like they're doing something righteous.

If the immigrants were Canadian, do you think there'd be so many Minutemen out there?

No! There wouldn't be any! There wouldn't be one. If those were blue-eyed blonds coming across the border, no one would even raise an eyebrow. Of course, they're doing this as a justification of the Homeland Security Act, but the people who came and attacked the World Trade Center came across the Canadian border. They didn't come through Mexico. It's just a cover for blatant racism and nothing else. It's racism. And somehow the hatemongers like Rush Limbaugh and, who is that guy…?

Lou Dobbs?

Lou Dobbs! They're getting people killed. They're the real terrorists because they're inciting anger by spreading lies and distortions. They're spreading all this wrong information and they're causing school children to be attacked on their way to school. It's a terrible thing. We need to organize a boycott of the sponsors of the Lou Dobbs show, because he's making things unsafe for our communities. He's doing a terrible disservice that's un-American, uncharitable, ignorant, and racially prejudiced. We don't have to put up with that.

Well, they're already organizing boycotts...

The Bastadobbs.com thing? Yeah…We Mexican Americans have great buying power in this country that really could influence the government. I saw a documentary of César Chávez recently, where he says he had a dream, and the dream was that the farm workers weren't being treated so badly because the bosses were so powerful, it was because [the workers] were weak. So we've being pushed around because we're weak, not because they have such power. We have more power than they do; we're just acting weak.

But I've seen too many Mexican Americans blaming the Mexicans for a lot of things.

They've probably been here for a couple of generations and are prejudiced against the newcomers. That's very widespread, and that's something that needs to be addressed. We all got here the same way, and we all need to help each other.

Anything else?

Come to the show, get informed about what's going on in the border, let's flex our vote and pocketbook, and let's do some progress and laws made.

Rumbo: The Remains of the Daily
(*San Antonio Current*, February 17, 2010;
Second Prize, AAN Awards 2011)

On October 8, 2008, at 9 a.m., the eight remaining employees of *Rumbo de San Antonio* received an ominous company email announcing a "mandatory" meeting at 10 a.m.

A Spanish-language daily newspaper chain first published in San Antonio in July 2004, *Rumbo* at its apex had more than 100 employees in SA alone before the owners turned it into a three-times-a-week tabloid and then a weekly. After four major layoffs in four years, I was one of the few employees left.

While we waited for publisher Bill Vincent, I turned to local editor Jesús del Toro.

"What's up, Chucho?" I asked him in Spanish. "Do you know anything?" He nodded.

"It's bad," he whispered. "It's very bad."

The meeting was short: *Rumbo San Antonio* and McAllen's *Rumbo del Valle* were dead. Del Toro and Houston-based sports and entertainment reporter Gustavo Rangel would remain as the sole staff of *Rumbo de Houston*, the lone surviving edition (the owners had closed *Rumbo de Austin* in 2006).

Today, *Rumbo de Houston* continues to publish, but Del Toro, Rangel, and the paper's logo are the only remains of the most ambitious Spanish-language newspaper chain ever printed in the U.S. This is its story.

***

Unbeknownst to each other, former *Wall Street Journal* staffers and Pulitzer Prize-winning journalists Jonathan Friedland and Edward Schumacher-Matos had been toying with the idea of launching an American Spanish-language newspaper. Friedland, a former *WSJ* Los Angeles bureau chief and Mexico City and Buenos Aires correspondent, decided to go to New York to share his idea with his pal Schumacher, whose response surprised him.

"I'm way ahead of you," Schumacher told him. While Friedland had been imagining a *New York Post*-style paper, Schumacher convinced him to produce a more family-oriented product, and they both agreed on four major points: It should be an all Spanish-language newspaper aimed at a first-generation Mexican immigrant population, it should serve as a guide to getting ahead in the U.S., it should hire the best journalists available and applying American-style reporting standards, and it should be an alternative to the dreadful Spanish-language publications already in existence.

"We chose Texas because it only had, at that point in time, small family-run newspapers serving the Hispanic community that were of extremely poor quality, journalistically speaking," said Friedland. The plan called for four initial papers in Texas and a rapid expansion, with four more publications in California the following year. "We were planning to expand big, get up big, get scaled, and then sell it. That was the idea."

The business plan Schumacher developed with head of advertising Jonathan Thompson, Colombian General Manager Giovanna Rueda, and Mexican Managing Editor Gabriel Sama convinced Friedland, and Meximerica Media was born in late 2003. Recoletos, a Madrid-based company owned by London-based Pearson P.L.C. — a media and education conglomerate which owns the *Financial Times* — agreed to invest $16.5 million to launch *Rumbo*.

The timing seemed perfect. Meximerica and the investors saw no warnings that the newspaper industry would implode soon after: In the previous year, six Spanish-language dailies and several weeklies had been launched in Los Angeles, Chicago, and new, growing Latino communities in Iowa, North Carolina, and South Dakota. The Tribune Company, which at that time owned the *Los Angeles Times* and the *Chicago Tribune*, expanded its *Hoy* chain from New York to Chicago and Los Angeles. Belo, publisher of the *Dallas Morning News,* began *Al Día* in Dallas, and Knight Ridder, owner of the *Fort Worth Star-Telegram*, turned the Forth Worth weekly *La Estrella.*

"In 2004, newspapers were still on an upward slope, and right then it tipped over and went downhill like a motherfucker," said Friedland. "Time proved that our timing was disastrous, but who could've known? On the other hand, I think we started the last [print] newspaper chain that will ever be started in the United States of America. I'm absolutely sure. English or Spanish."

Because finding available U.S.-based journalists was tougher than expected, *Rumbo* imported talent from Latin America. The paper was designed based on an original template by graphic-design guru Roger Black, former art director of *Rolling Stone* and co-founder of Danilo Black USA.

"We brought in the best people we could get, and we paid them decent salaries," Friedland said, echoing Schumacher's quote in the *The New York Times*: "We don't pay ghetto salaries."

On July 19, 2004, *Rumbo de San Antonio*, a 25-cent, full-color, five-days-a-week newspaper was born. *Rumbo de Houston* followed in August, *Rumbo del Valle* (Rio Grande Valley) in October, and *Rumbo de Austin* in November. The total circulation was 245,000.

"We launched four newspapers within five months, which I don't think anybody has ever done," Friedland said. "What we were able to accomplish was outrageous."

In *Rumbo* there was no question of scarcity. Good ideas were supported with full budget and corporate backing, and each person had a specific task to perform based on his or her specialization. For a long-time music writer used to fighting with Spanish editors who didn't understand why I wouldn't ask an artist what kind of underwear he/she wore, this was a dream job.

"I felt like one of the chosen ones," said former Travel/Life & Style Editor Tracy Barnett, who would resign in 2005 in order to save the jobs of the two writers under her care. "Our mission was to do two of the things I most believed in: Practice cutting-edge, award-winning journalism, and help the growing immigrant population to thrive in their new country. That mission transcended nationality and rank, and we developed a camaraderie that was truly unusual in an industry as competitive as ours. We were creating the best Spanish-language newspaper in the country, and we were doing it together."

Rumbo started accumulating awards for writing, design, and photography, often beating or almost beating publications that had been around much longer. In April 2006 *Rumbo de Austin* was chosen by the National Association of Hispanic Publications as the third best Spanish-language daily in the country, in a group that included L.A.'s *La Opinión* and NY's *El Diario/La Prensa*.

"With such a short life, getting to that level?" says Friedland. "Personally, I think our paper was way better than those two papers, but they had 100 years of history behind them." Too bad the recognition came three weeks after *Rumbo de Austin* had folded.

Even in *Rumbo*'s agonizing days of 2008, the Texas AP Managing Editors Awards gave the chain first, second, and third place in opinion, features, and sports categories, respectively. Notable stories included the coverage of Katrina (a photo by Alicia Wagner-Calzada's was chosen by *Time* as one of the best photos of 2005), an investigative series on irregularities at BexarMet, and a story about Salvadoran women forced to work at Houston nightclubs. In 2006, Designer Bruno García was chosen as Star Designer of the Year by Texas Associated Press Managing Editors.

But as *Rumbo* gathered public accolades, in private it was struggling. In March 2005, Schumacher summoned the San Antonio team and broke the news: Recoletos had pulled the plug on *Rumbo*, which was now looking for new investors. It came as a total surprise to the staff; just a few weeks earlier, Schumacher and Giovanna Rueda had shared, with beaming faces, how great sales were going.

"Our revenue projections were wildly optimistic," Friedland says. "The amount of money we thought we would bring from advertising was substantially larger than it actually was. [Schumacher and Rueda] were optimistic at first, and they weren't lying about it. But salespeople have to be optimistic, and they were getting optimistic reports from their salespeople."

Schumacher knew that Pearson and Recoletos were re-negotiating their deal, but, according to Schumacher, Pearson assured him in October 2004 that it was behind *Rumbo*.

"[Recoletos] had 90 days to close the deal [with Pearson], so they came to see me over the Christmas holidays in 2004 and said everything was OK," Schumacher said. "And then, about two months later, with two or three weeks to go, they said, 'Look, we're about to close the deal, but we're taking on more debt than we originally planned, and our lending banks are demanding that we get rid of everything that is not cash-flow positive and is not core.'"

In March 2005, Pearson executed a $1.2-billion management buyout of Recoletos, and Recoletos, after getting rid of other operations in Latin America and Europe, returned Meximerica's shares to its founders.

"The last thing on [Recoletos'] mind was to have a startup in the U.S. bleeding a million bucks a month in cash," Friedland said. "And good luck! So here we were, 100 percent of the shares back, but we had the burden of burning off over a million [dollars] a month, and revenues at that point of less than $200,000 a month. "[*Rumbo* was] totally screwed."

With Recoletos gone, *Rumbo* initiated the first of four layoffs, but three months after the announcement two new investors came to the rescue: Houston's Pinto America Growth Funding, and California's Rustic Canyon Partners put in $18 million. Problems persisted, however.

"I don't think that we ever got our act together on the sales side at all," said Friedland, who along with the other main Meximerica shareholders put in their own money to pay salaries and publish the papers until help arrived.

In January 2006, the new investors decided to turn *Rumbo* into a free, triweekly, and in March it closed down the Austin office, arguably the best of the four editions, editorially.

"[Gabriel] Sama and I were like, 'Dude, don't you think that if three times a week works, somebody else would've tried it in the last 300 years?'" Friedland said. "That's what we were telling them, and [Schumacher] went, 'No, it's going to work.' Ed's a sales guy, and at the end of the day he had to be optimistic — it was his baby!"

"Nobody wanted [to publish three times a week], but we were trying to find a formula that would work," said Schumacher.

"Once we went to three days a week, I knew we were done, personally," said Friedland. "And when we went to weekly, I decided to lay off the next big group of people, help them get jobs as much as I could, and then fire myself. And that's what I did."

With Friedland gone, the last remaining symbol of *Rumbo's* original Quixotic editorial spirit was Managing Editor Sama. He left in June 2006, shortly after Houston Editor Carlos Puig took editorial control of the papers. Puig would leave shortly after ImpreMedia, the owner of the largest chain of Spanish-language newspapers in the U.S., bought *Rumbo* in December 2007. Less than a year later, only *Rumbo de Houston* would still be alive. (In November 2009 ImpreMedia announced it was outsourcing all of its page design, formatting, and production to Monterrey-based publisher Business News Group.)

Behind the rapid reduction of its staff and the sales deficit was the fact that *Rumbo* had to compete with new publications that appeared shortly after, or just before, Meximerica launched the chain. In every city *Rumbo* was published, the local newspaper started its own Spanish-language or bilingual paper to compete with the new publication: the *Express-News* launched the bilingual *Conexión* in San Antonio two months before *Rumbo* appeared; the *Houston Chronicle* put more money into *El Día*; McAllen's *The Monitor* started *La Frontera* a month before, and the *Austin American-Statesman* began publishing *Ahora sí!* in August 2005.

"Quality wasn't the issue," says Friedland. "None of them gave a shit about quality, as you know. They just tried to set them up to fuck us. They didn't want us to grab that piece of the market, and they started offering deals to advertisers: 'Hey, if you come with us instead of *Rumbo*, we'll give you a free ad in our Spanish newspaper.' So basically they did everything possible to undermine us on the ad-sales front."

"If anybody tells you *Conexión* was a response to *Rumbo*, they're unequivocally wrong," said Robert Rivard, editor of the *Express-News* and a personal friend of Schumacher's. "It was in the market beforehand. But I do think that *Rumbo* coming into the market caused everybody to defensively invest, and as a result, *Conexión* got bigger. And as far as salespeople telling advertisers, '*Rumbo* is going out of business,' every day in this market advertising salesmen from TV tell advertisers 'newspapers are going out of business, don't advertise [with them].' That's the way salespeople are. But at the end of the day, advertisers are very shrewd and they know who is connecting them to their customers."

"I don't think the *Express-News* or anybody met at a table and said, 'Let's kill *Rumbo*,'" said Rueda, Meximerica's general manager from 2004-07. "But people talk [about *Rumbo*'s problems], and advertisers hear. Our salespeople would also bring up the fact that radios kept changing formats so that people would advertise with us."

Out of all the competing publications, none seemed more interested in *Rumbo*'s downfall than *La Prensa*. Ironically, it was founded in 1913 by Ignacio Eugenio Lozano Sr., who also founded L.A.'s *La Opinión* in 1926. Granddaughter Mónica Lozano is ImpreMedia's senior vice president of editorial, and publisher of *La Opinión*.

Early on, *The New York Times* stories quoted Kirk Whisler, president of Latino Print Network, saying, "Nearly every Spanish-language newspaper venture started as a unit of a foreign-owned company has failed in past years," and *Express-News* Editor Rivard warned Schumacher that San Antonio was the wrong city to start a Spanish newspaper. But Tino Durán, who took the reins of *La Prensa* in 1989, always went for the jugular.

"We were here yesterday, we're here today, and we'll be here tomorrow," Durán said in a *La Prensa* TV commercial that aired after *Rumbo* launched. "*No somos un periódico escandaloso*," ["We're not a scandalous newspaper"] he said in another, as if *Rumbo* were the *National Enquirer*. And, before *Rumbo* was even published, Durán was quoted by the *Express-News* saying, "The fact remains, if it's not relative to the community, it doesn't matter how much money is spent."

On February 2, 2010, I made an unannounced visit to Durán at the *La Prensa* office on Medina Street. I introduced myself and explained to him the reason for my visit.

"*Rumbo*? You're writing about *Rumbo*?" he asked. "*Rumbo* is gone!" He pointed to some of the countless pictures on the wall, in which he appears with artists, prominent members of the community, and politicians like former Mayor Henry Cisneros, former Vice President Dan Quayle, and Mexican presidential hopeful Luis Donaldo Colosio, who would be gunned down in 1994. "You see? You have to be culturally relevant or you die."

He apologizes because some people are waiting for him, but agrees to meet with me the next day at 10 a.m. The next day, I'm told that due to unexpected circumstances, he wouldn't be able to make it.

"[Durán] never hid his dislike of *Rumbo*," said Indra Castro, a reporter who left *La Prensa* in July 2008 to work for *Rumbo del Valle*. "After somebody got laid-off from *Rumbo* and wanted to come back to *La Prensa*, he wouldn't take him back, and tell us things like, 'You see? He left for the money, and now he doesn't have a job.'"

"Tino, for some reason, always had a hard-on for us," Schumacher said. "It's absurd, because we never saw them as competitors. They're mostly an

English newspaper serving the long-established Latino community, while we were an all-Spanish newspaper serving the new Spanish-speaking arrivals."

"With all due respect to *La Prensa*," Rivard said, "the quality of what *Rumbo* was doing — their graphic design, their use of photography and color, the talented people they hired, and how widely available they were in the beginning — was unprecedented for Texas. We've never had a Spanish-language newspaper like that."

As *Rumbo*'s salespeople kept changing, the staff, page count, and office space kept shrinking. In order to save costs, in late 2007 *Rumbo de San Antonio* moved from a full floor at the Milam building to a half floor, and two months later to a quarter of it, where it stayed until that fateful October morning.

"One of the things that I'm really proud about *Rumbo* is that we really improved the Spanish-language [journalistic] gene pool in the USA," Friedland said. "Those people are still here in various capacities, and some of them, if the world is a just place, will end up at a place of authority in news organizations of the U.S."

Some already are, here and in Mexico. Entertainment Editor (and my immediate boss) Ana Paula Ayanegui is an editor at *People en español* in New York; San Antonio reporter Manuel Martínez is the editor of *Esquire México/Latinoamérica*; Schumacher is a syndicated columnist with the Washington Post Writers Group; National and World News Editor Gabriel Rodríguez-Nava is online city editor for Univision Communications; and Friedland is vice president, corporate communications, for the Walt Disney Company in Los Angeles.

"I really miss *Rumbo*," said Fabiola Galdeano, a Monterrey-born waitress at a downtown restaurant. "I always read it to find out what was going on."

"I'm a *fútbol* fan and I read it every day backwards, starting with the sports section," said Rivard. "I enjoyed it, but it had the wrong formula, because we just don't have enough Spanish-speakers here. Maybe Chicago, or LA, or New York, but not here."

Schumacher says readership was never the problem, "and, advertising-wise, we always grew, but not fast enough." An independent media audit from winter 2006 ranked *Rumbo* San Antonio just behind *Conexión*, with 2.4 percent of the population, or close to 33,000 people, reporting that they read the last edition of the paper, compared to *Conexión*'s 2.9 percent.

"[*Rumbo* was] a newspaper start-up that at every stage of its development seemed to do exactly the right thing, often the seemingly brilliant thing — only to be forced to retrench again and again," wrote *Editor & Publisher*'s Mark Fitzgerald in February 2007, before adding that "*Rumbo* showed again that the readership is out there, despite the continuing spin of the radio and TV marketers who propagate the myth that Hispanics don't read."

"What happened to *Rumbo* — the layoffs, the loss of advertising — happened everywhere else, from the *Express-News* to the *Wall Street Journal*," said Rueda. "We just needed time, the same time those other long-running publications had, to firmly establish our growing readership."

"There were a lot of things that went wrong," Friedland said. "A lot of it was our fault, a lot circumstance, but yeah, we were a little arrogant, and I think the guy at *La Prensa* was right in that regard: We arrogantly came into San Antonio and immediately turned people off by basically saying we were going to kick everyone's ass. Not in so many words, but, you know, San Antonio is a very conservative place, and they protect their own. They don't like outsiders coming in and telling them what to do."

True, we might've been a little arrogant, but at least in those glorious, unforgettable first few months of 2004, we could back it up editorially, couldn't we?

"Absolutely, but I don't think anyone cared," says Friedland. "That was the problem. I'm so proud of what we did editorially, and it's kind of pathetic that good, solid reporting, isn't necessarily appreciated to the extent of financial support. The English-language press has gotten the same lesson; we just learned it in a particularly brutal and fast way."

Richie Havens: Still Using His Thumb at 69
(*San Antonio Current*, February 24, 2010)

After speaking with Richie Havens on the phone, I feel I understand more about his fiery opening performance and magical exit at Woodstock '69 — he *lives* in a trance.

He speaks slowly, thinking and relishing each word, but often interrupting sentences and starting over, not necessarily finishing nor following his original thought and topic.

His songs are simple and direct, and, over the past five decades, have strengthened his status as an American folk and rock icon.

Nobody Left to Crown is the 22nd album (not counting compilations and live recordings) by a man who started as a teenage doo-wop singer, turned beatnik, and hasn't stopped since his legendary three-hour performance at the greatest rock-'n'-roll festival in history.

For his San Antonio show, he'll be accompanied only by "Guild," his guitar.

"It'll be just the two of us," he says calmly, knowing well that's all he needs.

Even though you're a songwriter, you're known mostly for Woodstock and your memorable versions of songs by others. Yet, some people think singing a cover is a lesser art.

Long ago, when I stopped doing doo-wop in the early '60s, I stopped doing show business and began a career in the communication business. What I say, really, is, "do what you say and do what you love." I sit down to write only when it hits me. I decided I was never going to write a song again, if necessary, and I was only going to sing songs that were true to me. I knew that if I would get turned on by any song, then most people would as well.

One of your latest great covers is Pete Townshend's "Won't Get Fooled Again," which you transformed and made your own while keeping its original essence. I played it at the office and no one noticed it was that song. Always a sign of a good cover.

I see what you mean... (laughs) I have a lot of songs in my resumé, songs that I always loved, whether they were written by me or others. But I never say, "OK, for this album I'll do such-and-such song." No. It just happens, and it is what it is. This song fits perfectly for this album and this era.

"Say It Isn't So" is a wonderful anti-war anthem. When did you write it? Did you dust it off from the past?

No, it was recorded for the album.

It makes me think of November 2008, if you know what I mean...

No, I wrote it before that... (laughs) But isn't that so? That's what happens to me. Songs either from the past, or specifically written for an album, continue being relevant as times goes by.

Since we mentioned November 2008, aren't you a little disappointed that things aren't moving a little faster in Washington?

No, no, I'm not. Because the way they left it for [Obama] was as bad as it could be. I feel that he has the feeling and the vision to work with this, and ... [he pauses and starts laughing] Man, there are so many things I want to say, and songs come through my mind. I gotta tell my mind: "You gotta stop, let me get this one out first!" [he laughs and resumes talking on an entirely different subject] I stay loose because it's the only way the truth is going to come for me, you know? But now I have this whole teenage generation. They have hearts. What I mean is the heart of these songs are happening now. And [teenagers] need to participate on these songs, they should be able to see what I see, to push it forward.

In "If I," one of your originals in the new album, you sang *"If I could show the pictures/ of the faces I believe/ they'd all be children smiling/ with nothing up their sleeves."* What is it about children that inspires you so much?

I called them the Huggie generation... (laughs) I have five grandchildren, and I look at them and go, "look at these five kids, 16-18 years old," and the first thing they say [imitating a child's voice], "Can I have a hug?" You know? Male or female, it doesn't matter. They're here. They're already here. And I love it.

One more question: Are you still touching the frets with your left thumb?

Oh, yeah… (laughs) It's the only way I know how!

Gordon Raphael in SA: The Loser and the Lame
(*San Antonio Current*, December 22, 2010)

You're a 19-year-old aspiring musician who wants to rescue the San Antonio music scene from its perennial lameness and turn it into, say, the Seattle of the new decade, right? OK, here's what you *don't* do:

1. You don't bullshit the Strokes' management team into giving you producer Gordon Raphael's personal info. Yeah, *tha*t Gordon Raphael — the guy who produced the first two albums by the Strokes, including *Is This It*, chosen by *NME* as the best album of the decade and by *Rolling Stone* as the second best, just behind Radiohead's *Kid A*.

2. You don't bug the guy for two years, asking him repeatedly to set up a studio in San Antonio and, when he finally agrees, tell him, "Oh, by the way, can you bring some of your gear from Berlin? We don't have much stuff in here."

No, you don't do that, unless you're a complete nut. Or your name is Josh Villarreal.

Now 21, Villarreal plays guitar for local band the Lights. Two years ago he wanted to ask Raphael some questions about the vocals in *Is This It*, so he called the Strokes' management office and the scam began.

"Hey, is Ryan in?" he asked, even though he had never met the Strokes' manager. "I misplaced his email. Can you give me Gordon's email too? I need to talk to him. We're all supposed to have something going later this year, so..."

They bought it, and Josh got the info. Thus began a two-year conversation via phone, email, Facebook, and MySpace. Gradually, Raphael became intrigued about San Antonio's music scene.

"Should I open up a studio?" the producer asked one day, and all Villarreal could do was laugh — suddenly, it all made sense.

"I came to the conclusion that I had nothing to lose," says Villarreal. "So, I sent him an email and said, 'If you're serious about opening a studio I want you to know that I can help you and that I'm in 100 percent.'"

"We had a lot of talks, and he was very serious," recalled Raphael. "But my first thought was, 'Right, I'm gonna send my gear to complete strangers I've never seen in my life and they're going to steal it and sell it for drugs!'"

But it was something Josh said that made Raphael finally decide. "Gordon," Villarreal pleaded at one point, "the scene here in San Antonio is covered with gasoline, and we need you to be the match to light it on fire."

"That's very poetic, don't you think?" said Raphael. "That did it for me." After he finished recording Calendar in Argentina and the Plastics in South

Africa, Raphael was ready. He asked Josh to get him some bands to work with and, not surprisingly, they all agreed to work with the famed producer, who later chose Ill Prospekt, Education, Tangible Green, and the Lights to start with.

"OK, I bought a plane ticket," Raphael told Josh on the phone two months ago. "I'm coming. Let's do this."

Villarreal honed his skills as a benevolent con artist by paying close attention at the hotel where he works. "At the hotel, I watched every single person that came in and observed how businesspeople talked," he says. "I'd asked them about the economy, and what does this all mean? And I'd listen, and watch them, and watch my managers, and the accounting department, and see how they used their business strategy to make things happen. And I said, you know what? Fuck it. I can do this. So I put a team together and decided to do like a hotel site inspection. We're going to make Gordon love it here."

Raphael arrived in San Antonio on December 8, and Josh had everything ready for him. He put together "Team Gordon," as he calls it, a group of 20 or so local musicians and friends who all pitch in so that Raphael can have a place to stay, work, and have a good time. The group includes the "A-Team," a group of four stunning-looking marketing girls whose names, coincidentally, all start with an A, and whose job it is to wear Gordon Raphael T-shirts, follow him around, and tell people about him.

On December 10, I meet Raphael at the studio he set up near 281 and Nakoma, where he's working on Education's first full-fledged album.

The players from Education seemed at ease around him. "It's very easy to communicate with him and get along," says Brian Baker, who plays guitar and bass for Education. "He makes you comfortable. And what we've recorded so far is awesome. It sounds great, and we haven't even mixed anything yet."

"[Gordon] hears things no one else hears," says drummer Alton Jenkins.

"Last year I was listening to *Is This It* and thinking, 'Wow, it would be nice to be produced by the guy who produced this album," says Josh Huval, singer and guitarist for Tangible Green. "Now it's happening. Unbelievable."

"Most of the stuff I hear around the world, or in the radio, or in the media, just upsets me how bad it is," says Raphael. "But for some reason, whenever I get calls from bands the music is quite good."

That was the case regarding the three bands he's beginning to work with.

"I come from listening to long pieces of music and things with improvisation and space in them, and I heard that in all three bands, even though they're quite different," says Raphael. "Ill Prospekt does it with electronics, a groove, and a trance space; Education does it with a kind of rock 'n' roll with a Southern flavor, almost like a modern indie Allman Brothers kind of vibe. And I like Tangible Green because the songs I heard were very organic and evolving and have improvisational elements in them. It felt really free, and I liked their style."

Team Gordon's idea is to establish the studio so that local bands can record with him, ultimately making the studio a self-sufficient endeavor. Raphael has committed to staying in SA until mid-January, but everything else in Planet Gordon is up for grabs.

"If I'm only here for a month, the studio will last a month," he says. "If I'm here for three months, it'll last three months. If it seems that the scene can support a studio, I'll make a studio and leave it here and come back whenever I need to. By that I mean that I can take some of my gear back and they can get replacements of their own and the studio can make enough money to survive without me."

Despite his easy-going, playful nature, he's dead serious about the music. He doesn't believe the "in music, everything has been invented" mantra. "Bands try to be like other people, forgetting that the main object of creativity is trying to find what's special about yourself," he says. "I'm always looking for music that I haven't heard before, and I always find it. It's not impossible. We've been using the same scale for hundreds and hundreds of years, and there's always a band that comes up with a new way to make a melody, or a new beat, or a new sound, or a new set of lyrics, even new ways to dress! I'm really into originality and I think too many bands don't try to be original."

But why San Antonio, Lame Capital of America? Why not do this in a proven music capital instead of taking unnecessary chances? The way Gordon sees it, that's precisely why: there's a scene to be made here. And, as a native of Seattle, the capital of the '90s grunge explosion, the Gordon Raphael/SA pairing is a potential match made in heaven.

"'Keep San Antonio Lame'? I like that!" he says, laughing. "I come from Seattle, and our slogan in the late '80s and early '90s was 'Loser.' So you're lame and we're losers. We can make a scene here. I like scenes. I remember when the ['90s grunge explosion] happened in Seattle, it felt so good to have people working together and bands helping each other. It's a good feeling and I haven't felt it since then."

A couple of hours after my first interview with Raphael, the crew regroups at Vintage House, a Southtown clothing store owned by Villarreal and his wife, where Tangible Green and Ill Prospekt are slated to play as a sort of welcome party for Raphael, who would also do some deejaying. Midway through their second song, "Tree Song," Ill Prospekt was loud and smoking — so much so that smoke started coming out of one of the speakers. In a few seconds, flames appeared, and people began yelling, "It's on fire! It's on fire!"

A euphoric and clueless Raphael (who, I assume, wasn't referring to this when he said he wanted to set the scene on fire) had just emerged to tell me how the band had set their speaker on fire earlier at the studio. After a few moments, his jaw dropped. "They did it again?!"

After the fire was extinguished, he patiently explained how the group can solder a cheap fuse to the speaker to help avoid more meltdowns. For the rest of the night it was all DJ Gordon, playing everything from Traffic to Bowie to Pearl Jam. Ultimately, when the smoke of Ill Prospekt's speakers and Raphael's sudden appearance in SA clears, it all comes down to the music.

Personally, I don't give a feral hog's ass about "scenes." Austin is better known for the amount of concerts, festivals, and live venues than for the actual quantity of musical masterpieces it produces; even Seattle went back to loser status soon after the '90s grunge explosion died down. I would trade great albums for "a scene" anytime. And that's where Gordon Raphael can come in handy. His proven record of turning in solid albums on shoestring budgets, and the great chemistry he seems to have with some of our local bands could well be the beginning of a new era for rock in San Antonio.

"I definitely lit the match," said Raphael on December 13. "I worked with Education for the last four days and we almost finished a 10-song album, and it's really good. And I think when people hear this record a lot of them are going to want to come and record with me here, and Education will get a lot of respect and power to get their music out into the world. They're a really good band and the songs are amazing."

From here, either Raphael sets up a more permanent shop in San Antonio, or his disciples continue with what he started, or the whole venture crumbles: Raphael takes his plane back to Berlin, and San Antonio remains gratefully lame. Or...

No matter which way you look at it, Raphael's presence in San Antonio should, at the very least, produce Our Own Private Magical Moment, even if it's a fleeting one. After all, that is what Raphael is all about: he's a master of finding gold where (and when) you least expect it, and in the least amount of time. If you want to do take after take after take, get someone else. "As a musician, I find that the first time I play a song it's ecstasy," he said. "The second time, I'm studying it a little bit, I'm thinking about it. The third time it feels like a job, and the fourth time I'm angry.

"I want to catch it while it's ecstasy."

Slash on Lemmy, GNR and SA

(*San Antonio Current*, November 17, 2011)

Slash, the former guitarist for Guns N'Roses, Slash's Snakepit, and Velvet Revolver, will open for Ozzy Osbourne Jan. 24 at the AT&T Center. He spoke to the *Current*'s on Jan. 15, from his home in L.A.

I don't know about you, but it pisses me off when my fellow Latin Americans go see the so-called "Guns N' Roses" tour, and they eat it up as if you (and the others) would still be there.

It's no big deal, it's been going on for years. Before I quit the band it was understood that Axl [Rose] would keep the name and we came to an agreement, that we didn't want it and he could have it. He sees himself and whoever he hires as Guns N' Roses, and I don't think anybody really cares (laughs). I mean, maybe the public does, but as far as former band members, no one does.

So you're still haven't spoken to him since you left the band?

No, uh-uh.

And no interest whatsoever?

It just hasn't happened, you know.

Have you seen the *Lemmy* movie?

No, I haven't!

C'mon, man, he's one of your heroes and he sang in your album. Go see the poor man's film!

(laughs) He's one of my heroes, he's a good friend, and he is one of the great gentlemen in heavy metal. It was a huge honor that he found the time to record ["Dr. Alibi"]. And I definitely had him in mind for the song, right off the bat. It was a lot of fun. I played on Motörhead records as well, so I worked with Lemmy before. But to have him come down to my studio and put a vocal on one of my tracks was very, very cool.

Why do you say this is your first "real" solo album?

Slash was a whole completely different thing than any of the other records that I've done. It was a whole different production. I got the songs together, hired the guys to play, and then I got all the different singers on a daily basis. It was completely different than making a band record.

Just before *Slash*, you wrote and recorded the music for *This Is Not a Movie*. How did that happen?

That's an interesting project. When I got done with the Velvet Revolver tour in 2008, we parted ways with Scott [Weiland] and I felt like, "I need to take a break from this." We went in, we wrote some songs, we auditioned singers for a little while, and we felt nobody turned up to be a potential singer for the band. So I took a break, and I got a call from [Mexican director] Olallo [Rubio]. He said he was writing this movie, and we met and he showed me the script, and he wanted to have a score that was all guitar. I thought that was interesting. So I read the script and started writing music for him. He hadn't filmed anything yet, so I was writing from storyboards. It took me completely out of my normal rock and roll-writing pattern, and I started doing stuff that I didn't know was in me, sounds and styles and textures that just came out of me that I'd never done before. It ended up being a really interesting musical experience for me. And the film itself is very eclectic, very indie, cool, and interesting. I've seen the movie finished and the score came out really, really good. It opened up a side of me that I didn't know existed. Some of the songs in my record got their start in that score. I'd write something for the movie and think, "Hmm… This would make a great song."

Which ones, for example?

"Crucify the Dead" [sung by Ozzy Osbourne in the album] started in the score. "Beautiful Dangerous" [sung by Fergie] started in the score. And "Saint Is A Sinner Too" [sung by Rocco DeLucca].

***Time* magazine chose you as the second best guitarist of all time, behind Jimi Hendrix. That's a bold statement.**

You know, those kinds of things… It's really hard to respond to that. I never actually saw the article, but that's an impossible situation. Some of the guys on that list are guys that I grew up learning from, and the order [of the list] is all screwed up. I really shouldn't be in the list of *ten* best guitarists of all time. There are way too many names I would mention before I'd mention anything about me. It's very humbling, it's very flattering, but it's not really real. I don't put too much into it.

What's your perception of San Antonio? We like to think we're a metal capital.

I don't see it necessarily as a heavy metal town. It's just a great rock town, a great rock destination. One of the most enthusiastic rock towns *ever* in the States. I'm not just saying that because you're on the phone, but if anybody had asked me about great rock and roll cities in the US, I would've talked about a few of them, and San Antonio is one. It's as simple as that. It's a great all-around rock and roll town.

Why do you say that? Memories with Guns N' Roses?

Anytime you go to a city where the fans have a great, deep appreciation for what is going on [onstage], you remember that. There are places where you play in front of an audience and it clicks, but you just don't feel it as much as in other cities. I played San Antonio probably about a dozen times or more and it's one of those places where after the first couple of good experiences you look forward to going back to.

That's great to hear.

But it's true, though!

OK, one more: How many snakes do you have now?

Just one. I had like 80, but gave them all out to the zoo and other organizations. When my first son was on his way, and my wife was on her last trimester, I started to realize that the dynamics of having 80 10-feet or larger snakes in the house with a newborn probably wasn't a good idea. And it turned out it was a wise decision, because my eldest son is very precocious and some sort of accident along the way would've happened. (laughs) But I'm so busy now that I don't know how I managed to keep 80 snakes in the first place. So I just got one now, and he's great.

Chaplin vs Keaton
(*San Antonio Current*, February 16, 2011)

Who was the greatest silent comedian of all time?

The Texas Public Radio-sponsored screening of Buster Keaton's *The General* (1926) and Charles Chaplin's *Modern Times* (1936) reignites the debate Saturday at the Bijou. By calling the bill "Chaplin vs. Keaton," it urges you to take sides. I know it's just a promotional hook, but they got me thinking.

As a boxing match, Keaton's *The General* would possibly beat Chaplin's *Modern Times* on points in a great fight. *The General* is Keaton's most spectacular, ambitious film and is hilarious as hell, as all of Keaton's best movies are. The highly enjoyable *Modern Times* (Chaplin's best overall are *City Lights* and *The Kid*, with *The Circus* arguably being the funniest, and I don't care if Chaplin's personal favorite was *The Gold Rush*) is actually two movies: the first part is a funny and lethal left-wing critique of the dehumanizing effects of the industrial age, including several classic scenes (Chaplin on coke, the automatic feeding-machine, the protest leader); the second part involves a string of isolated brilliant gags featuring Chaplin's Tramp character and co-star (and then-wife) Paulette Goddard. *The General*, however, is a perfectly constructed film from beginning to end.

But the match-up is good enough that audiences will be able to appreciate the best qualities of both comedians. Even though in *The General* Keaton is not in his usual porkpie-hat character, his legendary stone-faced demeanor (in contrast to Chaplin's all-out, first-class pantomime, which detractors call overacting) is an amazing example of how, with minimalist perfection, he was able to communicate all sorts of emotions. Why anyone wouldn't automatically fall in love with both characters has always been a mystery to me. But I've come to realize that it's not Chaplin the comedian some people don't like, but Chaplin the man.

While Keaton was a humble, baseball-loving All-American boy with no formal education who lost his first marriage and his own studio to booze, Chaplin was a rich, cocky, left-leaning, womanizing, sophisticated Brit. "Charlie's tramp was a bum with a bum's philosophy," Keaton said once. "Lovable as he was, he would steal if he got the chance. My little fellow was a working man and honest."

Chaplin, on the other hand, would wipe his face with someone's beard, kick a policeman in the ass, make playful faces to a baby and then steal that baby's food, and even knock someone unconscious, tuck him into bed, and then kiss him on the forehead.

Don't get me wrong: all the accolades Keaton has received (especially after his death in 1966) are more than well deserved. But Chaplin's detractors are making a big mistake by saying that Keaton was a far better director. Keaton was more subtle and technically innovative, but Chaplin's directorial skills are generally underrated. No one could make the last scene in Chaplin's *City Lights* (one of the greatest endings in all of cinema) without knowing exactly where to place the camera and when to use a close-up.

Keaton repeatedly referred to Chaplin as "the master," as everyone else did. But some think it was only a façade. "In public, Keaton was careful to genuflect before Chaplin as the greatest comedian who ever lived," wrote Marion Meade in *Buster Keaton: Cut to the Chase*. "Not only did he dislike Chaplin personally, but he also despised his Communist politics. His antipathy for Chaplin was rooted in something a great deal more personal: Chaplin's intellectual pretensions inflamed Keaton's old insecurities stemming from his lack of formal education."

Chaplin was no communist. A socialist, maybe. He cared about human rights, and thus opposed Hitler before it was fashionable to do so. And he made lots of money for the U.S. government selling war bonds during WWI. But his arrogance also took the best of him — in his otherwise brilliant autobiography, Chaplin spends pages describing early obscure romances, but he doesn't once mention Keaton, his only true competitor.

In the documentary *Charlie: The Life and Art of Charles Chaplin*, daughter Geraldine remembers how she once took a boyfriend to have dinner with her and her dad, who was already living his later years in Switzerland. The boyfriend happened to be a Keaton fan, which was "*not* the thing to do," recalled Geraldine. The boyfriend started talking about Keaton "and my father started getting smaller and smaller, and he shrunk, and he was so hurt, as if someone had stabbed him." Chaplin became very quiet, didn't speak for the rest of the dinner, and sat quietly in front of the fireplace. "Then, suddenly," she says, "he looked at my boyfriend in the eyes and said, 'But I was *an artist*. I gave [Keaton] work." He was referring to a memorable scene in Chaplin's *Limelight* (1952), the only time the two geniuses shared the screen.

Yes, Chaplin was an artist. But so was Keaton. And the best way to enjoy and honor both is by receiving their art without any preconceived notions or denying either half of the story. While your personal tastes may lead you to decide for yourself who is "the best," I recommend you embrace both.

Me? I'm a Chaplin man. But I couldn't live without Keaton.

Emerson, Lake & Palmer: Punk's Illegitimate Dads
(*San Antonio Current*, February 22, 2011)

In the excellent *Westway to the World*, a Clash documentary directed by Don Letts, bassist Paul Simonon recalls the music his brother would listen to in the '70s.

"He'd listen to stuff like Yes, with birds chirping," he said, "and I would go, 'God, what are you listening to?!'"

He could have been speaking about Emerson, Lake & Palmer as well.

The British trio (Keith Emerson on keyboards, Greg Lake on bass/guitars and vocals, and Carl Palmer on drums) were the first commercially successful progressive supergroup. They've sold more than 40 million records and, in the '70s, only Led Zeppelin attracted more fans in concert. Today, except for diehard fans, they're all but forgotten.

With all due respect to the New York Dolls and the Ramones, I boldly declare: without ELP, there would be no punk. Strictly from a musical point of view, that so-called punk DIY rebellion we all talk about was a direct reaction to the opulence and virtuosity of groups like ELP, which only needed three guys to produce fireworks with such a level of musicianship that it was impossible to reproduce by anyone else.

I understand the critics, though. In the middle of his live version of "Karn Evil 9," Carl Palmer starts one of his trademark solos and goes on forever. When you think he's about done, he starts playing symphonic gongs. By the time he ends up playing a bell with his teeth, I was thinking of Nigel Tufnel in *This is Spinal Tap*.

ELP could slow down too ("Lucky Man," "From the Beginning"), but when you think of the trio all you get is the flawless, highly complex interplay between Emerson and Palmer in "Pictures at an Exhibition." Impressive, yes, but how long can you sit in awe of these guys? That's the great thing about punk music: it was a way to say, "Forget about this shit; I can't play, but I'll play anyway."

Growing up, walking with a vinyl copy of *Trilogy* under the arm was a sign of sophistication, a declaration of principles. "This is what I listen to. Don't bother me with your crap." Today, even musically knowledgeable young people I talk to don't have a clue about who or what ELP is, and that's a shame.

The P in ELP hasn't gone anywhere, and now Palmer is back with an instructional drum DVD, which was an excuse to talk on the phone to one of the greatest early drum heroes in rock history.

Why did you choose those particular solos for your DVD? ["Karn Evil 9" solo from the California Jam TV show in 1974; "The Heat Goes On" solo with Asia in 2008; and "Fanfare For The Common Man" solo with Asia in 2009]

I chose solos that I thought people would enjoy, historical solos people talked to me about throughout the years. It came about very organically, and I felt it was what other drummers wanted to hear and see again.

How is the DVD structured?

We structured [it] in such a way that each solo could be reduced in tempo. You can go from 100 percent down to 25 percent. You can understand each solo in a very slow format. Each solo has a PDF you can print out and actually see the notes I'm playing and what drums I'm playing. Once you get better at playing it, you can speed up from 25 to 50, and then up to 100 percent. The actual idea here is to learn everything very slowly, playing it very slowly from the DVD and speeding up when you are ready. Each solo is transcribed note-for-note, and you don't have to buy an extra book — it's all on the DVD.

What is it about a drum solo? Is it just technique? Is it about the ability to improvise? Why even bother with a drum solo? Just to show off?

A drum solo has to be three or four things. It needs to be entertaining because, number one, the problem with a drum solo is the fact that it starts and people get bored immediately. Who wants to hear a drum solo? So a drum solo's got to have creativity, it has to look good, to please the eye, and it's got to please a person who isn't a drummer. Obviously, if you can play interesting things and excite drummers in the room, isn't that fantastic? But at the end of the day, it has to be as visually exciting as it is from a technique point of view. The technique, obviously, is very, very important, because that gives you the longevity in the solo and enables you to play more things. That's the beauty of a good drum solo.

What drums are you using now?

The drums I use now were built for me as part of the 100th celebration of the Ludwig drum company. They made me a stainless-steel drum set, which is what I've always played. I have one in Europe and one in America. And they've just released a Carl Palmer snare drum. (Go to carl-palmer.com for more info.)

In "Toccata," you were the first drummer ever to use synthesized drums.

That's correct. The sounds in the middle of "Toccata" are very atmospheric, and people thought they were generated by a keyboard, but that was wrong — they were actually generated by electric drums I had made at the time. I had eight synthesizers made the size of a cigar box for each tom-tom. And I could trigger this cigar box synthesizer from an internal microphone I had in each drum. The sounds you hear in the middle of "Toccata" are produced that way. It was the very first electronic drum solo recorded.

The 1970 Isle of Wight festival was a big turning point for the band.

You have to understand something: before the evening of Isle of Wight, we played at a small center in Plymouth called The Guildhall, and then Emerson, Lake & Palmer were known as individuals, not as a group. The minute we played at Isle of Wight we became an international group. That's what the Isle of Wight festival did for us, overnight.

I'm sure you've heard this question many times before, but I've got to ask you: how did you guys react to the advent of punk rock, which, in great part, was a direct reaction to the so-called excesses of bands like ELP and Yes, for example?

It was obviously a problem for us when punk rock came along because, at the same time — and not because of punk rock — American radio had changed. American radio was not ready to play pieces of music 15-20 minutes long. So that's the first thing. The second thing was that there was a strong rebellion against anything that was extravagant, such as ELP putting on big rock shows which required us to begin setting up in the next town before we finished playing on the previous one. None of this related to what was happening in the streets, and that was called punk. So there was a bit of a backlash that we got from that.

Basically, the music is the music; if you liked it, you liked it. But we were no longer played in what we called drive time; we were now played at 2 or 3 in the morning, and that was a problem, not only for ELP but many bands. Of course, as we know, punk didn't last as long as one would've expected it to. But the music of ELP and many of those prog-rock bands has stood the test of time because it is quality music. That is not to say that certain punk bands didn't have a certain amount of quality, but I think that prog music, ELP, for example... We had songs like "Lucky Man," "Still You Turn Me On," "From the Beginning," "C'est la vie," and on top of that we had technology in the form of Moog synthesizers and all these things, so we had a slight edge on most bands and our music had endured the pass of time, unlike a lot of punk bands.

Yet, lots of young people don't know you exist or have forgotten you while you can feel the influence of punk all the way to now, especially in the '90s. Don't you feel that?

I don't feel that personally, but if you feel something has been forgotten that's your prerogative, you're allowed to.

I mean, for some people…

[gets mad] I can't talk for some people, Enrique. All I can tell you is that our catalogue still sells. It doesn't get played on the radio that much but it still gets bought, we still get downloads, so that's where we are. Next question!

You were mentioning about the backlash the group started suffering towards the end of the '70s. But that backlash started *after* you became huge. Until then, the critics didn't mind what they would later call "excesses." They loved it! It's not that you suddenly changed your sound, you were always bombastic. But sometimes critics feel that, after a band becomes huge, it is their duty to destroy them.

Some people do that to bands, and some bands like Queen never got attacked [I wanted to interject, because Queen did get attacked, especially after *Hot Space*, but I let it pass], they were always thought of as a sensational group, sensational songwriters, and great performers. Unfortunately, some bands do get attacked, and you're absolutely right: ELP got attacked not only in the U.K., but also to a certain extent in America. But I have to say that the American audiences were always much, much stronger than the U.K. audiences, though the U.K. audiences for the first few years always stood by us and they are still with us even today. We just played last year on the 25th of July for 18,000 people. The people in the U.K. had stayed by the band, but journalists started attacking the band when we were four years old, in 1974, or late '73. We always had that, but we had less of it in America.

Again, another question you've probably heard before: What's the true story about Mitch Mitchell and Jimi Hendrix? Was Hendrix ever going to join ELP and thus give birth to "HELP"?

Hendrix was *never* going to be part of ELP. That was a complete fallacy, basically put together by journalists who wished it would happen. Hendrix never played at the rehearsal, never came down to see the band, and I never saw him once during my existence in the band. Mitch Mitchell was the first drummer to be chosen for ELP, but he didn't pass the audition and they decided to get rid of him and call me in, and I got the job.

So, all that about "HELP" is just a myth.

You got it: It's all rubbish. None of it is true. You're speaking to the man, Enrique, this is the story.

Finally, where is your head and your heart right now? ELP? Your DVD? The Carl Palmer Group? Asia?

All of the above. I played in America last October and November with the CPG, and I'm coming back this year in October-November. Then I'll play with Asia [Palmer, John Wetton, Steve Howe, and Geoff Downes] April through May, and we'll make a new album next year, celebrating our 30th anniversary. So I can tell you that my heart is in many corners of the room. I do lots of things and need lots of things to keep me interested. In February I played in Mallorca and Barcelona, Spain, with my band. I'm always doing something.

Exene Cervenka on the new rebellion
(*San Antonio Current*, March 23, 2011)

In Los Angeles, everyone knows Exene Cervenka was always many things.

For the last 35 years, she's done it all — music, poetry, art, film — but she's best known as the co-singer of X, the seminal Los Angeles punk band formed in 1977. Yet, despite her six solo albums (not counting collaborations), all of which could not sound more unlike X, some might be surprised by the sound of her latest solo release.

The Excitement of Maybe, released March 8, is a jewel of alternative country, full of vocal harmonies and love songs of light and darkness, "just like love itself," as she told the *Current* on the phone from L.A. It is the second album she has released since she was diagnosed with multiple sclerosis in 2009.

"I'm doing really well, actually," she said. "I don't let that diagnosis..." Then she stops, and it's obvious she doesn't want to talk about it. "Yes, I've been diagnosed with MS, but I'm doing really well."

After performing in Austin with her band during South by Southwest, Cervenka will visit San Antonio March 26 for an intimate performance, just her and her guitar, at The Ten Eleven (with Kevin Seconds from 7 Seconds). "I'd like to play my songs and talk to the audience, tell stories, interact with them," she said. Expect a conversation about the state of real punk, the one that's coming back.

"Early L.A. punk was all about love, freedom of expression, individuality, loving each other, and helping each other survive outside of the corporate structure," she said. "Now it's 2011 and everyone in the country better learn how to do that, or they're going to be screwed."

Cervenka says the best of the musical and social scene from 1975 to 1982, unlike '50s or '60s music, was not allowed to be heard on the radio or seen on TV, and what you did see had nothing to do with punk.

"It all became a cartoon," she said. "Fashion, fascism, redundancy, all your songs had to be played fast and had to be played by men, with the girls on the sidelines and the guys at the mosh pit. And that thing was exactly what real punk was against. That's the punk I'm talking about, and that's coming back out of necessity. And it doesn't matter if you play bluegrass, or folk, or punk, or hippie music, or whatever music. If you got that same ideal, it is punk."

X was — and still is — the embodiment of that punk spirit Cervenka talks about. Without a clear front person, it was the union of four talented people from different musical backgrounds who mixed punk sounds with anything from rockabilly to blues to folk. It was part of a scene that, unlike most of its English counterparts, was more than just attitude and DIY ethics — it was musically challenging, and X was among the most challenging of all. *Los Angeles* (1980) and *Wild Gift* (1981), both produced by the Doors' Ray Manzarek, were chosen by *Rolling Stone* as two of the 500 greatest albums of all time, while *Pitchfork* chose *Los Angeles* as one of the top 100 albums of the '80s (*Wild Gift*, by the way, was "Record of the Year" in everybody's list).

"In 1978, in the USA you couldn't find two punk bands who sounded alike," she said. "[Austin's] Big Boys didn't sound like the Replacements, X didn't sound like the Plugz, or the Weirdos, or the Cramps, or Blondie. All those bands were completely original. Everybody was scary and smart. That's the way it should be, and that's the way it's going to be again."

The Excitement of Maybe is mellow in nature, but all the songs carry a good punch and could be played by any punk band.

"*Any* of my songs could be played in X," she clarifies. "I guarantee you any one of the songs on my solo albums could be X songs... but that's a whole other subject of why X isn't recording new material. I have song after song after song, so many songs X could do and that I haven't recorded yet."

When I ask her whether she would like to record them with X, she screams the answer.

"I would loooove to!"

So what's the problem?

"You know, it's an internal problem [with] the band, let me just put it this way," she said. "There's no consensus that making a record is a good idea. I think it is, but the consensus is not there."

But is it a disagreement about the sound, or is it about something else? Is the band afraid she will make X sound like one of her solo albums?

"No, I think if we went to the studio to record an album with X we would sound like X and make a kick-ass record," she said. "I think X could make a *great* record right now. But not everybody is ready to make that move.

"I give up... I have no idea what will happen in the future, but nothing surprises me. But hey, I'm happy. The album came out today, I'm talking to you, you like it, I'm going on tour... What more could I ask for?"

Fuck, the Movie
(*San Antonio Current*, May 24, 2011)

F**K: A Documentary
Dir. Steve Anderson; feat. Drew Carey, Billy Connolly, Bill Maher, Hunter S. Thompson, Ron Jeremy.

"We're going to murder those lousy Hun cocksuckers by the bushel-fucking-basket." — **General George S. Patton's address to the troops on the eve of D-Day, 1944**

If Patton can say it, why can't I every once in a while?

Unlike anything in my native Spanish language, the word "fuck" is a marvel of versatility. You can use it when you're happy, sad, angry, horny, and mean a different thing each time. Its myriad possibilities and real-world uses suggest "fuck" may be the most widely used word in the English dictionary — now that it's in the English dictionary.

But, where does the word come from and why are some people afraid to use it? Even 2005's *F**K: A Documentary*, premiering on TV on the Documentary Channel in the early morning of May 28, has a tagline that says a lot about the word's power: "The film that dares not speak its name."

What's the big fucking deal with "fuck"?

Using stock footage and exclusive interviews (Bill Maher and the late Hunter S. Thompson, among many others), the movie explores the origin, meaning, and consequences of the word and its usage.

From the urban-legend file on entomologies: Fuck has been wrongly rumored to be an ancient British acronym for "fornication under the consent of the King," meaning that no one in ancient England could have sex unless authorized by the King, unless he was part of the Royal family. "Does that mean we'd be supposed to ask permission from George [W.] Bush?" asked Hunter S. Thompson in the movie. The existence of the supposed law being hard to document, it is widely accepted that the F.U.C.K. theory is a bogus one.

According to one of the interviewees, Jesse Sheidlower, editor-at-large of the Oxford English Dictionary and the author of *The F-Word* (not related to the film), the term was first used in writing in *Flen flyys*, an English satirical poem from 1475. "They're not in Heaven because they're fucking the wives of Ely," says the poem.

It would be nearly 500 years later that it debuted in a major Hollywood film (Robert Altman's *MASH* in 1970). In music, it was Eddy Duchin who used the word in his rendition of Louis Armstrong's "Ol' Man Mose," long before the advent of hip-hop. (He says "Ahh, fuck it!" even though some maintain he said "bucket".)

J.D. Salinger's *The Catcher in the Rye* includes six references to "fuck." Three years earlier Norman Mailer had to use "fug" in *The Naked and the Dead* instead: "Fug you. Fug the goddamn gun."

The documentary also explores how Federal Communications Commission complaints exploded during George W. Bush years. In 2000 there were only 111 complaints, but by 2004 there were 1,068,802. During this period fines went from $48,000 to $7,928,080.

Ironies abound in fuck's history. Dick Cheney used the word on the Senate floor (telling Senator Patrick Leahy: "Go fuck yourself.") the same day the Senate passed a broadcast decency bill (the "Defense of Decency Act") by a 99-1 vote. Dubyah wasn't immune to the word either, famously saying, "Fuck Saddam; we're taking him out." The President even showed his middle finger on camera in a video that first surfaced in 2006 before going viral.

If you really want to insult someone, "at least be creative," suggests Pat Boone, the King of Clean, offering the following put-down alternatives: "You ragged cod piece." "You pile of excrement." "You're an excretory sphincter, you know that?"

Mmm... I don't know, Pat.

"In fact," Boone continues, "I've turned my own name into my most used cursed word. When I hit a bad tennis shot or I make a bad mistake, I say, 'Oh, Boone!'"

That makes sense.

But is fuck necessary? Is censorship ever justified?

"A man curses when he can't find the right words to communicate," Malcolm X once said. "Free speech is important, but not everything is helpful for the human consciousness," says a Hare Krishna interviewed in the movie.

What makes even more sense is Lenny Bruce's take. Arrested nine times and convicted twice for obscenity, few are more qualified than the late comedian to explain the power and the reasons behind the puritan's fear of the word. "Take away the right to say 'fuck,'" Bruce said, "and you take away the right to say 'fuck the government.'"

Shawn on Doug
(*San Antonio Current*, May 31, 2011)

When Doug Sahm unexpectedly died on November 18, 1999, he left a huge hole in the Texas music scene. Besides being the undisputed leader of the Sir Douglas Quintet and the Texas Tornados, his work as a solo artist, session musician, and producer is impressive and well documented. But seeing Sahm live, in concert, was *it*. He called the shots, no matter who he played with. In 2009, 10 years after his father's death, the *Current* talked by phone with Shawn Sahm, the son who now carries his dad's torch.

What are your earliest and latest memories of your dad?

If you look at the cover of *Rolling Stone*, in 1968, I was on the cover with my dad when I was three. I remember running around in California with Dad. When I was a kid, I always wanted to play his gold records. He had a "Mendocino" Gold record, and I always cried because I wanted to play it on the turntable (laughs).

The actual Gold record?

Yes! As a little child I wanted to put on the Gold record, and he would say, "No, no! You can't do that!" Me, Dawn, and Shandon, the three of us and my father were really close.

And the latest?

Right before he passed away, when he was heading out to Taos [New Mexico, where he died in 1999]. This story has gotten changed around a lot, as it happens with people as times goes by. The story gets changed a bit, embellished, but the truth of the matter is this: I live off Hwy. 10, you take 10 all the way right to Taos and right to California. He came by my house on the way to Taos. So my latest memory is him sitting there at the table with me. We were talking about everything, from personal to business stuff, because we had a company together. I remember asking him if he was OK, because it dawned on me that he looked like he didn't feel well. We thought he might've had the flu, and he said, "No, no, I'm fine." And then he continued on to Taos after staying for a couple of hours. That would be my last memory of him. I remember looking right in his eyes, man.

I remember seeing him twice in L.A. We had gone to see Flaco Jiménez, but your dad stole the show both times. He was amazing.

You know? Flaco is so awesome about giving Dad credit for introducing him to the rock 'n' roll side of things. My dad took Flaco up to New York in 1972 or '73 for the Doug Sahm and Band record, with Bob Dylan and Dr. John. That really introduced Flaco, and these are Flaco's words, that really introduced him to a whole new world. He said, "Shawn, your dad was the one who said, 'You can take what you do and bring it into my world and play the rock 'n' roll with the accordion. The accordion is an instrument that has no boundaries.'" When you think about it, Dad and Flaco getting together, having that conversation, that was a quintessential little moment, wasn't it? Of course, Dad and Augie [Meyers] were doing that for a long time as well. You can hear tracks like "Nuevo Laredo," from the [Sir Douglas Quintet's 1970] *Together After Five* album... Those were quintessential Tex-Mex songs. We still play "Nuevo Laredo" today, and that's Tex-Mex to the bone.

Musically speaking, what did he teach you, specifically?

Honestly, at the end of the day, I got it all from him. You learn from a variety of sources, you always do. I learned from the Rolling Stones, Led Zeppelin, the Beatles... Hell, old-school Elton John! I'm trying to paint different pictures of music styles. I like all kinds of different styles. But the things you grow up with seem to be the things that matter most. And I would be lying if I said that it wasn't Doug Sahm's music that has been embedded the deepest in me since I was a child. I mean, the first song I learned to play was "Mendocino." You can see my baby books, where my mom would write it. I was just obsessed with my dad's music. I always wear his influence on my sleeve, and rightfully so. It's my father, and it would be ridiculous for me to deny it. At the same time, I also think I have my own things to say, and I write my own songs. Me and Daddy used to write songs together all the time. He used to call me his "own little songwriting machine." One day I had this song, "One and only," that the Tornados cut. The very beginning of the song was very similar to one of his songs. So he said, "Hey, son, that's a great song, man! I think you got that one line from me, man!" I said, "Pop, you kidding? I got them all from you, man!" So he hugged me and said, "That's my boy!" He'd also tell me, "When we sing harmonies, it all sounds like just one voice." And I would say, "Well, it is, pop!" And he'd give me a hug.

What do you think would have been you father's reaction to the new Tornados album you produced?

That's a very good question, and me and Augie had this conversation before. We both think Dad would freak out, he would absolutely love it. When Freddy goes... [he imitates Freddy Fender's singing], Dad would just be jumping around the room. He would've loved this record.

The album includes an unreleased song by your dad. Any more unreleased tracks for the future?

Oh, yeah... but we don't just want to put stuff out: We want to put great stuff out, and we have plenty of them. It will all see the light of day at the appropriate time.

Augie told me that your dad had high blood pressure, and...

Well... that's kind of assuming a lot. Augie has been telling the story that [Doug's] girlfriend called and there was no answer... I'm actually the one that called his girlfriend and gave her the news.

You know better than me: Augie loved your dad. But his memory sometimes...

Oh, no, me and Augie are family too. We're real close. But sometimes I have to tell him, "No, Augie Boogie, it didn't happen like that..." And he goes, "Oh, Shawnee, OK." Sometimes stories get turned around. The truth, or the simple version of the truth is this: Remember that I told you that at my house [Doug] looked like he had the flu? Well, he'd been sick all week, apparently. Here's the real version. I mean, yes, he did sit in a hot tub, but it was more than just that.

But he did have high blood pressure, right? I'm asking you because I have high blood pressure myself, I want to know!

In hindsight, he may have, but he never discussed this with us. A lot of the shit we found out kind of, you know... He had a little problem with his finger, little issues. We never knew Dad was sick. He was telling Augie he was sick. The truth of the matter is that none of us knew. No one can tell you they knew Dad was sick and that he was going to pass away. It was a shock to all of us. He had some little health issues, and age and the flu partly contributed to them. But the truth of the matter is that he was sick from the time he left my house to the time he got to Taos. It was a series of things he did that didn't add up correctly. He went all week with being sick. I remember him saying, "I'm feeling better." I even offered to come get him a couple of times, and he would say, "Oh, yeah, I might let you drive me back down," and then he would say, "No, I'm OK." He did have some health issues, but overall he was healthy. It was getting close to 60 [degrees] in Taos, it was getting hot, and things started happening. But none of us knew there was anything wrong like this.

Mötley Crüe's Tommy Lee: "I'm definitely not a Nazi. No fucking way."

(*San Antonio Current*, June 6, 2011; abridged version)

Mötley Crüe *is celebrating 30 years of rock and roll with Poison and the New York Dolls. The show is Thursday, June 9 at AT&T Center (7pm, $25-$95 plus fees, attcenter.com). A few days ago, drummer Tommy Lee spoke to the* Current *on the phone from Dallas.*

How's the tour going?

It hasn't started yet. We're in the middle of pre-production, working on the new set, the dancers, a 360-degrees drum roller-coaster and fucking you-name-it. It's insane!

Well, it has to be big. It's your 30th year on the road, isn't it?

I think.

You don't even know!

[laughs] I guess it is.

What's the secret, man? You guys have been through it all, and you're still standing.

I don't know if there is a secret. I was just telling somebody else that what's really cool, one of the exciting things about now is to look into the audience when we're playing and... You know, when we were coming up, you'd look into the audience and there were all people your age. Now, you see people your age with their kids. There's a whole new generation of kids wanting to see us. That makes me very happy, because it's a nice sign that lets you know you're going to be around for a while. That's really cool. But it doesn't feel like 30 years. That really stupid cliché of "time flies when you're having fun..." I guess it's really true, because, fuck, 30 years, man! It's incredible. I had two children not too long ago, and they're already 14 and 15, and I'm like, "Fuck, man!" Time is just flying by! It's incredibly fast.

Another cliché: Now that you're older, you're wiser. Can you see things more clearly now?

Oh, yeah, of course! I guess that's true to a point. The other cheeseball cliché is that "some things never change," and that's true too. We're older and wiser, but we're still fucking retarded. You know what I mean?

But not to the point of throwing TV sets from the hotel window, like you used to...

Yeah! We still do that dumb shit, you know? We still get in trouble, we still have the big parties after the show backstage, and we still do a lot of the same dumb shit. Sometimes I think we'll never grow up, and that's fine too. It's a nice balance: some things haven't changed, and other things are exactly the same!

What's the latest craziest shit you did?

Flying around upside down on a fucking roller coaster trying to play drums. [laughs] Last night.

Onstage?

Yeah! The drums are on a rollercoaster.

Fuck!

Yeah, fucking insane, dude! The road crew guys are looking at me and saying, "Dude, you're out of your fucking mind! What is wrong with you?"

Describe to me the stage: you mentioned the dancers, the roller coaster... What else is there?

There's everything, man! Everything you ever wanted to see is going to be there. Trust me. I don't want to mention everything. Fuck it. It's just so loaded with so much fun shit. It's going to be a fun summer, let's just put it that way.

When you released *Dr. Feelgood* you said it was the best album, because you were all sober when you did it. I don't know how sober you are now, but you've been on both sides, so let me ask you: Can you still make good music without any shit? If you can do it sober or high, what would you choose?

Uh, well… That's an interesting question, because you can make pretty wild music both ways. I don't know if that's going to be easy for me to answer, because we've done it both ways, and they're both good and they're both different. It depends of what you're after, what kind of vibe you're looking for, what kind of sound, what's inspiring you, you know? That's a really hard question for me to answer.

OK, answer this: when Vince Neil left the band in 1992, did he quit or was he kicked out?

I don't even remember, and I don't think it's even important.

Well, it is important to me. It's history. What's the big deal? The official story is that he quit, but he said he was fired. So, what is it?

I think at that time we weren't getting along with Vince very well and he wasn't showing up to rehearsals. If I remember correctly, we, er, asked him, uh, you know… we were going to look for another singer. And that's when he walked out. So I guess we sort of inspired it by saying, "We're not happy, we're having a new lead singer." And he said, "Well, fuck you, guys, I'm out of here." So I think what went down was truthfully a combination of things. We weren't happy and he bailed. That's the truth of what really happened, but everybody will give you a different version. "He quit." "No, I was fired!" But, really, that's what really happened. [laughs]

The fans chose the bands you tour with and the songs you're going to play. Are you happy with their selection?

Yes. They're coming to see you, so you might as well play what they want to hear. Just when you think you know what the fans like, you know, sometimes you don't. Some of the songs they pick we never play live. There were some bizarre choices, and that's cool.

How many times have you played in San Antonio?

So many times. I love it there, man. Just a cool vibe. Texas has always been good to us. And San Antonio has a good vibe. I always head down to the Riverwalk. It's so beautiful to have a river running through the middle of the city.

And you can walk there, just like that? The people let you?

Hell, no! [laughs] I end up going for a little while and then head back to the hotel. But I always try to go, because I think it's just so pretty. It's gorgeous. Nice vibe, and the people are cool.

You're a big Queen fan, but Queen is a band often dismissed by metal-heads. Did you know Queen's first five albums have been re-mastered and re-released with bonus tracks?

Wow! Fuck, they're amazing, man! And it's cool that they've re-mastered and re-released those records. I had the pleasure of meeting all of those guys. It was a band that really influenced me growing up. I like them a lot. Their drummer sang and inspired me to sing. A very talented group of guys.

Besides the singing, did Roger Taylor influenced you as a drummer?

Yeah, he did, maybe not so much in his technical playing, but in terms of sound and how he played into the music. He's an all-around talented drummer.

Are you still associated with PETA? Are you a vegetarian?

I still help those guys, but I'm not a vegetarian. I tried to go vegetarian for a while and I did pretty well for about a month and then... I don't know, man... I found it very difficult to stay vegetarian. I got bored with eating vegetables only. Shit, and when a couple of guys showed up eating hamburgers and shit I went, "Oh, man!" But my girlfriend is vegetarian and, to tell you the truth, I'm eating less meat. We cook together and I don't cook meat, because she doesn't eat it. So I'm eating a lot healthier, for sure.

You got a lot of flak for wearing a tattoo of a swastika once, but I just want to set the record straight: The swastika symbol has nothing to do

with the Nazis. It is actually a Hindu symbol that Hitler altered and adopted as his own.

Thank you! Hell, no! As a matter of fact, it's a Buddhist peace symbol [it is also used by Buddhists, but its origins are Hindu]. I got so much flak I just covered it up. Lots of ignorant people out there. It's a fucking swastika, but if you flip the symbol around it looks like [a Nazi symbol]. I just said fuck it, and I covered it. But I'm definitely not a Nazi. No fucking way.

Julio Iglesias:
To All the Songs I've Screwed Up Before
(*San Antonio Current*, July 12, 2011)

When Julio Iglesias' PR people told me he would only answer questions in writing due to the fact that "he's traveling in different time zones," I was disappointed. In my 32-year career, no interviewee was ever funnier and crazier than Julio. I knew I had to ask him something that would force him to call me.

"Are you aware of the fact that most touring acts I interview call me from different time zones?" was my first question, followed by, "Do you promise to be as much fun in writing as you are in person or on the phone?"

A few days later, my phone rang.

"I know you, but my PR people didn't have the slightest fucking idea," Iglesias said in Spanish from Punta Cana in the Caribbean. Despite his clean-cut, suit-and-tie look, Iglesias is a prankster at heart and never worries about "protecting" any image. "When I saw your questions, I told my wife, 'Look, this is Lopetegui, the little fairy.'"

That was *my* Julio. So, as usual, he starts by taking over the interview, asking me all sorts of questions, from the most personal to the most banal. He talks about soccer, family, and housing ("I was going to buy a house in San Antonio, but then I realized I don't even have time to live in my own house."). He finally asks, "What do you want to know?" and, for a second, I thought he was serious. I ask him whether this tour is more of the same (him singing the hits that allowed him to sell more than 300 million albums worldwide) or if there would be some new stuff.

"No, now I come out onstage naked," he says, without missing a beat. He was on a roll. "The first half of the show I'm all dressed up, and the second part I'm naked." Twenty minutes into the interview, he finally gets serious. "Soul-naked. I'm traveling with 30 people, many of them new. There are always changes. I have less hair and more desire to sing, but the same passion."

And, according to him, he's singing better than ever, and he's not just saying that. He's so convinced by the subtle improvements of his voice that — besides touring — he's been hard at work for the last couple of years (and expects to remain so for the next year and a half) re-recording of all his hits for one or two albums to be named simply *Número 1* (or just *1*).

"I'm re-recording all the songs that I sang badly, meaning all of them, from [1969's] 'La vida sigue igual' to [1996's tango] 'Uno.'" The first of those albums, which he is producing, will be released worldwide in September. "I've already recorded 60 and there are 60 left." The final song list is not ready, but "Hey," "Nathalie," "Abrázame," and "Un canto a Galicia" are sure bets. Will he include "To All the Girls I've Loved Before," his career-changing duet with Willie Nelson that peaked at #5 on the *Billboard* charts? He won't say, but in an email sent after the interview, he praised the track and Willie.

"It's a key song in my career, the one that opened the doors for me to the Anglo-Saxon world," he wrote. "I'll be forever grateful to authors Albert Hammond and Hal David for having thought of me to sing it. ... Even though it happened [in 1984] every time I sing it on tour I feel people dig it like on the first day. Besides, it was a pleasure working with Willie Nelson, an exceptional artist."

In a career that spans 77 albums in 14 languages, Iglesias is one of the top 10 sellers in history. But there is one thing he hasn't done. "I'd love to make a Christmas album in five languages," he said, sending me looking for the nearest toilet bowl. "The most important Christmas songs in Spanish, English, French, Italian, and Portuguese. Twenty-five or 30 songs that define Christmas' culture in the Western world."

When I share my phobia for anything Christmas-related, he predicts: "Now that you have a daughter you better get into it. I know what I'm telling you — I have eight kids."

And none of those kids is more famous than his son Enrique, the only singer he loses sleep over. "He's the one [singer] I like the most," he says. "Enrique is a champion, and he did it all himself." (When Enrique told him he wanted to sing, Julio said, "Fine, but don't ask me for any help.")

Yes, he loves what his son does, but deep down he still feels he's the best. At 68 (which he will be in September), he leads a disciplined life and keeps in shape, but how strong is Julio Iglesias' voice, really?

"Don't they say, *'Gardel cada día canta mejor'* in your country?" He's referring to Carlos Gardel, the greatest tango singer ever, who died in a plane crash in 1935. Tango fans always say "Gardel sings better every day," even though the guy's been dead for decades. "Well, the same thing happens to me, without false modesty. I know people are going to say it after I'm dead. So, I just prefer to say it now, while I'm alive."

Elvis Costello's *Spectacle*
(*San Antonio Current*, August 2, 2011)

After a few seconds of a Hammond-driven version of U2's "Mysterious Ways," Elvis Costello puts his guitar down, grabs the microphone and, while the band keeps playing the song, transforms himself into *Spectacle*'s MC. He's equal parts preacher, rapper, and circus ringmaster.

"Long ago, my friends, giants and monsters walked the Earth," he yells loudly, delivering each line in sync with the band's backbeat. "There were Beatles, there were Stones, the Who, the Where, the Why, and a Zeppelin of Led, and the faithful worshipped at their feet. But, in time, giants grow old. And the people asked, 'Who shall join their company? Who shall climb up and take their place on the mountain?' Four lads pushed their way to the top of the mountain and said, 'Let us try to go up the mountain.' And the wise among us laughed, 'Ha!'"

Costello then jumps to the song's "It's alright, it's alright" chorus, but before the "she moves" part, he goes right back to the intro.

"Were they brave? Were they blessed? Or were they simply barmy? Because they kept on climbing, even when their fingers slipped on the dark and howling night, they kept on climbing... Ladies and gentlemen, please give a warm welcome to the last rock stars... Bono and The Edge!"

Between 2008 and 2010, the two seasons and 20 episodes of *Spectacle: Elvis Costello With...* (co-produced by Elton John, who was the first guest) was the smartest music show on TV, but chances are you missed it unless your cable company carried the Sundance Channel or you are a frequent YouTube surfer. With the release of the show's complete second — and, as of today, last — season on DVD, you can now discover this gem and even see extras that were not shown on TV. According to the show's publicists, there won't be a Season Three (Season One was released on DVD in 2009).

Spectacle was unpredictable, but it usually began with Costello performing his own version of a song by the show's guest, followed by a hilarious and informative guest introduction, a smart conversation, a song by the guest, and a duet. Despite the notoriety of the guests (besides Elton John, Season One featured, among others, Lou Reed, Rufus Wainwright, James Taylor, the Police, Tony Bennett, and even former President Bill Clinton) this wasn't a star-driven show — the songs themselves, and the things that triggered the artists to write those songs, are the real stars of the show.

"My wanting to sing and play came from being a fan," Lyle Lovett told Costello, who always found a way to ask simple questions in ways that made the guest dig deeper. "Lucinda Williams, Guy Clark, Townes Van Zandt... just the great thinking that exists in their songs made me want to try to write something. ... They taught me songs could have a narrative quality, that you could paint these wonderful pictures and find yourself inside these stories, living in the song. That's a very powerful thing."

Highlights within the consistently gorgeous sound and images of Season Two include Bruce Springsteen and Costello's funny (and ultimately failed) attempt at Roy Orbison's "Oh, Pretty Woman," an exhilarating version of U2's "Stuck In A Moment You Can't Get Out Of" (by Costello, Bono, and The Edge), a not-seen-on-TV bonus version of Costello's epic "I Want You," and Ray LaMontagne's accurate description of the art of creation.

"Writing is such a strange thing," LaMontagne tells Costello, speaking on songs' elusiveness. "Oh, they're tricky, they're so tricky... Those little sons of bitches."

Apollo 18 Actors Wish They Could Remain Anonymous
(*San Antonio Current*, September 5, 2011)

After refusing to screen the film for the press (a move usually reserved for studio execs who know they have a bomb on their hands) and delaying the release of *Apollo 18* six times, Dimension Films' head Bob Weinstein was quoted as saying, "We didn't shoot anything, we found it. Found, baby!" Ha-ha.

Apollo 18 is being marketed as "the truth" as to why we never went back to the Moon. The film uses so-called found footage chronicling what supposedly happened to the last three astronauts to go up in 1974. For months and months, the names of the actors weren't revealed because, you know, this is supposed to be real! These are not actors! And even now, only the names of two of the three actors are easy to find. Like we give a shit. Worse still: After the movie, the closing credits invite you to visit a website. If you're that easy to manipulate, you get what you deserve. The site claims to have been "forcibly shut down." How clever.

Any nefarious plots suggesting the use of the astronauts as guinea pigs or claiming those rocks we brought were good for anything besides presents for foreign dignitaries, is barely touched upon. Instead, the movie relies on pure atmosphere and increasingly loud second-rate scare scenes in an attempt to try to keep you awake as time ticks by.

Then the movie is over. Just like that. After almost 90 minutes of cheap thrills you can see coming from clear across on the Moon's darker side, this bogus *Alien*-meets-*The Blair Witch Project* affair disappears from the screen and from memory faster than you can say "NASA." Unlike the perfectly paced, genuine tension of *Alien* (where there is a reason and consequence for every turn), the "horror" in *Apollo 18* is no more than a gratuitously claustrophobic succession of shocking gimmicks that were old — and better — in the '80s.

Too bad, because the film's visuals effectively recreate an updated version of the early days of the space program (at one point we hear *Aqualung*-era Jethro Tull, in case you forgot we're talking about 1974) and the three actors (especially Lloyd Owen) do the best they can with lines like "There is something out there," "Those Russians could be anywhere," and "What was that?"

According to an industry pre-release survey, *Apollo 18* was probably going to earn the number one spot among releases of Labor Day, traditionally one of the slowest movie-going times of the year. Allow me to give you a small piece of post-release advice: Don't bother.

Apollo 18 (PG-13)
Dir. Gonzalo López-Gallego; writ. Brian Miller, Cory Goodman; feat. Warren Christie, Lloyd Owen, and another guy lost in space.

Lost in City Limits:
Could San Antonio become a live-music capital again?

(*San Antonio Current*, September 6, 2011)

Pick a day. Any day. Check out what bands are coming to, say, Austin. Then look to see what other cities they'll be visiting. Most won't be coming to San Antonio. They'll go to Austin, Houston, Dallas. Even Edinburg. But SA? No way.

England's Yuck played Austin, Dallas, Houston, and even Chapel Hill, NC. No SA.

Penguin Prison went to Austin, Dallas, and Houston.

Matt White? Austin and Dallas.

Moondogies? Austin and Dallas; same as Destroyer.

Seattle's The Head and The Heart prefer the triple treat: Austin, Houston, and Dallas. Fuck San Anto.

There are exceptions, of course. We Came As Romans put San Antonio on their to-do list. Mexico's rock powerhouse Zoé hit SA's Club Río last week. And Santana regularly plays both Austin and SA. As do the Misfits.

Just when you start feeling better about things, you read that the Robert Johnson Big Head Blues Club tour headed by Big Head Todd & The Monsters' Todd Park Mohr went to Dallas and Austin but skipped the very city where Johnson recorded 16 of his 42 songs, arguably the most important recordings in the history of the blues.

Worst of all: Arcade Fire played Austin, Houston, and Dallas earlier this year, and will return to Austin for Austin City Limits on September 18. Screw San Anto. The South By Southwest spill-over phenomenon won't be happening then — most of ACL bands won't be coming to SA.

Some say there are not enough people in San Antonio for Arcade Fire. Really? The seventh largest city in the U.S. doesn't have enough people to see one of the most beloved bands in the world? We're lamer than I thought. Perhaps we've been a "secondary market" operating in Austin's shadow for too long. Or maybe, as some think, our promoters are just too cheap and lazy.

"Secondary markets have secondary-minded people, while primary markets have primary-minded people," said a national booking agent from a major L.A. firm who asked to remain anonymous. "Almost every time I'm booking a tour, it's easier to get Austin to react than it is San Antonio. It's much easier to get a quality offer in Austin."

Better venues with more money means "a better class of promoters," he said. Better promoters put pressure on the clubs to up their game. "And the cycle grows."

Austin, the L.A. promoter continued, "represents a number of large-scale festivals. Conversely, there are no major festivals in San Antonio that are on my radar."

It wasn't always this way.

Margaret Moser, long-time music writer for the *Austin Chronicle*, keeps at her desk a poster from 1969 that says it all. It features a cartoon drawing of the state of Texas as a woman holding two men labeled "San Antonio" and "Austin." It reads: "Open Air Concert, Sunday, September 21. Austin and San Antonio are getting together at the Sunken Gardens Theater. From Austin — The New Atlantis and Plymouth Rock. From San Antonio — Virgil Foxx and Doobey."

"Austin and San Antonio once had a very close relationship," Moser told the *Current*. "In the '60s, when this poster came out of, San Antonio's rock scene was much, much stronger than Austin's. Austin bands regularly came to San Antonio, much more so than the other way around."

But then, San Antonio musicians began to move out. "Being the late '60s and the early '70s, let me tell you, every place was calling but Texas, pretty much," Moser said. "People either ran off to California, like Doug Sahm did, or they went up to Austin… like Doug Sahm did!"

But before you start blaming Sahm, consider the politics (and cops) of the time. Says Texas Tornados' Augie Meyers: "Yes, San Antonio used to be a stronger market, but Doug [Sahm] and I got tired of being busted for smoking pot. And many venues [in SA] stopped booking us because we were busted. L.A. and Austin in those days were freer than San Antonio, so people started moving out."

In the time since, Austin has developed a strong sense of local music, which is reflected on the local dial. "On San Antonio radio I can't get a sense of what San Antonio music is," said Moser, "while Austin does very much support the sound of its town."

Then there's the infamous radius clause, which makes it hard for bands to play both towns. In fact, most touring acts playing Austin are not allowed to play anywhere within 90-300 miles, depending on whom you ask. Why is it, then, that Das Racist, scheduled to play San Marcos on October 27 and Austin the next day, was planning to skip San Antonio? I brought this up to Erica Vigliante, whose Twin Productions books touring bands at the White Rabbit, Sunset Station, Backstage Live, and other local venues. Days after we spoke, she had secured Das Racist for October 30 at the White Rabbit. Bingo! It *is* possible to book good shows in San Antonio. It only takes a little bit of extra effort, with or without the damn clause.

"Whenever I [tell booking agents], 'Can I please get such-and-such band?' it's always the same answer: 'No, they're in Austin. There's a radius clause.' That has been engrained in my head in 15 years in this business: 'There's a radius clause. There's a radius clause,'" said Vigliante.

C3, a major Austin concert production company, would not agree to an interview about the practice. Instead, they had a PR person refer us to another company. "C3 does not promote any shows/venues in the SA area, so it will be difficult for them to comment on this," the flack said.

But even radius rules are not written in stone, as we saw with Sleigh Bells, who sold out Austin first and then nearly sold out the White Rabbit in April. "Oh, I begged for that show," Vigliante said. "I begged." Then she blamed politics for the state of affairs: "Anaheim and L.A., for example, are the mecca for labels, big managers, big business, and big promoters, so the tolerance to have shows that are close together is higher for those cities. Promoters in Anaheim and L.A. are very, very well connected."

There's no logical reason why it couldn't be the same here. Vigliante has been pushing the issue for years. "When I put my offer in, I don't care if you played Austin," she said. "You know why I don't care? Because I have faith in San Antonio. We are the seventh largest city in the country. [Austin draws] from us. This has been engrained for years, because promoters in Austin started doing it before any of us promoters here started. This is a much, much bigger city. So Austin needs us. This is the crazy part about it. ... People are trained to drive to Austin. Don't go. Don't go."

San Antonians, it seems, need to stop and ask themselves: "Why can't that band come here?" and then work to make it happen. If Austin is holding San Antonio fans captive with this radius clause, why aren't we organizing to turn the tables and force those bands to come here, instead? How much power do we really have?

Not much, according to Roland Fuentes, owner of Nightrocker Live and a contractor with Live Nation. "You're talking about what, honestly? Twenty people, 50 people, 100 people going to Austin?" said Fuentes. "And maybe a little over 1,000 for a major show?" The numbers don't support the argument.

But if Austin could survive without us, why is there a radius clause in the first place? It's a combination of things: Major Austin promoters needlessly pissing on their territory like greedy cats, struggling SA promoters unable or unwilling to do the work necessary to dismantle the radius clause, and SA fans more willing to drive to Austin than attending local shows. "I'm sure Arcade Fire was willing to come to San Antonio, but they wouldn't give up Austin to come play in San Antonio," said Scott Andreu, owner of Texas is Funny Records and part of the Drunken Monkey Promotions team. "I can understand that."

So can Fuentes.

"We're a city of almost 2 million people, [but] the most people you can get for an Alamodome show or any kind of major rock show is 8,000 people, where everywhere else they're doing 15,000 to 20,000," said Fuentes. "And these baby bands, the club acts, they play elsewhere in the States for 500-800 people, but they come to San Antonio and do 100. Being a talent buyer, I can't pay the prices that they command just an hour down the road."

The turnout for recent shows by CJ Ramone at Nightrocker and Nashville Pussy at White Rabbit back him up. "CJ Ramone is good for 4,500 people, but we had less than 200 in my club," Fuentes said. "And Nashville Pussy, a big club band that tours the world and draws 1,000 people in any city, [attracted] less than 100 [at the White Rabbit]. And we and the White Rabbit do everything by the book: We have full-page ads in the newspaper, the *Current*, radio ads, the press releases, all that kind of stuff. No use."

It's certainly not a problem of venues. San Antonio has venues of all sizes. Many cities with fewer venues than us still bag more and better shows. It's the fans that don't show up. "We have plenty of venues," Fuentes said, "but honestly I don't want to take the risk because I don't see the support. Why should I risk my time and money for a show that attracts thousands elsewhere, when I know beforehand in San Antonio, with luck, I'll only attract a few hundred fans?"

Of course, there is not as much disposable income in San Antonio, either.

"People in San Antonio make less money, so they can't afford higher tickets. But the promoters want to charge the same amount they charge in Dallas and Houston because San Antonio is a big city," said Lisa Morales, of the recently de-coupled duo Sisters Morales. "But there is another thing that we saw, at least in the Americana scene: maybe 1,000 out of a million will come to see original live music. People don't support. They consume movies more than music here. Which is weird, because this is a town known for its music."

While Don Foose (of hardcore bands Spudmonsters and Foose) says he doesn't like to play in two cities separated by less than three hours, most acts like to play in as many places as possible. "I always go there. I always thought

San Antonio was one of the major markets," said Mexican rock superstar Julieta Venegas.

Both her and Colombia's Juanes — two of the world's biggest Latin acts — opt for San Antonio over Austin, which makes sense, considering the fact that the Latino population is much greater in San Antonio. "I played [TV's] *Austin City Limits*, but most of the crowd was Anglo," said Venegas. "When I rely on my Latino fan base, I think San Antonio, not Austin."

It's not just Latino artists, either.

"It's a great all-around rock 'n' roll town. I played San Antonio probably about a dozen times or more, and it's one of those places where after the first couple of good experiences you look forward to going back to," Slash said recently.

"I played San Antonio so many times," said Mötley Crüe's drummer Tommy Lee. "I love it there, man. San Antonio has a cool vibe."

"I play wherever," said Carlos Santana, who will perform in both Austin and San Antonio (the later at AT&T Center on September 11). "I go wherever God takes me."

So why don't more acts come here more often, then?

"It costs more money that you can imagine to get a band on the road," said Exene Cervenka, the iconic singer for the L.A. punk band X who stopped both in Austin and San Antonio on her last solo tour. "Almost every penny you make is spent. You usually don't come home with anything. You have to play cities that can pay you enough for you to keep going. So, if a city offers you $1,000 and Austin offers you $5,000, you might skip San Antonio because there is not enough money … But I love going to places like San Antonio, and Oklahoma, and Memphis, and Little Rock, and Boise. I don't want to just play Chicago and Minneapolis, Denver, and Los Angeles. I want to play in all the cities."

But is it her decision or her manager's or booking agent's?

"It's my direction to my booking agent," Cervenka said. "I tell her: 'This is how much money I need to break even, and this is how much money I need to keep afloat. Any place that can come up with the minimum amount, say yes.' And that's what she does."

***

Dan García, founder and CEO of LiveIn210 Presents, has been successful doing what many other independent promoters have been unable to do — luring in big-name acts to SA.

"When I first started LiveIn210, that's the same question I had: 'Why don't bands come to San Antonio? And the longer I've been doing this, the more I've discovered it's [due to] a lack of promoters going after the bands."

After realizing that most adequate San Antonio venues already had an in-house promoter, García made a deal with Josabi's (in nearby Helotes) and since December 3 has presented nine shows there. Six have sold-out (Ghostland Observatory, Lauryn Hill, Ryan Bingham & The Dead Horses, Gary Allan, and Matisyahu), and even the Bob Dylan show he didn't book but helped promote at New Braunfels' WhiteWater Amphitheater in July was well-attended — García says more than 4,000 tickets were sold (the venue's capacity is 5,500). But it wasn't easy for García to get established.

"I started LiveIn210 in January 2010, and it took me almost nine months to confirm Ghostland Observatory," García said. "That was our first show, and I had to convince [the band's booking] agent to let them play here. And we sold out. More than 3,000 tickets sold. I couldn't believe it. More and more agents are seeing the success of our shows and are now giving us the opportunity to book more indie/alternative shows."

Booking agents like my anonymous L.A. contact are all ears for San Antonio offers.

"I would love to have more happen in San Antonio and would love to have our bands play there and I encourage the managers of our bands to play there," the L.A. booking agent said. "As I am not a promoter in San Antonio, my hands are tied until more offers actually come in from promoters in venues in San Antonio. I would like to think that there is more than enough of an audience there."

García agrees with that, but even he, sold-out shows and all, has to battle the well-meaning skepticism of some who think he's paying too heavy of a price for his success.

"When the bands finally do come here, that means somebody is paying them a whole lot more money," said Vigliante. "I don't want to bribe bands into coming here."

"We're really getting the same price or right around it," counters García. "But some of the agents understand that this is a new market for these bands so they understand I'm not going to take as big a risk as maybe Austin would. You book Interpol in Austin, that's an instant sell-out." In San Antonio, however, you just have to work harder, and García — often seen himself distributing flyers of his shows in different venues around town — feels he found a formula that works for him. "It just seems that the guerrilla marketing that I've been doing is working and proving that there is a market for more alternative and indie music in San Antonio."

Despite the fact that most of his shows are selling out, some off-the-record critics are still skeptical, claiming that "García is not making much profit, once you consider his expenses."

Only in San Antonio would you hear comments like this. In all my years in Los Angeles (19) and South America (19), I've never heard anybody dismiss a promoter who has sold-out shows for "not making enough money." Even if García were broke after every sold-out show, the fact that he keeps coming back with more quality music should be applauded and supported. We need more people like García. Of all the independents, only García's LiveIn210 is determined to bring mainstream, quality acts, even if he, as some claim, has to pay more than Austin for the same band.

"Don't get me wrong," says Vigliante, "I love what LiveIn210 and the others are doing, because everybody is trying to find a way to bring more music here. What makes me angry is that we all have to do more than other cities to get them here."

Vigliante's quick reaction when I mentioned to her that Das Racist was playing both Austin and San Marcos, but not San Antonio, gives me hope — she quickly booked the band, which proved that, in enough cases, it is possible to fight our way through unfair clauses and financial hurdles to bring quality acts to our city. García's success with LiveIn210 has raised the bar for local promotions. We may be entering a new era in San Antonio's live music.

Filled with enthusiasm, I decided to put García in touch with my mystery L.A. booking agent. "This is the guy you need to talk to, man," I told my own Deep Throat. "Offer acts to this guy and let's make a strong scene here."

No luck. Months later, the booking agent sent me a note. "Remember the guy that you said was worthwhile, your promoter in San Antonio? Never responded past one email," wrote the bookie. "That statement in itself should tell you EVERYTHING you need to know about your own market."

Just before press time, I check again with García. Did he ever get in touch with my man in L.A.?

"Yes, [he's a] good guy," García said. "Talked to him the other day. Going to start looking at [his] artists."

In L.A., the booking agent sounded relieved.

"Yeah, he's starting to respond," the L.A. man said. "Coolio."

García has already announced two more shows at Josabi's: Thompson Square on October 13 and Stoney LaRue on November 5.

"Our plans are to expand to venues within the San Antonio city limits, which will be seen in later 2011 into 2012," he said. "I believe San Antonio will be considered one of the greatest live music cities in no time. We are proving that there is a market here for bands that usually skip over San Antonio."

I'll give it a year. Then we'll see if this is more than a promoter's wishful thinking.

Santana: In Metraton We Trust
(*San Antonio Current*, September 6, 2011)

Has everything been invented in music? Yes and no. You can always trace what anyone is doing to an earlier master, an earlier sound. But every decade has new waves of music that change the musical map thanks to the inspiration of people who listen to their own muse. Or their own angel.

On August 16, 1969 (the second of the three days of the original Woodstock), Carlos Santana and his band stopped the show with a performance that catapulted him to Guitar God status. And even though the mix of congas, electric guitar, and Afro Latin rhythms (African, if you ask him) had been toyed with in different countries, none had the power, skill level, and influence of that fierce rendition of "Soul Sacrifice." But then and now, Santana refuses to take credit.

"God invented everything, we discovered," he told the *Current* on the phone, back and forth in Spanish and English, days before his Sunday show at AT&T Center. "I just always kept my ears open."

He's touring for *Guitar Heaven: The Greatest Guitar Classics of All Time*, an album where he and guests cover songs like "Little Wing" (sang by Joe Cocker, another Woodstock veteran), "Can't You Hear Me Knocking" (Scott Weiland), and "Whole Lotta Love" (Chris Cornell). After the tour ends, he'll release *Shape Shifter*, an all-instrumental album of mostly originals that, judging from the quality of its title song, is the most challenging and least commercial Santana album since the '70s.

"I'm finally ready to do something like that," he said. "No singers, just the band and my guitar."

Santana has kept busy ever since the San Francisco *tardeadas* in the '60s opened his eyes and ears to a musical universe he internalized with integrity. He'll never forget the day he saw a mariachi orchestra, a salsa band, and a rock group playing in three different sections of a park in the Bay area.

"People would choose who to listen to, but I heard all three at the same time," he said. "Then I began to integrate B.B. King with Tito Puente, Cuco Sánchez with Ray Barreto, and Mongo Santamaría with Miles Davis. People said that it was something new, but for me it was only natural."

The most popular names of the era (Cream, Jimi Hendrix, Led Zeppelin, the Doors) were basically playing the blues, only increasingly louder. They were taking inspiration from the same blues and rock 'n' roll artists admired by the young Santana. "The only thing that was different was that I began to listen more to Tito Puente, Miles Davis, and [John] Coltrane. I began to integrate the thing with more latitude. Instead of being a one-trick dog, I learned the whole book."

But he has always known where it all comes from. He not only refuses to take credit for it — he doesn't want anyone besides the true owners to claim ownership either.

"Ninety-nine percent of my music comes from Africa," he said. "Sorry, Puerto Ricans, and sorry Cubans, who think they invented it. But those are lies. They didn't invent chicken broth. Chicken broth was invented in Africa. Danzón, cha-cha-cha, mambo, bolero, cumbia... I can name 1,000 rhythms — they all come from Africa. The only thing that doesn't come from Africa is *Riverdance*. Even polka can be integrated with ska. A lot of people get mad at me and say, 'Why do you give so much credit to the *negros*?' Because it's their music! If I play at all, it's thanks to them! Thanks to them I have what I have! That's why I send a lot of money to Africa, because I clearly articulate the music of my African brothers."

While every one of his albums until 1984 had enjoyed some level of success, afterwards he became a thing of the past. That's why Clive Davis, the man who signed him to Arista in 1969, went to see him live at New York's Radio City Music Hall in the late '90s to change his life. Again.

He wanted Santana back on the charts. To do that he first needed to know if the musician was willing to work with some of the better-known names of the time. "[Davis] said, 'What you do live is incredible, but to enter the ring of radio is another thing. Are you open with willingness to play with Rob Thomas, Dave Matthews, Lauryn Hill, and Wyclef Jean and write songs with them?'"

"Yes, I'm not afraid," Santana replied. "I'll open my heart and complement what they give me, no matter what they bring."

They brought pop songs, and Santana made them explode.

Supernatural sold more than 27 million copies and won nine Grammy Awards, including Album of the Year. But don't credit Santana or Davis — credit Metatron, the Biblical angel some believe is the person who stopped Abraham from sacrificing his child.

"That [*Supernatural* success] was something God wanted," said Santana. A year before he and Davis reconnected, Santana says he began consulting with the angel Metatron. "A lot of people think I'm crazy, but I don't care. They say, 'You say you speak to Metraton and the Virgin of Guadalupe, how can you say that?' And I say, 'How can you believe in God and not be able to speak with Him? You speak to Him but He can't speak to you? What kind of relationship is that? That's fantasy.'"

It was through those conversations that he knew it was time to up his game, he said.

"Each person, you and I, have a lot of voices, like monkeys yelling, that make us criticize, be afraid, and all that. But we also have another voice, more calm, lower, but more clear than all those monkeys. That's the voice I've followed from an early age, and that's why I am who I am and I am where I am."

Eddie Palmieri: The Sun of Latin Music
(*San Antonio Current*, August 25, 2011)

A chat with the master days before JazzSAlive Fest 2011.

What went through your mind when you found out NARAS had eliminated the Latin Jazz category, for which you fought so hard for many years?

What went through my mind was that I thought the French had gotten rid of the guillotine. Because they just cut everything off without letting anyone know. They did it in a terrible way. It was preconceived for the last two or three years and in the last minute [the National Academy of Recording Arts and Sciences, NARAS] announced that they were going to 12 states they had chapters in to explain why they did it. All we had was one day to get prepared for it here in New York City. It was a terrible way to do it. [When the category started in 1995] we were so elated. Before that, you were quite honored to be selected and put in the jazz category. But if you're a young Latin pianist coming in and recording a fine CD, you were going to be put in the jazz category, which meant you had to go against a Herbie Hancock, Chick Corea, Keith Jarrett, McCoy Tyner… Or, if you were a saxophonist like David Sánchez, you still had to go through Wayne Shorter, Branford Marsalis… There is nothing wrong with being in the category and fighting to see if you get the nomination, that is wonderful. But the odds were so against you. So we needed our own category. And sure enough, look at the jazz players that are now in our category. A lot of the jazz players are now recording their own style of Latin jazz, so they are falling in to the Latin jazz category. With all that said and done, they chose to remove it because they figured that it wasn't getting the attention that it should've had, not getting what they called "submissions" coming into that category, and they decided to abolish it completely and put restrictions on it and make it more difficult for any young artists to be able to be nominated in that category [NARAS rules require at least 25 submissions in each category to be considered for nomination].

Did anybody consult with you?

Nobody consulted me about getting rid of the category. They were applauding as we slept. It was a very terrible thing, and it will be there forever. They will never change it. When I was a governor at NARAS, they came up with the idea of LARAS [the Latin Recording Academy]. Then I said, "Whoever came up with that idea, let's surround him and kill him," because that was a quote from the retired general Colin Powell referring to the Iraqi army. Once they allowed that to happen, they were phasing us completely out of NARAS. LARAS is now viewed as such a successful program, but it has nothing to do with the essence of the best albums. It's really a hit parade.

Unlike NARAS?

No matter which one, they both turned into hit parades. By having LARAS, they're telling us, "What's the big deal? You have a Latin jazz category in LARAS." No matter what you try to do, it won't work. They are trying to sue them and all these kinds of things [on August 2, Latin jazz musicians Ben Lapidus, Mark Levine, Eugene Marlow, and Bobby Sanabria sued NARAS for the reinstatement of the category]. It's all worthless, going nowhere, because LARAS exists. *Mira* [look], there's not two Oscars, two Tonys, or two Emmys. Why do we need two Grammys?

For me LARAS works because, when you only have one Grammy, there's not enough room for all of our categories.

What we needed to do was expand the categories in NARAS.

But still, how many categories can they extend it to? They can't extend it to 48 categories. And even if they did, we would be lost, especially on the TV show. It's all about the ratings.

We don't have any new categories in LARAS. It's the same thing. There's no extra categories there. The only thing is that it features more of the Latin artists, mostly the Mexican Tex, Tex-Mex, whatever it is. That's all fine and good, but still all that could have been put into NARAS because that's the real Grammy-type situation. By having LARAS, you see what's happened to the categories that we had and that we fought so dearly for. You can't fight something that's successful, and LARAS has been successful. It's the most viewed program to go out to the Latin American countries, but that's not the real essence of the Grammy and of the award. It comes from here, NARAS, and when you go into LARAS, it's another ball game. It's never going to be the same to certain artists, me included. It should've been amplified in NARAS and not get involved with LARAS because now, whatever we do and whatever they take us out of, they go, "What's the big deal? You still have it in LARAS." But that's not the deal.

OK, let's move on to the San Antonio show. What will we see?

We are bringing La Perfecta II there. We are doing classics and some we didn't record. "Muñeca," "Azúcar," and others.

Is this the format you're most comfortable with nowadays?

I just got back with a [jazz] quartet from touring all over Europe. So we are doing all kinds of presentations, but when I do Latin, we have the big band. I have a DVD coming out at the end of the month, my first. There will be a DVD release party at the end of this month. It's the 50 years of Eddie Palmieri. It was [filmed] about four or five years ago in a concert in Connecticut. My son has been handling it, and it is about time that we release my first DVD. The only problem is mathematically I do not know how it works out, because it says [it is] my 50th year and I'm only 24 now.

Really…

[laughs] It's because "Chocolate" Armenteros, the Cuban trumpet player, taught me that after 50 you start counting by one again. I would tell everybody that I was born in 1898 and that I was a friend of Tito Puente then. And Tito would say, "Eddie, don't say things like that!"

Do you think the 9:35 "Azúcar" was to salsa what "Hey Jude" was to rock?

It wasn't just the length of the song. There we broke a precedent. I was already recording a little longer. Remember, when I started to record you could only record two minutes and 45 seconds. And when "Azúcar" came out, it began with a typical number and after the piano solo it turns into what I call "instrumental mambo." You didn't utilize the word "Latin jazz" then. It was "instrumental mambos." They were exciting during the time of Machito, Tito Puente, Tito Rodríguez… They were very exciting arrangements for the dancers. Within "Azúcar" you had the typical, the expanded piano solo, and then the instrumental, which was in a Latin jazz format. It's piano and flute solos while the trombone player is holding firm on a typical basis. It's a combination that had never been heard of, in my opinion, had never been done in that form and it became something very special. It became a tremendous hit. It helped us tremendously. It established a precedent, in my opinion, on how to use an orchestra that would give you two different types of sounds in one, one typical and one taking the Latin jazz form. And at the same time, we were quite honored with the Library of Congress taking it in as one of the greatest recordings. I'm quite proud of that, too. That song was very special because I wrote it two years before I recorded it. It was a hit in the street. That's how I landed up with Roulette Records.

Once and for all: Were you born in Puerto Rico or New York? I've seen conflicting stories.

I was born in Manhattan. My mother arrived in New York from Puerto Rico in 1925 and my father in 1926. They got married here. And then my brother [musician Charlie Palmieri, who passed in 1988] was born in 1927. And I was born in 1936, on 112th street between Madison and Park. And by the time I was about five to six years of age, we moved to the Bronx and I was raised there.

So… When did you live in Puerto Rico?

Much later in my career, in 1983. I had gone there naturally a few times but not to stay. I went there to take care of my mother when my brother had his first heart attack. My wife sold our second home in Long Island, and then we moved to Puerto Rico and I formed one of the greatest orchestras that I've ever had with Tito Torres, *el gran trompetista* [the great trumpet player] of Puerto Rico, and that orchestra was the first orchestra that traveled from Puerto Rico on an extensive European tour. It was really my first European tour, even though they had been looking for me for about 15 years to travel to Europe. And that's the orchestra that won three Grammys for Fania [Records] in 1984. We were the first band, period, to win a Grammy from Puerto Rico.

What about new music? Are you recording or about to record anything?

The problem is that I have so many different ventures and different bands that I do not know which direction I should take. And now I just got on with a quartet. We were traveling with a quartet throughout Europe. That was the first time I had done that. Never was I playing as much piano, my brother. We went all over Europe. Well, we didn't do all of Europe, but we mostly did Italy, Switzerland, and the North Sea Jazz Festival in Holland. We also played in a place called the Umbria Jazz Festival in Italy. Such a special place to play. I had never played that festival and it was about 10 days of music coming in and out and people walking up there. It was up on a mountain. It was really a way to close out. It was just gorgeous. Chucho Valdés was there with his presentation and so was Michel Camilo. And we had three pianos. I opened up the show, Michel came in second and Chucho closed the show. It was really a night to remember there and never forget. So, they are talking about recording the quartet. They are talking about recording the big band again, which is three trumpets and two trombones with vocals. I won't do La Perfecta again. But either the big band or the quartet or the Latin Caribbean jazz ensemble, which can be a sextet, septet, or octet.

Last one: Are you willing to fight for the re-instatement of the Latin Jazz category at the Grammys with the same intensity you fought for its inclusion?

That's not going to happen. They already made their decision. They cut it out. And it's fruitless to try to go into any discussion on that. I see that you are very up on LARAS. I wish you the best, I wish you can enjoy the program every time it goes on, every year. To me, [the Grammy and Latin Grammy Awards] are both hit parades. It shouldn't be about who sells the most records. It should be about who makes the best recording in their genre, and they took that away. It's very sad.

Debating Vikki Carr
(*San Antonio Current*, October 16, 2011)

*V*ikki Carr was euphoric. Talking in English and Spanish on the phone from Orlando (where she was doing the Spanish TV rounds), she shared with the Current her enthusiasm for the public's reaction to Viva la vida, her first album since 2001. But gradually the conversation — which took place days before the first presidential debate — turned to politics. Here's the whole conversation, which begins with her return to music and ends with a spirited defense of her man in November: Mitt Romney.

Congratulations on your return to Sony and to recording in general. It was about time!

I came back home. I feel like Judy Garland when she told her aunt, "Oh, Auntie Em, there's no place like home," because I had been without a record company for many years. After I got married I was in San Antonio with my grandkids, and now they're grown up and I was happy to take time for myself and my husband. [Dr.] Pedro [De León] kept saying, "Honey, you've got to get back. People are waiting for you to come back, and you're singing better than ever, so do it!" I was without a record company at the time. It was very difficult because, after the success that I had, record companies were not that interested at the time. So I decided to invest in myself, I borrowed money, and contacted a friend of mine in California, [Mariachi Sol de México founder] José Hernández. He's been a very good friend for many, many years. I asked him if he'd be interested in being my co-producer, and he said, "Yes!" The album was initially recorded three years ago for my 50th anniversary of being in the business. It was my way of thanking all of my public, all the *mexicanos*, and all the Latin American countries for the success that they have given me. And to tell them that God continues to bless me with the gift of my singing and that I will be continuing to sing for everybody. So, [Hernández] got some songs that were original and some that had not been done in about 75 years.

Were the originals done especially for this album?

Yes. One in particular is "A mí no me importa" ["I Don't Care," written by Hernández and José Alfredo Jiménez Jr., the son of Mexico's arguably greatest composer], which talks about me singing to the people. I don't care about time, yet I'm 72.

No way...

Yes way! [laughs]

You look younger than me!

Oh, c'mon...! Thank you, darling. As I was saying, the lyrics [of "A mí no me importa"] are *"Camino, siempre camino/llevando el amor en mi alma/y en mis manos corazones/sin dejar a nadie atrás"* ("I walk, I always walk/taking love in my soul/and hearts in my hands/without leaving anyone behind"). I'm singing for all those who have given their hearts to me. And I'm saying, "I don't care about time," because I'm still going to be here for all of you, and my way of thanking you is my singing. Then there are some songs that were written by [Argentine songwriter] Roberto Livi for me, and also one by [Argentina's] Leo Dan ["Amante peligroso/Dangerous Lover"] that says, "Yo sé que fui muy celosa" (I know I was very jealous). A part of me that maybe I never would have wanted to admit, but maybe at a point in my life I was. We all have our insecurities.

José [Hernández] has been very successful on his own. His Mariachi Sol de México is widely considered the top mariachi in the US. He's been busy. Yet, he found time to work with you. That must've felt great.

Oh, I know. He's incredible.

He was just in town playing with Luis Miguel.

Yes! Did you see him then? I went to see him. I know, he's very busy. And he's very talented. And to be my co-producer? Ha!

What's the deal with Sony now? Distribution only or what?

Well, the album was presented to them. We were getting to the point of, after waiting for three years, "Forget about it!" If we couldn't get someone interested in a finished product with album cover and everything, then we'll just put it out ourselves. My manager got it to Sony, and the people at Sony, when they heard it, they absolutely flipped. They loved it. They wanted to be involved. Yes, initially this is a distribution deal to them, but we're already talking about other projects in the future. They're excited, and I'm excited. It's wonderful after 53 years of being in this business, to be with a company that is young but is excited that you're back home where you have had your success. So, I'm thrilled. I've been here at the office. I've met everybody. We did [Univisión's] *Despierta América*, with an amazing response from people that have missed me so much! It's wonderful. They've missed my songs. And so many of the young people that are working now at Sony were raised with my music, so it's been a love-in. That's all I can tell you.

At the time you started singing in Spanish, you already had an incredible career in English. Do you feel at all that, because of the success of your Spanish career, people forget that you were already successful before you became successful?

You're right. They do forget it but, you know, the amazing thing is had I not had the success in English first, I wouldn't have had the strength to insist with the president of my record company at the time, that I wanted to do this album in Spanish. It was like pushing something that I knew was going to be successful. It was also suggested by the Anglos in my audience, because I would always include at least one or two songs [in Spanish]. I would tell the audience what the songs were about, and then they started mentioning to me, "Gee, why don't you do an album all in Spanish?" I said, "Well, isn't it going to bother you that you're not going to know what I'm singing about?" They said, "No, because when Vikki Carr sings we understand everything." You realize music is the universal language. People can tell when it was a love song, and it gave me a chance also to introduce beautiful music *en español* other than the same things that we had heard over and over. And to showcase other great composers like Armando Manzanero and José Alfredo Jiménez... I'm so glad we did, even though the company dropped me and stayed with [Barbra] Streisand, because of that fight to do the first one [in Spanish]. That was when Columbia México came to me and they said, "We want Vikki Carr because we know that she can sell records." They had known me in México and Latin America for "It Must Be Him," for "With Pen in Hand," for "I Got My Eye On You," and I still sing those songs for them, because I cannot deny who I am and the success that I have. It's beautiful now to be accepted. The biggest frustration to me, Enrique, was after having success in English, and in concerts, and then being in Mexico, and having that incredible success, and three Grammys, it was amazing for me to come back and work in the United States, and then have your agents have a stupid mentality. They'd say, "Well, is she going to do her Spanish show? Or her English show?" All of a sudden, I was put into this category. What do you mean? Why can't I just be Vikki Carr? I am everything in music. I am in the Spanish, and I am in the English. But that was the stupid mentality, I think, at that time.

What will happen now? Are you going to tour? With only this new album, or with, uh... *all* **the Vikki Carrs?**

Of course I'm going to tour! I'm going to tour as Vikki Carr. There is no "all the Vikki Carrs." There's only one Vikki Carr. One who has been blessed to have success in both. In my English show I've been doing the retro stuff. We go back to the music that made me who I am, and I wind up doing it maybe a little more differently, just to give it a little more life. Then I share with them all of my success in Spanish. Thank God I draw an audience that is equally balanced between the Anglo and the Hispanic. That, I thought, would be an incredible selling point for Vikki Carr. Be it symphony shows or whatever in theaters. If you're going to be thinking, "I'm only going to draw a *mexicano* or Latino," you're making a big mistake! It's like having a jewel in your hand that has just now began to be polished, and to be able to shine for everybody. Here's a woman who has done everything. I have even recorded in Japanese, and I've recorded in Portuguese, in Italian, but the thing is that I am known for the English and the Spanish. And plus, I have a great sense of humor. I'm a comedian. Before, I had been kind of guided in my career like, "They pay to hear you sing, not to hear you talk." And now I'm at a point where I feel I have a lot to say, and I am funny, and the people love it!

I have conflicting information about something: do you or do you not play guitar?

No, I don't. I did take lessons, but I wouldn't say that I play guitar. I was given an incredible, beautiful guitar that I still have. My ex-husband, my first, on our fifth anniversary, he came into the bedroom with this humongous big box, and he told me to open it. I opened it, and it was a beautiful handmade guitar. I looked at it and I said, "Oh! A guitar!" He said, "Yeah." And I said, "You got me, for our anniversary, a guitar?" But he was so cute. He said, "For the fifth anniversary, it's wood." So, he got me the guitar. And I had that, and it was very beautiful. I still have it. Then, I started taking some lessons from some of the musicians that I worked with, and I said, "Oh! This would be kind of cool if I could really accompany myself." But I never really went further with it, other than to hold it, and to strum a few chords.

OK, let's play a little game. I'll give you some names that were important in your life and you tell me the first thing that comes to your mind. Let's start with Johnny Carson. [she was a guest host at *The Tonight Show* in 1973 and sang for the presidents mentioned, except Obama]

Very funny.

Richard Nixon.

Someone that really… OK… Richard Nixon. He was, actually… Hmm… Richard Nixon…

OK, we'll get back to him later [I forgot to get back; sorry]. Gerald Ford.

He was a sweetheart.

Ronald Reagan.

The best that we've had, and I wish he were back.

George H. W. Bush.

A great gentleman.

Bill Clinton.

A great talker.

[San Antonio's] Holy Cross High School.

The importance of education.

Did you ever meet Obama?

Nope.

You were born in El Paso but have lived in San Antonio for many years. What do you think of our city?

I first went to San Antonio in '68 to perform at HemisFair, and I fell in love with the city. I said, "Gee, I love this city. I'd love to work here one day," and it did come to pass. But, you know, I wound up marrying someone that I had met in 1971 [in San Antonio], and over 30 years later we got married, and that's why I moved here. I love San Antonio! Are you kidding? There's nothing nicer than to go into the mall or go to the market and everybody calls you, "Vikki!" and they'll tell you, "Thank you so much for what you did for Holy Cross, you helped my brother." I've come across former alumni of Holy Cross that say, "Thanks to you! You are our Angel." But I only went to do the [benefit] concert; it was the people of San Antonio that really supported something so very important.

Thanks, Vikki. Anything you want to add?

Viva la vida, the name of the album, can be translated as "live life," and it's also kind of geared more toward the Mexican people and all of the horrible problems and situations that they are in right now. They must have faith and unite, because it's pretty frightening what is happening, and what has happened to them.

Based on your take on past presidents, I suspect I know who you're going to vote for...

You can ask me about the election now. I don't mind. It's Romney for me.

Do you really believe what Romney has to offer is what the Mexicans need right now?

Yes, because I feel [Obama is] only placating and playing up to a Latino. Meanwhile, he's put out in immigration... How many people has he already deported? He knows what to say to get votes. And I feel that he says the things, my darling, that the people want to hear. But I remember a country where we really worked and nobody gave up anything. I'm not saying that some of the benefits and things that have come about are not important and were not given to people that really needed it, but I feel truly in my heart (because I know personally from relatives) that they have abused it, OK? And I resent that. Because I have worked so hard for 72 years, my father worked so hard, my mother worked so far, and I was a Democrat until I started to work, and then to read and to find out really what is going on... The thing that frightens me the most, is [that Obama] is appealing to those that are afraid that they're not going to have somebody take care of them.

Are you saying that, if I vote for Obama, I do it because I'm afraid no one's going to take care of me?

You're going to vote for Obama because that's whom you want. That's what's so great about this country, Enrique.

OK, but you just said Obama appeals to "those that are afraid that they're not going to have somebody take care of them." You're generalizing, just like Romney did when talking about "the 47 percent."

Doesn't Obama also do it? "The rich. The rich. The rich." Do you want to know who that one percent is? It's myself and a small company that I'm trying to keep going. And I'm going to have to pay more taxes than the 35 percent that I do now.

Do you make more than $250,000 a year?

Es junto con mi esposo [along with my husband]. He works his butt off! And they don't pay doctors what they used to pay. Congress has stolen from Social Security. They've stolen from Medicare. Why do we have so many programs? And where do you think the money is going to be coming from, Enrique?

Oh, Vikki... We could go on forever. But I respect the fact that you're talking with your heart and standing up for your ideas, unlike many of your colleagues who are unwilling to risk any political opinion for fear of losing fans.

I have to, hon, because a lot of people before would say, "Don't say anything. Think about your career." If I had to do that, I never would have taken the first stand against smoking, OK? And I was blackballed in Nevada because of that in 1974, but I also was the Chairman of the American Lung Association. I fought for the first all-Spanish album; I fought to give scholarships to young Latin-American kids that needed help in East L.A.; I fought to do Holy Cross. So, a lot of things that I've believed in, I have fought for.

That's true. But everybody fights. Everybody works hard. Not just the rich.

We agree there. But don't you think everybody would like to be working now?

Of course, but a lot more people *are* working now than in 2008. I'm one of them. In 2008 there were layoffs all around me. I don't see that happening now on a massive scale as in 2008. For your information: I'm not that thrilled about Obama either, OK? I enthusiastically voted for him and felt somewhat betrayed. And the only reason I'm going to vote for him now is because I saw the Republican National Convention and said, "No way!" But you have to give it to the guy. Am I better off now than in 2008? You bet. And most of my friends are now working, unlike four years ago. Things are still bad, but don't you sincerely think things are a little more stabilized now?

May I say a couple of things? We often complain about 2008 and what happened. But everybody forgets there's no other president that went through what President Bush went through. When they went into two towers.

Right: they went into the towers under *his* watch, and after his administration ignored signs of a possible attack.

Who said that? Where is the proof?

Where is the proof? Didn't you see Condoleezza Rice's testimony before the 9/11 Commission? I can send you the video.

Hindsight is great. Who would have believed that this was going to happen? And why didn't [Bill] Clinton take out Osama Bin Laden when he could have? He blew it there.

Well... At least he tried.

We can keep going back and keep going over cases and cases. But the thing is, you forgot that there was a war. That we had a president that had to stand up for our country, and that's the only time that everybody was united. Now, here was a president (and I'm talking about Obama) who said, "I am going to unite everybody, not divide them." Our country is more divided now than it has ever been. Every time the Republicans could have helped with an idea, he shot it down.

Vikki! It's the other way around! The Republicans are the ones who said, "Our number one priority is to make sure Obama is a one-term president." And…Oh, never mind. Vikki, I still love you, OK?

OK, Enrique. I love you too. And I'm glad this was a nice, heated discussion and debate. I liked it.

Girl in a Coma's Return
(*San Antonio Current*, October 25, 2011)

Girl in a Coma broke my heart. Jenn Alva (bass) and Phanie Díaz (drums) are eating meat again.

"Oh, c'mon…" says Phanie. "It's hard when you're on the road." Jenn tries to make me feel better: "We're still not eating beef."

But the more road-friendly diet is a small thing compared to the many deep realizations and adjustments this group went through on the way to the making of *Exits & All The Rest*, a triumphant work and the trio's fourth album. Not surprisingly, the album is dedicated to Ernestine Davis, Jenn's mom, who passed away in March. But it is also dedicated to San Antonio, "for being our inspiration."

At a time when bands routinely leave town as soon as they get a taste of success, Girl in a Coma don't ever see themselves living anywhere but the Alamo City. What is it about San Antonio that inspires them so much? I asked the girls to show me around those places that nurtured them growing up and continue to provide nourishment. Weeks before their free CD release party at the Pearl on Saturday, Girl in a Coma showed up at the *Current*'s office in their 15-passenger, 2005 Ford van they call "Big Bertha," and took me on a trip into their past.

***

"Romance us!" says Jenn, standing in front of the van. It's a code phrase meaning, "Whoever has the keys, please open the van." There are no automatic locks, so things have to be done the old-fashioned way, by hand. "We call this 'romancing,'" Jenn says as she (the band's official chauffeur) gets behind the wheel. Phanie is to her right. I have the honor of sharing the second row of seats with vocalist/guitarist Nina Diaz — this is her spot, typically nobody rides or sleeps back here but her.

The van is a mess. Clothes, shoes, papers, flyers, CDs, you name it, litter the floorboards and seats. I notice a huge pair of red boots cast to the side. "They're Jenn's," Nina says. "Badass, right? Jenn's Bigfoot. Dang, right? I'm like 6 1/2."

"I'm 10 or 11," says Jenn.

"Petite feet," sings Nina.

"Feminine step…" Phanie responds, referencing a tune by Tim and Eric from Cartoon Network's Adult Swim. Jenn smiles and keeps on driving. The girls are in a great mood.

It's the day after Steve Jobs' passing, and I comment on the iPod plugged into the dash.

"Oh, there's a song there from when Nina was 12," says Phanie. When I ask to hear it, Nina rolls her eyes. "Oh, I sound like a chipmunk," she says of the track, recorded by a friend who was still learning her equipment. "I was singing loud, and she told me, 'You're not supposed to sing so loud when you're recording,'" Nina says. "So I was backing up on it, but now I've learned: You can sing loud."

Our first stop is a vacant building at the corner of McCullough and Dewey, the site of the recently closed Klub Atomix. When the trio — then still known as the plural Girls in a Coma after the Smiths' song "Girlfriend in a Coma" — was first getting off the ground, it was known as Sin 13. "We played our very, very first show here," Jenn says as she approaches the entrance to peer through the glass. Unlike other bands who had to prepare press kits and hustle their way into the scene, the trio's best calling card was their live shows. "We never really had to give press kits to different places," Jenn says. "There weren't many all-girl groups anyway, so they started calling us to come play. We were lucky."

That was 2002, the same year Jenn slipped a cassette tape of their songs to Morrissey in El Paso, not knowing that in 2008 they would be invited to open for him. "We always wanted to do that stuff, but we never thought it would actually happen," Nina says. "It's pretty crazy."

A passing car stops and a woman starts screaming. "Girl In A Coma, right?! Y'all are fucking awesome!"

"Thank you!" the girls reply in unison. They seem genuinely surprised and humbled. The woman gets out of the car and starts spitting out her words rapid-fire. "We were going out to lunch, and I was like, 'There's no way. There's no way!' We turned around, and I was like, 'That has to be them!' We totally need a picture. Y'all are fucking awesome, I swear to God. I know I'm not supposed to be cussing."

Far from adopting rock-star postures, the scene here on the street is no different from what I've seen at concerts time and time again: Girl in a Coma and their fans talking like friends on equal footing. "Yeah, it's nice," says Nina, as we depart. "But I also understand that there are going to be people who don't like our music, and that's fine. The only thing I want people to be aware of is that we're not rich. We're not well-off. We pay our rent, we get some food, we're still struggling artists. Nothing has been given to us."

The group's status as San Antonio's greatest contemporary rock 'n' roll export was sealed in 2006 when Joan Jett signed them to her Blackheart label. You've heard the story: While recording the pilot for SíTV's *Jammin' in New York*, the three were told that one of their musical heroes was planning to drop by. The shows' producers gave them some hints, so that they wouldn't completely freak out.

"We were putting clues together," says Phanie. "We were like, 'Well, she's a female who lives in New York and owns a record label.' So we suspected Joan Jett, but we didn't know until the last minute."

"We kind of knew before, but as soon as we saw her, it was just kind of surreal," says Nina. Even more surreal was what happened later.

"I was just supposed to meet them, watch them rehearse, say hi and all that stuff," Joan Jett told *VenusZine* in 2008, "but I thought they sounded great, and I wanted to see the gig." After watching the rehearsal, Jett checked out their performance at The Knitting Factory. The rest is history. "I was very impressed with them," said Jett, who signed the band to her label the same night. "I thought they'd be great to have on Blackheart. … We really want [the label] to be a place where girls feel comfortable to come play their music, because it was so hard for me."

Four albums later, both Jett and Girl in a Coma are thrilled to have each other.

"We're good friends with her, and we can call her up if we need something," says Phanie. "She's just great."

In a statement sent to the *Current* last Friday, Jett ratified her opinion of the trio, calling them a perfect example of how a band can grow together. "Since they've been with Blackheart, they have toured the U.S. and European continents, have played to bigger and bigger crowds, winning over fans across the spectrum. The musicianship has gone from pretty damn good to really, really good! I am so proud of them and all their very hard work."

***

We're on our way to Hogwild Records, a seminal local music store that has served as a watering hole for the San Antonio indie rock scene since the early '80s. But more than that: this is the band's "favorite record store ever," Phanie says.

This is where the group would hang their show flyers and check to see what other bands were playing around. "This is before MySpace, so we used to come to find bands to play with," says Jenn.

"Look! Here's a Pop Pistol flyer," says Phanie. "They're still putting up their stuff. I think a lot of bands forget [that] you need a flyer."

A good chunk of the group's influences can be traced to the bands they discovered first here. "Man, we would order imports, whatever," says Jenn. "It was always a big competition between [Phanie] and I with albums. I'd be like, 'Oh, I got the new Nirvana import.' You know, UK edition. We'd just order a huge Morrissey poster or a T-shirt. I was always excited when they'd call and said that, you know, 'Your poster's here' or 'Your record's here.' It was awesome."

"I watched them grow very organically from a local band into a very successful national act," says Hogwild's owner David Rischer, hidden behind the register. "I couldn't be prouder of them. Did I envision their present? No, but I'm not in the 'envisioning' business. It's a tribute to their talent and hard work."

A guy selling incense is smitten by Nina (when she paints her lips red, she has one of the best mouths in the history of rock 'n' roll). "Who is this beauty?" he asks. Nina smiles and buys $5 worth of incense, then goes to the register to pay for a Howlin' Wolf vinyl.

On the way to Jefferson High School off of Fredericksburg Road — Nina's high school and the site of Jenn and Phanie's freshman year — Jenn remembers how she "saved" Phanie. "She was in marching band and I told her, 'Phanie, get out of that nerdy shit. Let's start a real band."

"Yeah, but that nerdy shit taught me how to read music, and I'm the only one that can do that," Phanie replies, smiling with pride.

"Yeah, good for you," says Jenn, turning to me while pointing at Phanies' legs. "And she has monster calves from marching band."

"That's a really random fact," says Phanie. "But yes, that's true."

Jenn and Phanie are excited to be back at Jefferson, but Nina whispers, "This is weird. I feel I have to go back to class at any second."

They show me the steps where they took their first-ever band photo in the mid-90s, when they were called Sublimaze, in those pre-Nina days. Since then, the band went through multiple lineup and name changes: Lady Dick, D.O.R (Day Old Rice), Ordinary Girls, Girls In A Coma, Sylvia's Radio, and, finally, Girl in a Coma.

***

Nina remembers always being "the weird girl" at school. Once, after they put up posters for one of their concerts in the school auditorium, a girl tore it and sprayed it in chocolate milk. "That was harsh," Nina says. To get back at her they used to stuff the girl's backpack with bread rolls and fish nuggets.

"She was like, 'Stop throwing stuff in my backpack or I'll tell my dad!'" says Jenn. "We were like, 'Whatever.' She would call us 'lesbians' and run away. At the time we were like, 'We're not lesbians!'"

The band still feels they have a lot to prove, and not just musically.

"Beyond Texas, people don't want to take us serious because we're all girls," says Phanie. "The fact that we're three Latinas, the fact that Jenn and I are gay, the fact that we don't look like a cookie-cutter band: We're not these girls in mini-dresses and high heels. We're just three real girls from San Antonio, Texas, and it's hard for people to accept that."

In the school's cafeteria, I sit down with Phanie while Jenn and Nina clown around with the videographer who has joined us for the day. I comment that Phanie seems to often be the "voice of reason" for the trio. "Yeah, I think that's always been my role in this band," she responds. "Somebody to keep them level-headed when things get crazy."

Phanie is the group's rock. She's the one who taught Jenn how to play bass and switched from guitar to drums so Nina could play guitar and sing. To this day, Phanie is the one to bring them back to reality "when they get distracted or weirded out."

When I turn back to the others, I notice Jenn is crying. "What the hell happened?" I ask. "Are you alright?" It turns out Jenn has been acting. She had been bragging on her four years of theater training in high school and the videographer challenged her.

"I was just trying to show him I could cry on the spot, and I did," she says, a bright smile betraying her tears.

Jenn, a visual artist and creator of the video for their cover of Patsy Cline's "Walking After Midnight," tells me about the many changes during the recording of *Exits & All The Rest*. "I always told myself, if the band doesn't do well, I'm going to have to do Plan B or something," she says. "But the band's been doing great, so that's weird. That's a big change going from your 20s to 30s and playing music."

When Jenn's mother died in March, it was both a personal blow and a potential obstacle to the new album. "You start to realize that the big exit, whether it be death, a change in career, whatever, that's a major thing," Jenn says. "Everything else is just… whatever. When I lost my mom, that's a big exit. And that's what the [album's] title represents: don't sweat the small stuff."

Even though she was asked if she needed more time to record the album, she didn't want to slow things down for the others. She's glad of her decision. "I hope it does something," she says. "We've put even more of ourselves into it. We're growing as musicians and as people, so I hope this is the one. We'll see."

Then there's Nina.

In early 2001, when Phanie and Jenn were 20, a 12-year-old Nina, Phanie's little sister, heard the other two were looking for a singer and asked to audition.

"We thought, 'OK, whatever,'" says Phanie. "We were not thinking anything of it, but as soon as she hit that first note we were amazed. We thought she was showing us a cover song but it was a song she wrote. Regardless of her age, we knew she was to lead the band. I later learned she had been practicing starting a year earlier in her room. She had to build the courage and confidence leading up to that moment where she sang to us on the front porch of our mother's house."

I'm not sure how aware Nina is of this, but she's a world-class singer. Nina's voice is the backbone of the group; everything locks into place when she starts singing. And she's never sounded better than on this album. All you need to know about her talents is in the closing track, "Mother's Lullaby," arguably her best vocal performance ever. When she sings, "And now I'm aching for you" in the chorus, it is the sound of someone finally excising years of pain and confusion.

I tell her how much I like this album, but that hearing the stories behind it reminds me of that Bob Dylan line on "Where Are You Tonight?" in which he sings, "If you don't believe there's a price for this sweet paradise/ just remind me to show you the scars." Then I notice scars on her left wrist.

"I have scars," Nina says. She doesn't try to hide them, but speaks as someone who knows the worst is over. "Every young girl has her silly little moment of self-mutilation. I just would always have a problem with anxiety to the point of..." She pauses. "It was another form of numbness, something to avoid the actual truth of what you need to work on. If I [had been] really trying, I would have gotten it right."

Considering Nina has been with the band since she was 13, her growth could not have been more public. "People have seen me go through my different things, my different relationships. They've seen me at my best, and they've seen me at my worst. You know, the jail thing."

On March 22, 2009, an altercation with two off-duty police officers at Chances, a Houston nightclub, led to Jenn and Nina spending a night in jail. It started with an argument between Nina and an ex-boyfriend. "He was really jealous, and he got really upset about me and [Jane's Addiction's] Dave Navarro, because Dave had a crush on me," Nina says. "I never did anything with [Navarro], nothing at all, but he just had it in his mind that I was doing something."

The discussion got bigger than it had to. Phanie went to get Jenn. "There's trouble in the other room," Phanie told her. Jenn slipped on some beer on the floor, got pissed, and next thing she knew she was fighting with a guy who happened to be a cop. He hit her with a baton and smashed her against a glass window. Both Nina and Jenn spent the night in jail, and a good chunk of the band's savings were consumed fighting third-degree felony charges of assault on a public servant.

"That really sucked," Jenn says. "I felt I was being attacked and I was strong, but Nina was only mouthing off and as a punishment [the cop] lied and wrote that she had hit him too." After a Houston grand jury heard all sides, the two were no billed and the matter was dropped.

For Nina, the incident turned out to be a blessing in disguise. Though the root problem was a man's jealousy, it was fueled by alcohol, she says. And from that moment on she has tried to stay sober. "I've had slip-ups, but I don't want to have them anymore and I'm determined to stay sober," she says. "It's a Pisces thing… We have a tendency to overindulge in certain things." Tell *me* about it.

"I see it all the time," Nina continues. "Men saying, 'Why are you looking at him?' And women saying, 'Why are you looking at her?' It just gets so annoying. Why do you even drink if you're going to end up arguing over something stupid? That silly Houston incident was the beginning for me, and this album was the ending of [the old] me. When you hear the album, you can tell there's a little bit of something waiting to come out."

At the end of "Sly," another album highlight, Nina sings, "Drink your bottle of wine. Feel how high you fly."

"It's like, 'Go ahead and numb yourself. See how far you're going to get with that kind of thing. You're not going to get very far if you keep doing that.' I'm talking to myself as well as others."

***

Next, we go to Nina and Phanie's mom's house, where they rehearse. No beer here — Topo Chico water is the drink of choice. After running through "Smart," the first new single, Nina explains how the lyrics evolved. "At first, the girls didn't really like it because I said 'sunshine' in the lyrics," she says.

"Nina would be like, 'Did you ever see the sunshine?' And it sounded too commercial to Jenn and I," Phanie says. "We were like, 'What are you talking about?' She changed the lyrics, and then we got involved."

Nina changed the "sunshine" line to "don't you ever start to wonder what it's like to be alone," and this living-room performance adds rawness to the most radio-friendly song on the album.

When Nina talks about the other songs she has building up "for other things," Phanie teases her: "Yeah, for a detergent."

Performing as Sylvia's Radio last Thursday, the girls tried out the new songs at a not-so-secret concert at Nightrocker Live. They blazed through a dynamite set that included eight of the album's 11 new songs and a few older gems, like a cover of the Beatles' "While My Guitar Gently Weeps," which they dedicated to its author, George Harrison.

Whether the album will be merely treated as another "promising" work by Girl in a Coma or serve as the long-awaited breakthrough that will take them to new heights, no one knows. But no matter what, we'll always have them with us. "When we were younger, we thought we had to leave in order to make it," says Jenn. "It took our first tour for us to realize, 'God, we have a really good thing back at home.'"

"This is a unique city," says Phanie. "There's a lot of art and culture, lots of hidden talent, it's very united, and everyone has each other's backs here. I have no intentions of ever leaving or moving anywhere else."

"I've always liked Los Angeles or New York," says Nina, "but San Antonio is always my home. I'm never going to say, 'Oh, I'm from L.A.' or 'Oh, I'm from New York.' I'm from San Antonio. I was born and raised here, and I want to stay here."

But with those songs and that voice, will Nina ever release a solo album?

"Yeah, I've thought about it," she says. "It would be something just for fun. It wouldn't be now, nor anytime soon. I do have songs [set] aside that aren't necessarily Girl in a Coma songs. I'd also like to do an all-Spanish album [with Jenn and Phanie] someday. Unfortunately, I'm part of the younger generation that wasn't really forced to learn it. Now, I regret not paying attention in Spanish class."

Phanie says that she and Jenn support side projects. "If she wants to go and try some stuff out or release a record, we'll support it. And I think even Jenn and I talked about doing a side thing. But Girl in a Coma will always put out records and will always go on tour no matter what happens in our brains."

"Yeah, I'm hoping that we're going to end up being 40-, 50-year-old ladies still playing in a band and putting out records," says Jenn. "When they ask, 'Who influenced you?' people can be like, 'Oh, Sonic Youth,' and another will say, 'Oh, Girl in a Coma. They've been doing it for 40 years.' It'd be so rad to be able to do that."

"We'll be like Aerosmith or the Stones," says Nina. "We'll always be together, and there will always be Girl in a Coma." She has the conviction and enthusiasm of someone who has never seen things so clearly and doesn't have any more time for silly bullshit. "I'm starting to get very, very focused on little details, like on certain pedals I need to use, and I'm starting to write songs for the next album," she says between sips of her Topo Chico.

"It's real. If I get stressed out or get writer's block, I know it passes. I don't have to do anything to pass the time except letting the time pass. I think it's going to be great. Everything's going to be OK."

Public Enemy's Chuck-D: Fight the Power
(*San Antonio Current*, November 3, 2011)

Public Enemy will be at Austin's Fun Fun Fun Fest's Blue stage on Friday, Nov. 4, at 8:30pm. For those outside of Austin, Pitchfork will be streaming the festival live starting at noon on November 4-6. The following is a phone chat with Chuck-D, who was driving somewhere in Brooklyn.

Man, you won't believe the crap I have to hear. Why do most young, up-and-coming rappers seem unable to take the Public Enemy-approach to hip-hop to new heights?

(laughs) Yeah, I know, I know… Once the corporations started dangling their money on top of the art form, it turned the "we" into "I." When you care about "we" you care about what affects "we" and the community and the people, so therefore you make songs that we and the community can relate to. I have nothing against these [new] songs, because people want to actually get away from what affects their everyday life. They want to have a good time and drink and stuff like that, but there [used to be] a balance when it came down to Black music, and that's where we come from. Somebody's got to protect the door at the party, you know what I'm saying?

Today I was reading a quote by Malcolm X where he says that, if we're not careful, the media will make us hate the oppressed and love the oppressor. The current political climate seems made-to-order for Public Enemy.

Yeah, pretty much. This is the silent sea of media in the United States. For example, you have so many people who are anti-immigration that come from immigrants. It's a damn shame. They don't even understand the true histories of this land, and that's why we put things in our music. I have a song from last year called "Tear Down This Wall," and it takes Ronald Reagan to tear down that wall, but you know what? The United States has spent billions on a wall between Mexico and the United States that makes no sense in the modern day. You can go check it out on publicenemy.com or just put down "Tear Down That Wall." My statement is, we got to occupy hip-hop.

How do you do that?

You occupy hip-hop by supporting many of the artists who make songs that support the people of their community instead of the corporations trying to get money from the community by any means necessary. I think that's a good way to start. Support the artists that are saying something, and there's plenty of artists who are doing it on the Internet. We can occupy hip-hop by supporting those that are speaking for the people instead of against the people.

Fortunately, there are still some people doing good things. What contemporary rappers do you like?

I have a radio show. I play people like Common. I support the Roots. I support Lupe Fiasco, who's saying some things. Also, Dead Prez has always been strong and powerful, but they've been kept out of mainstream opportunities. People like J-Live, Immortal Technique, KRS-One have always been fantastic and great. These guys don't get worse; they get better.

Do you see any chance for Obama in 2012?

He's a great driver on a bad vehicle, like a good captain with a bad boat. I think the two-party system in America is outdated. I think it does nothing for the people, and the politicians have to spend most of their time fighting each other for position. This is why you see these occupy movements come out. The politicians and corporations seem to be moving further away from the needs of the people. I don't expect miracles from anybody in government.

But Obama blew it with all of his conciliatory bullshit…

That's a bad position to be in. The minute that you get into office, you're going to have to be on the defense. When you talk about the people, the people have to be fought for. A job can't be defended more than the people. That's the issue.

Bad position for him or me to take?

I think no one could do a good job in that presidential suite. The only thing you can do in that presidential suit is do worse, and you have to say basically, "Fuck the people" and "Fuck the world," like Bush said, and then you can probably be successful at being a US president because you followed the American agenda. Is that too strong for you?

It's pretty hopeless…

When you have people sitting in the same section who are anti-immigration law, I don't understand what that's about. I have no idea what that's about. This is one world, and countries and governments are just like corporations. They control people. The fact that you have to ask permission from a government to go to the world that God gave us is actually ridiculous to me. Maybe I'm a believer and a purist, but that's the way I feel, Enrique. That's the way I feel.

So, what should we do in November 2012?

I'm going to vote for Obama again. I don't want no cowboy up in there like Governor Rick Perry... I don't expect miracles by any of these people. I just think that we should be able to do things [for ourselves]. I don't rely on government for anything. I believe that most Americans, if they're able to work with the world, they would be able to do better. But America doesn't serve us the world. It just consumes now. It's just some individual, selfish bullshit to me.

I don't understand: you admit even Obama can't do shit, that's the nature of the position, but you're still going to vote for him? I'm not saying we should vote Republican, but there's a third alternative.

What third alternative?

Democrats always get away with murder because they know most (true) liberals would never vote for the GOP. But what Obama did is incredible. He had the momentum, the popularity, the mandate, everything served on a silver platter, and he kept "negotiating" with people who told him on his face their main goal is "to make sure he's a one-term president." We should fuck the Democrats until they learn they have to deliver what they promise instead of trying to be like Republicans. At least they should *try*. We should vote for a real socially conscious third party. And if the GOP wins, fine — I survived eight years of Bush, I can take four more years of whatever clown the GOP nominates. What I can't take is Obama shitting on all of us who were hoping for him to stand up for what's right.

I don't know, man... To me, it ain't no baseball game. I mean, I think the two-party system in America is bullshit. Maybe it needs to be one party. Everybody knows that the party comes along and you end up voting for the person inside the party. Look, the Democrats are damn near Republicans and the Republicans are Democrats in some kind of way. The Republicans seriously want to get into the dynamic of identity, and they're Klansmen. But I don't even want to get into that. It's all one big political game, and people don't want politics to play with them like it's a big game, and they can't help it.

OK, I'm pissed now. Let's change the subject. Tell me about the new album you're working on.

It'll be called *Most Of Our Heroes Still Don't Appear On No Stamp*.

That's based on a line from "Fight the Power," right?

Yes. I like making one song at a time to make it very relevant, but I am committed to doing this album because it's a project, but it's still a band project to show how things are put together in a digital type of way. I'm committed to making an album. It's going to say a lot of things. It's going to be a concept album. We'll see how it goes. I'll tell you, I have always started making one song at a time because you can make a song based on how you feel at the moment and then release it the next day if you need to. That's what I like, I like the fact of making things a capella and letting it out there and seeing remixes come back with something.

But will it be singles, an EP, or a full album?

It's going to be a whole album. I just told you what I like. I like making one song at a time and releasing them separately, but I'm going to release an album. It's going to be fun, but I enjoy making new roads with new music. That's what I enjoy. I think that's really exciting, knowing that you can put an a capella out there and see what comes back.

Were you surprised by the impact of *It Takes a Nation of Millions To Hold Us Back*? Why is it so powerful? It still sounds great.

As far as hip-hop, the album format was new. It was a new expression at the time, and we knew that very few people had tackled an album that actually meant something, with strong topics, and we took to that task. We wanted to make an album full of up-tempo fight songs. That was our goal, and we knew it wasn't being done. We just said, "OK, let's do what isn't being done." That was new and refreshing at the time. What challenges me is doing something new that hasn't really been done. That's what I like.

Once and for all: What's your take on homosexuality?

My whole take is people should not have anybody telling them what to do with their lives. Whatever goes on in their lives, why would a government have the final say on whether you should get married or not, whether you should be with someone or not? I'm very strong about people having their human rights and sexual rights, and leave it at that. I really don't care what anybody does.

What about lyrics like "Man to man/I don't know if they can/From what I know/the parts don't fit," for which you got some flack in the past? (From "Meet the G That Killed Me")

I was addressing the germ that I think was created in a lab. You can call me crazy or whatever, but I think that AIDS was biological warfare on people designed by some person in some kind of laboratory. You know, it's affected gays, it's affected a lot of different people, so therefore I was addressing that in my song. [The "G" in the song title] could be replaced with God, girls, gay, germ, but it basically shows how something was created to take the whole area of love and use the area of love. Look, you can't get no more diabolical than that, because it can't get better than [having sex]. So if they can figure out a way to have you die doing something that natural, that's a diabolical war. When I made it, it basically talked about how the germ was transferred. At the end of the song, Flavor goes up and introduces me to some girl that he's with and goes, "Hey Chuck, meet this G that killed me." It could have been, "Meet this girl that killed me, meet the germ that killed me." Basically, at that particular time in 1989, if you caught the germ, it was automatically and socially instant death. That's what the song "Meet the G That Killed Me" [means]. It was basically talking in past tense. I was very angry at the fact that this germ, I thought, was manufactured to kill people. [I'm still angry] to this day, there's not a legitimate answer to any of this. It's mind-boggling. One of the big discrimination areas in hip-hop and music is discrimination against women and gays. We built shemovement.com as that portal that really has women making music on their own terms without having a man dictate what kind of music they should do or what kind of art they should do. I think that's the biggest crime going in hip-hop right now — the destruction of groups, collectives, and the destruction of women [making] music on their own terms.

Was Flavor Flav ever out of the band?

People would come to us and be like, "Oh, we hope you get back together." And I'd say, "Who the hell thought we broke up?" They might have said it when they saw Flavor on a TV show, "How could he do a TV show and still be in the band?" It only takes two weeks to film one of those things that last all year. So he has to deal with the ignorance of people that don't know the industry, that'll just throw anything at us. And we have to be like, "Well, where'd you get that from?"

Twenty-five years later, things are different. Hip-hop is dominated by corporations and Public Enemy is not an as influential as it used to be. Do you agree?

Well, we're not mainstream. Never really were. We never had a record that was in the top 20. Never. Never had any Grammy awards. Never had no *Rolling Stone* covers. We had to fight for our influence. These other guys, instead of having to fight for their influence, just happen to be mainstream and successful. We can't even be put in the same category. We're more like pioneers of what we did instead of being [influencers]. Our influence is in the creation of these acts, not trying to be influenced so people can say, "Oh there's Public Enemy; I'll go hang them up on my wall." We're way past that. Look, would you say the Beatles are influential?

Yes.

Would you say they're more influential than Eminem?

In the big scheme of things, probably. But I think *It Takes A Nation Of Millions To Hold Us Back* is the *Sgt. Pepper* of hip hop.

Most people say *Fear of a Black Planet* was. We're happy to have two.

Do you feel 2007's *How You Sell Soul To A Soulless People Who Sold Their Soul* is underrated? I believe it should have had more of an impact.

We don't really look at other places for respect. We play those songs off that album, either we smack the crap [unintelligible] or we don't. That's what we do. We don't really care what anybody thinks. When we come live and perform, when we come down to Austin, we're going to give a show that, if somebody sees us for the first time, they're going to say, "Oh my God." That's our only goal. A song can be anything, but if you can't perform the song, what good are you? We don't need no explosions. We don't need none of that pyrotechnic shit. What we gotta do is get down.

Movies and Booze
(*San Antonio Current*, December 13, 2011,
and *Orlando Weekly*, February 8, 2012)

It's hard to believe but, even in 2012, the film industry continually faces a villain more arch and stubborn than pirates, bored patrons or "sequel-itis": teetotalers. Whether on the screen or in the seats, alcohol is an issue — at press time, battle lines have been drawn regarding beer and wine in movie theaters all over the continent, from Vancouver to Levittown, NY, where one local official was quoted as saying, "If movies booze, families lose." The movies do, indeed, booze: One of the buzziest films that came out of the Sundance Film Festival in January was a darkly comic hit called *Smashed*, about an elementary school teacher's battle with alcohol addiction.

We say long live the potentially flammable (and always entertaining) mixture of celluloid and cocktails. From Pathés' anti-drinking documentary *Les victimes de l'alcoolisme* (1902) to *Sideways* (2004) and beyond, the devil's drink has been a frequent guest on the big screen with actors delivering some of the medium's most memorable lines (and gags) when a bottle was nearby.

Best gag: *The Idle Class* (1921)
"I will occupy the other room until you stop drinking," reads the note signed by Edna (Edna Purviance), the tortured wife in Charlie Chaplin's classic short. After reading the note, Chaplin — playing the Tramp as alcoholic husband — looks at a portrait of his wife, starts weeping, and turns his back to the camera as his crying apparently becomes inconsolable. But when he turns back to face the camera, we meet the husband shaking not from grief but from mixing himself a drink.

Best unsolved vomit: *This Is Spinal Tap* (1984)
On the death of former drummer Stumpy Joe:
Derek Smalls: "The official explanation is that he choked on vomit."
Nigel Tufnel: "It was actually someone else's vomit."
D.S.: "They can't prove whose vomit it was. They don't have facilities in Scotland Yard."
N.T.: "You can't really dust for vomit."

Most accurate ETA: *Leaving Las Vegas* (1995)
Ben: "I came here to drink myself to death."
Sera: "How long will it take you?"

Ben: "I'd say about three to four weeks."

Best toast while falling off the wagon: *The Shining* (1980)
Jack Torrance: "Here's to five miserable months on the wagon and all the irreparable harm it has caused me."

Best discriminatory moment: *Sideways* (2004)
Miles Raymond: "If anyone orders Merlot, I'm leaving. I am not drinking any fucking Merlot!"

Best tolerance: *Who's Afraid of Virginia Woolf?* (1966)
Martha: "Look, sweetheart, I can drink you under any goddamn table you want, so don't worry about me."

Best indication you should not date that guy: *The Lost Weekend* (1945)
Don Birnam: "What kind of party did you say that was?"
Helen St. James: "A cocktail party."
D.B.: "In that case, I'll join you."

Best case for drinking: *The Lost Weekend* (1945)
Don Birnam: "It shrinks my liver, doesn't it, Nat? It pickles my kidneys, yeah. But what it does to the mind? It tosses the sandbags overboard so the balloon can soar. Suddenly I'm above the ordinary. I'm competent. I'm walking a tightrope over Niagara Falls. I'm one of the great ones. I'm Michelangelo, molding the beard of Moses. I'm Van Gogh painting pure sunlight. I'm Horowitz, playing the Emperor Concerto. I'm John Barrymore before movies got him by the throat. I'm Jesse James and his two brothers, all three of them. I'm W. Shakespeare. And out there, it's not Third Avenue any longer, it's the Nile. Nat, it's the Nile, and down it moves the barge of Cleopatra."

Best case for not drinking: *Leaving Las Vegas* (1995)
Ben: "I don't know if my wife left me because of my drinking, or I started drinking because my wife left me."

Best case for drinking part 2: *Barfly* (1987)
Tully: "Why don't you stop drinking? Anybody can be a drunk."
Henry: "Anybody can be a non-drunk. It takes a special talent to be a drunk. It takes endurance. Endurance is more important than truth."

John Swenson: The Music Writer
(*San Antonio Current*, July 16, 2012;
transcribed by Tori Sommerman)

John Swenson, one of the deans of music journalism, is coming to town. The former Crawdaddy, Creem, *and* Rolling Stone *editor (and current editor of* OffBeat *and a renowned sportswriter) will be hosting a music writing workshop on July 21 at Gemini Ink. He'll walk you through an interview, read your writing, and tell stories of his accolade-filled career. Days before his visit, Swenson spoke with the* Current *from his home in New Orleans.*

How is your workshop going to work? What should we expect?

I have no idea what the composition of the people who are going to attend the workshop will be. So I will definitely approach this on an individual basis. I have a few exercises that will apply to whomever might show up. I am going to talk about some history. I am going to demonstrate interview techniques with local recording artist Bett Butler, who is also a historian. There are two parts of the seminar that will take place during the day, and during the second part Bett is going to sit in and allow herself to be interviewed by the entire group. We'll discuss techniques for a successful interview during that process. But I want to keep this as open-ended as I possibly can and involve the participation of those attending the seminar as much as I can. The one thing that a one-day event will limit is how much I can review whatever writing people are interested in showing me. So what I am going to offer whoever is involved is a follow-up where they can either bring to the class what they want me to read of their writing, or they can email me later and I will offer them feedback on their work. In my ongoing capacity as an editor, you know, I am always looking for new writers. So, that might be part of it. To answer your question more specifically, it is going to be open-ended depending on who shows up.

After being in the business since the beginning of rock writing, do you agree that, except for some honorable cases, most music writing today is entertainment rather than journalism?

There is no question about that. Certainly, mainstream entertainment reporting has become almost entirely celebrity based. This is a process that's been slowly going on since the '70s. However, I do think that the entire music industry and entertainment industry is going through massive changes that are precipitated by the democratization of the Internet; through blogs people are able to write some very interesting things. I mean, the downside to that is, a) you don't get paid for that and, b) it's a somewhat limited audience. But you know, it's still in its infancy. I think that the people who have something interesting to say have a forum to say it. Serious journalists aren't being paid for their work in the way they used to be. Unfortunately, we are reaching a point where being a serious journalist is something that you have to do in your spare time, while you have a day job.

What would you say are the most common mistakes new, young music writers make?

I think that biggest mistake young writers make is to fall in love with their words. Writing is a job, it's hard work. Revision is... I may have known only one or two writers in my lifetime who were automatic, that could sit down and write and never have to revise.

Anyone famous?

Well, Lester Bangs was like that.

Who was the other one?

Oh, I would say it would be wire service journalist Bruce Olson. He ran the City desk at United Press International during the 1980s. But that was a specific type of discipline, writing wire service copy. It had to be written fast and he was a machine. Completely different from Lester Bangs. But I think that, for most people, writing is something that requires revision. You need to really work and hone the craft until you get everything right. I am sure you agree with me, being a writer yourself.

Totally. But, as you well know, one of the consequences of downsizing is that writers are busier than ever, covering more than one beat, and the turnaround is faster than ever.

Obviously, I've had to write some things hurriedly. Downsizing only places more deadline pressure on a writer and, like any artisan, writers have to weigh a tricky balance between speed and excellence. More pressure means more mistakes and less fully realized thought. Pausing for reflection shouldn't have to be a luxury but, unfortunately it has become one. One advantage of online writing is that it can still be edited after it's posted. But even then, you have to have the time to go back and think about it.

Besides the writing part, there's the question of ethics. I am very anal, very old school about not accepting trips, taking photos with the people I write about, or hanging out backstage unless I really, really have to. But there are cases like Lester Bangs: he would accept a trip to interview the Clash, come out of the plane completely wasted, and then write an absolutely memorable piece about them. What are the limitations? What are the do's and don'ts of any serious music writer?

Well, certainly I don't think you should take junkets as a music writer. I have to admit I have done that, but it was a really long time ago and I never let it affect me. I don't think too many people are really paying their way into coverage. But you bring up another point and that is that some people basically write about their friends. Now is this a matter of ethics or is it just a matter of being a fan rather than being a professional? That's a really open question. I think that the nature of the Internet coverage creates a situation where a lot of even some of the best writing about music is done by fans now rather than by objective journalists. So, [it] becomes a grey area at this point.

So, taking certain ethical licenses are only really valid if you can write like Lester Bangs or people like that?

Well, only Lester could write like Lester. I think it's a big mistake to try to imitate that style. Everyone has to develop their own voice and Lester's voice was perfect for its time. But I doubt that Lester would still be writing like that today if he were still around. I knew him very well and I think he would have gotten tired of writing that way, personally.

Worst first questions in any interview.

"How did you start?" "How you doing?" Probably not a good idea to start like that. Serious artists expect serious questions.

How important it is for a music writer to know music or to make music himself/herself?

Not important at all and, and here is why: I think it is a real fallacy for people who are music students or musicians to get too involved in the technical part of what they are writing about (unless, of course, they are writing for a technical journal), because the audience is not composed of musicians. So, they're not going to know what they're talking about. And I see this a lot, particularly with jazz writing, where the writing gets to the point where there are too many technical issues being discussed rather than aesthetic issues. For the most part, the general audience is interested in aesthetics rather than matters of technique.

From all the writers that I have read, it seems to me that only the late Robert Palmer [1945-1997] was the ultimate example of someone who didn't just know about Anglo rock 'n' roll and jazz, but he was well-versed in all sorts of music, from classical to World. Some people stick to one type of style and become experts in that field. Shouldn't everyone, not only writers but readers as well, listen to as many styles as possible?

I think that is a healthy thing to do. You've named probably my favorite writer in history in Robert Palmer, God rest his soul. What a tremendous thinker. Now, here is someone who was a musician and understood the technical aspects of music but also understood how to talk to a general audience about music and how to relate different styles across the differences between the styles. He could talk about jazz or rock or hip-hop, because he did write about early hip-hop. He could pretty much relate any kind of style to its root elements. Music is music. The one phrase that you'll hear from all the greats over the years is there's only two types of music: good and bad. Obviously, some people prefer a certain style of music. You know, Frank Zappa famously said that music, for most people, was a lifestyle choice like fashion.

He also said (and I'm paraphrasing) that "music writers are people who can't write, writing about people who can't play, for people who can't read."

(Laughs) Very well recalled on your part. Well, there have been a lot of people who are really just posers or masquerading as journalists, just pretending to be music writers. Anyone can declare themselves one, you know. There have been a lot of bad ones over the years. They tend to disappear, but that's why people like Frank Zappa built up such a poor opinion of them. Historically, the music industry has been a very big powerful money industry populated with very clever publicists who manipulated a lot of the writers who wrote about it, in ways the writers weren't even aware of in many cases. This is a byproduct of this industry. You know, a lot of this hype is simply publicity and, you know, a lot of it was bought. I hate to single out *Rolling Stone* for this because it was a thing that happened pretty much across the board, but certainly there were instances where five-star reviews were literally paid for in the magazine. So this is built-in, it is cooked into the stew. You have to be aware of that throughout the history of music criticism.

The Making of Los Lobos' *Kiko*: A ~~Chicano~~ Rock Masterpiece

The Complete Louie Pérez Q&A
(*San Antonio Current*, August 21, 2012)

With the August 21 20th anniversary edition of Los Lobos' masterpiece, *Kiko* (1992), the East L.A. band celebrates two decades of an album that defined them as a band. The celebration includes the simultaneous release of *Kiko Live* (recorded at a concert at the San Diego House of Blues in 2006), available on DVD and Blu-ray. The *Current* spoke to founding member Louie Pérez on the making of the album and the "identity crisis" the band went through after reaching the top of the charts with "La Bamba."

Tell *Kiko* I said happy 20!

Thanks! Here is the real kicker: this November we are going to have our 39th anniversary. And in November 2013 we are going to be 40 years old.

Why November?

We knew the band started at around that time, so from the very beginning we have always picked Thanksgiving to be our anniversary. We would get together and have a barbecue. Now the years go by and it's like, "Oh, yeah it's our anniversary. Hey, what time is the flight tomorrow?" (laughs) But it's great. It's going to be 40 years and we are going to do a lot of stuff.

And with the same lineup for most of those years [saxophonist Steve Berlin joined in 1984].

Yeah, it's the same set. I don't know if we hold the record for the original members from the very beginning.

It's amazing.

(Sighs) I don't know... Well, remember we were a band for 10 years before we ever had a record deal or before anything else ever happened to us. The first year was, I think, 1983, with our first record with Warner Brothers [the 1983 EP ...*And a Time to Dance*]. That was to kind of legitimize ourselves after doing *Just Another Band From East L.A.* on our own in 1978. So, it's not like we were a brand new band. We were already adults when we became "rock stars."

The band is almost 40 and *Kiko* has just turned 20. Do you ever listen to it?

If I never even put the record on or never even listened to another note since [it came out], then it would still stand out in my mind. It was a life-changing experience as a songwriter. Something happened. Talk about blowing minds — that album did it. I don't even know. Everything just kind of lined up and something happened. I hate using "magical," but something otherworldly happened in the studio during that time. And, yes, I have listened to the record. To me, it's as if I hear it and I'm like, "Wow." It still holds a big place in my life as a songwriter and in the lives of this band. And something happened during that time that I really can't explain. All I know is the events leading up to it. We released a bunch of cool records and then "La Bamba" happened and we became this big thing. Nobody knew everything else. It almost eclipsed everything else that we had done before. In my own opinion, I think the band went through a little bit of an identity crisis because here we were, "The 'La Bamba' Band." And we had been together for so many years before that.

Was it a bittersweet success? I mean, you become number one all of a sudden, but for all the wrong reasons.

It was the right reason, because we paid tribute to the legacy of Ritchie Valens. He brought name and prominence to Chicanos. It was Chicanos back then that were doing radical things. I mean, no one had ever taken a 100-year-old *canción folclórica* and put it to rock 'n' roll, and this was [1958]. That was way, way radical. But I guess what happened was that we kind of sacrificed ourselves for it. At the time, we didn't think it would become as big as it was. And at the time, a lot of people would expect [us to do] "the Ritchie Valens Show," but we didn't do that. We didn't turn ourselves into "The 'La Bamba' Band." We just did exactly what we had been doing for 15 years at that point.

Did you ever purposely refuse to play the song live after its success?

I think a little bit of that has been sensationalized. Somebody might have said something once, and then somebody told somebody else, and then it would spread out. But we never willfully said, "No, we are not doing it anymore. We are boycotting it." We just didn't play it that often anymore because, as part of our set, we didn't always play it. We would play it every now and then or play "Come On, Let's Go." We were supporting other records. It wasn't a part of what we did all the time. So, it really didn't change much. We wouldn't play it a lot once it became a hit, but later it just became part of our repertoire. I think it would be a little bit insulting to our legacy to say that we refused to play it. But that wasn't really the case.

So, you do play it now?

Jimi Hendrix played "Purple Haze" and "Foxy Lady." And the Doors had to play "Light My Fire." And on, and on, and on. Bands always have that one hit that they are expected to play, and they will play it because people respond to it. Yesterday we played in Seattle at the zoo and there was a bunch of people, families. It was sold out and we played "La Bamba" because we know that everybody is going to get up on their feet and sing along. So, we never had any bad taste about "La Bamba." It really put Los Lobos on the map. After that, though, we had to work on getting ourselves back on track and getting our audiences educated on the fact that we were more than just "La Bamba." And we had an identity crisis because, right after the song happened, we may have been expected to do "La Bamba No. 2" to chase after that hit song, and then do something like it. That wasn't what we were about, though. We already had a very rich history of original music and had two or three critically acclaimed records. So after "La Bamba" happened, we went to the extreme and released an album of *música folclórica*, *La Pistola y El Corazón*, and everybody thought we were crazy. Journalists from coast to coast, all over the place, were saying that Los Lobos committed commercial suicide.

So, you needed to stop and regroup.

That's exactly right. At that point we were saying, "Ok, who are we? Are we "The 'La Bamba Band' or are we this?" So, we went into the attic to find out who we were. We opened it up to find out who we really were. And right inside there was a cardboard box that had our whole Mexican heritage, so we decided to focus in the music that really means something to us. And that was *música folclórica*, because that was the music we started playing as Los

Lobos. This was a way for us to pay tribute to our roots and to expose it to a larger audience. I got such a huge smile on my face when I found out people in Helsinki or Tokyo were listening to *son jarocho*. It was a really important statement for us to make. We were kind of just grounding ourselves after that big hit.

Then came *The Neighborhood*.

That was going back to our roots as rock 'n' rollers. And after that, we were thinking, "What do we do next?" We already had grounded ourselves and had our originals back on track again. I think a lot of what happened with *Kiko* was that we were opening up ourselves to a lot of possibilities. At that point, David [Hidalgo] and I just started writing down some songs and it just went somewhere else. There were no more rules. We went into the studio to not even try. We were just going to let things happen. Mitch Froom and Tchad Blake came in and they were having a similar situation with them too. They had just come off working with Crowded House, a real hit. And they too, as a team of producer/engineer were thinking, "OK, now that we are commercially successful producers, what are we going to do?" We all found ourselves in the same mental place.

You started working in a shitty studio, and then somebody at the label suggested you give Froom a call. That's when things *really* started happening.

Yeah. [Froom and Blake] brought everything that they had. They put everything into it and we put everything into it. [They] created this environment for us to be comfortable, where we could just try things and do things that were different. And once we got in the studio it was like, "OK, we got a bunch of crayons, and we have a lot of paint. So let's just make something." We were open to everything that was going to happen, whatever experiences, discoveries, or music. We had nothing to prove anymore. No one has to tell us if we have a single in here or, "What is this?" We looked at it as just one big piece of canvas and threw all the paint at it to see what came out. It was just a transcendental experience for us. The record almost seemed to make itself. We had no control over it.

I never heard a cumbia like "Kiko and the Lavender Moon." It has a jazzy, psychedelic feel to it, especially when the sax appears.

You are right. When David [Hidalgo] came up with the basic idea he was thinking of a cumbia. But the introduction is a Duke Ellington sort of thing. There is sort of a jazzy element to it. And then we brought it together and the imagery that I wrote was this magic realism sort of thing and it happened without even trying. I just painted this picture with a song and it sounded like a jazz-based cumbia.

And the video is superb.

That was really interesting. We looked at a bunch of different videos of artists and there was a Czechoslovakian filmmaker [Ondrej Rudavsky]. This guy was like avant-garde and a good video artist. A lot of those effects that he did were all done mechanically. He took a record player turntable and cut out figures on it and he filmed those things going around on a turntable. That's what I mean by mechanical effects. It was very beautiful.

Let's talk about the percussion on the album. Right off the bat, with "Dream in Blue," you can tell something's going on here.

There is a lot of groove on it. The very first track, "Dream in Blue," has that drum figure. Pete Thomas, from the Attractions, played on most of the record and he could actually pull off this groove. So we told him that there was a song to where this could fit. That groove comes actually from a Jamaican ska tradition. And then you look at something like, "Wake Up, Dolores," and the percussion on that is more tribal because the theme is of an indigenous, Mexican culture. And then when you look at, "Saint Behind the Glass," it is a *mezcla* of *son jarocho,* and the approach there was different for percussion. The songs were recorded song by song and we would move on only after a song was finished. Songs were being written as they were being recorded, and new ideas were coming up every day. Tchad Blake was just a genius in the recording studio and was trying all these different techniques. He would take a Shure [SM]57 mic and put it in the bottom of a trash can. We wouldn't overthink it too much. And although everything was very lush, nothing was over-produced. It was like a painting where you lay down the first colors and then you start to make a shape and then you add other colors when it starts to take form. And musically it was the same: we let the background of the music lead the way. We didn't rehearse anything.

"Whiskey Trail" is a simple, fierce rocker that ends with a bunch of effects, including what I think is a woman screaming. What the hell was that?

Wow, I don't remember that.

Hold on, let me play it for you. [Pérez listens through the phone]

(laughs) I don't know what that was. I do remember that there were a lot of things that Tchad [Blake] brought in because he is a collector of sounds. And somehow that ended up on there. Even if you listen to "Wicked Rain," the tape machine is just starting up. There is a lot of that on the record where we are revealing the process of recording. In the whole record there is evidence of being in the studio.

I don't know, man... *Kiko* was such a radical change that I can't help thinking, "These guys were really having fun there." *Sgt. Pepper*'s was supposedly the Beatles' acid record. Did altered states have anything to do with how magical *Kiko* came out?

I don't think that is something you would ask Gabriel García Márquez. It's like asking him, "Were you on drugs?" No, I wasn't on drugs. Where did that thing come from? I don't know. I just really don't have an answer. All I know is that we just got to that point where it became a sort of transcendental sort of experience. And I still look for that when I write. When I am working on a song, there is another place that I go to, and a lot of artists and writers probably do the same thing. They go to another place where there is no time. It is just a zone I get into. When I'm writing a song, I have no sense of time or anything. All of us went into this chamber of altered states.

Not only the music, but the lyrics are different as well.

Even "Wake Up, Dolores" had all those images. I look back at that record and think, "Wow, how did I do that?" And every time I sit down to write it's almost terrifying because, how could I ever write "Saint Behind the Glass" again? I'm kind of daunted by that. Whenever I think back about that album, I think someone else was at work there. We opened up this connection and power that was greater than ourselves and we allowed it to all just come in. I'm not trying to seem like we went into the studio and meditated and lit incense or anything. The only mystery was, how did it all just come together so perfectly? It's really difficult to describe. Even when we finished the record and listened to it from start to finish, we didn't say anything to each other. We just got up and walked to our cars and went home. It was so surreal. I've been trying to find it again. I found a little bit of it with *The Town and the City*. It's like when you look at these artists or painters or musicians and they reach a place where everything just seems right, and everything just comes out. It's the master at work on the masterpiece. It's where artists hit this one spot where something else just takes over and then they try to chase after that again. It's been really difficult for me to find that place again. I've come close to it, but I haven't found it entirely. It's similar for everyone where a particular album was "it" for the artist.

It was the band's peak, in a sense.

That's what I mean, even though I didn't want to say that because whenever you think of reaching a peak the only place after the peak is down. So, I'm afraid of using that word. Everyone has said *Kiko* is Los Lobos' masterpiece work and that nothing can ever reach that. It's very difficult to accept that as an artist.

It's difficult but it's a damn good album, isn't it?

No shit.

And then you do *Kiko Live*, which is a completely naked version of *Kiko* that proves the songs were there. It wasn't only about studio wizardry.

That's an excellent way of looking at it. The recorded version of *Kiko* was just this dense, organic, and psychedelic album, but it wasn't just all this studio stuff. When you look at *Kiko Live* and *Kiko* studio together, you really see how all the songs were really there. That's what I'm really proud of. When we decided to do the shows for *Kiko Live*, I think we decided to do seven or eight of them. It was also shot in a film as well. When we set out to do the tour, we were just only going to do it for a handful of days. It crossed my mind as to how we were going to reproduce it and recreate that, but once we entered into the rehearsal studio, we started these songs and thought that, "No, we can do this." Another thing is that, when we started putting the songs together for the live tour, the songs held up on their own. It's not really a big departure.

OK, let's look beyond *Kiko*. I always wanted to ask you how you view San Antonio. You guys have a strong connection with San Antonians like Flaco Jiménez, Max Baca, and Steve Earle.

When we first toured the US, the St. Mary's Bar and Grill was the very first show we did in Texas, I think. Of course, SA is one of the cities that are predominantly *mexicano* and Mexican American. I love San Antonio. As a matter of fact, a good friend of mine, Oscar Garza [former editor at the *Los Angeles Times*] is from San Antonio. I got San Antonio music coming in and out of my ears all the time, with *conjunto* and all of that. It has such a rich culture there. Some people I talk to are like, "Ah, I don't care too much for San Antonio." Personally, I don't see what is not to like about it.

You're in the middle of two completely different figures like David Hidalgo and César Rosas. Two superb guitarists and singers, but completely different to one another. How would you describe them?

I've known them since the very first day in 1973 when we were learning *música folclórica*, and there has always been this interesting balance. Vocally they are completely different. César can sing the boleros, while David can sing the *huastecos*. As a *rockero*, César can sing more of the really John Lee Hooker blues, and David can break your heart and sing "A Matter of Time." And as songwriters, César offers up the cumbias and the blues tunes and David and I share more of the dense-cerebral stuff. Somehow, we throw them in there and it becomes the sounds of Los Lobos. I can only describe it as a marriage between the two styles, and it works.

And as guitarists?

David [Hidalgo] is a sound-shaper, and César is more of a blues/rock 'n' roll style. David can shape these sounds, he's a phenomenal guitar player. And César also plays so well. They're equally soulful, but César offers more of a gritty rock style. I'm the man in the middle.

Yeah... But you can play everything, man, even drums. By the way, who's playing drums now?

We have a new drummer now. He is from Monterrey, Nuevo León. His name is Enrique González. They call him "Bugs." Do you remember that band from Mexico called Jumbo?

Of course! Don't tell me you got Jumbo's drummer.

Yeah, we got the drummer.

How did that happen?

Cougar Estrada, who had been with us for about 10 years, recently became a father for the first time and got married. Things really changed for him and he really just wanted to stay at home and raise a family. You can't argue with that, so he left and then we found Enrique, "Bugs," through Steve [Berlin], who had worked with him on something else. We brought him in and he immediately just fell right into place.

Are you now concentrating on guitar?

I've been in the front playing guitar for many years now.

Yeah, but I always see you changing instruments.

Yeah, I move around. For the Tex-Mex stuff I play drums. But mostly I'm upfront and play *jarana*, and every now and then solos on the electric guitar. It feels like I'm back in 1973 again.

John Lydon and Judge Judy's Eyes
(*San Antonio Current*, October 30, 2012)

John Lydon's life could have been a lot easier right now — all he had to do was keep the name "Johnny Rotten" and squeeze every single drop of juice out of the Sex Pistols brand.

"Tell me about it!" he said to the *Current* on the phone from London. "I think I put my head on the chopping block now almost continuously. But that's all right, it's a good place to be."

Instead of perpetuating his Pistols persona, he created a band, Public Image Ltd (PiL), which could not have been more different than the Pistols. With PiL, he released eight albums in 1978-1992, after which he published his must-read autobiography (*Rotten: No Irish, No Blacks, No Dogs*) and reunited with the Pistols for the infamous "Filthy Lucre Tour" in 1996. In 2009, Lydon revived PiL and in May of this year the band released *This is PiL*, its first in 12 years. It is the album they will be presenting 7:50 p.m. Saturday at Austin's Fun Fun Fun Fest.

"We are a very fine combination of live acoustic and syncopated electronica," said Lydon, who believes this is the best PiL lineup ever. "In terms of electronica, we created many of these, shall we say, demons now that lesser acts don't quite understand."

Lydon has evolved and mellowed out a bit, but only a bit. When describing PiL's music as "folk" ("music by folks for folks") he takes the opportunity to praise a band that he loves and to lambast two of today's biggest groups.

"Los Lobos to me is folk music," he said. "I have a love for them. … The songs are absolutely relevant to the situation they live in. To me that is vitally important. That is good art. Whereas in Coldplay or Radiohead it's not good. But then again, people born wealthy have a message too. It's just not one that I can relate to."

One thing he can relate to is San Antonio and the whole South of the USA. But talking about the Sex Pistols' SA show at Randy's Ballroom on January 8, 1978 (shortly before the band self-destructed), is a tricky issue — Lydon is never fond of saying more than what's strictly necessary about the Pistols, and his publicist warned the *Current* about going there. But Lydon was in a good mood, so I went ahead. Was the show really as chaotic as the British press described it?

"I remember [the SA show] being a wonderful gig and a brilliant relationship with an audience that had very little understanding of us," Lydon said. "I remember the only people that misbehaved and didn't understand how great that gig was the British press who turned up just deliberately to write rubbish and create fiction."

Yet, on the internet you will find a video showing that, towards the end of the show, Sid Vicious hits someone in the audience with his bass. Lydon saw that. He was right there. But he only remembers Sid, his late buddy.

"Poor old Sid was a very weak character and had the tendency to over-perform," said Lydon. "He did well and I miss him dearly. He was a very close friend of mine."

Now completely independent (the new album was self-released), PiL is still led by a man who is rarely intimidated. But there is at least one person who put the fear of God on John Lydon: Judge Judy Sheindlin.

In 1997, a former bandmember sued Lydon for assault, battery, and breach of contract. The case ended on *Judge Judy*, and the video of the show went viral. She sided with Lydon, but...

"Take a look at Judge Judy's eyes," said Lydon. "I tell you, man, she has the most beautiful eyes, and they are utterly ferocious. It's like trying to stare down a puma."

La Presy: Rediscovering San Antonio's gift to flamenco

(*San Antonio Current*, January 8, 2013)

Priscilla Treviño Lozano left San Antonio 33 years ago and never looked back. She sporadically but regularly kept in touch with her family, but only visited on a couple of occasions. For the most part, she devoted herself fully to her mission: to live, breath, dance, and teach flamenco in Granada's historic Sacromonte neighborhood, one of the main hearts and breeding grounds of Gypsy Spain.

Named "La Presy" (a rendition of "La Prisci," as she was known in San Antonio) by legendary singer-dancer-actress Lola La Faraona (Lola Flores, 1923-1995), she died penniless on December 25, 2011 at the age of 59, but only after becoming one of the most respected flamenco teachers in Granada.

Instead of the usual dresses, her signature look was pants (as inspired by the great Carmen Amaya), white shirt, and black vest. She was an aggressive dancer who worked in the U.S., Spain, France, Italy, and Switzerland, and her intense style resembled that of *bailaor* (dancer) Manolete, the man who convinced her to stay in Spain.

A little over a year after her death, La Presy's work is beginning to pay off: two of her best and closest students, Lara Bello and Patricia Guerrero, are traveling the world sharing the art they began learning with her.

Directly or indirectly, most San Antonio flamenco schools are related to La Presy, whose legacy is also a vindication for the work of a local scene often dismissed in favor of "the real flamencos from Spain." Yet, very few people know of La Presy in the Alamo City.

"Because she left and was in Spain for so long, everybody here forgot who she was," said Chayito Champion, the daughter of Teresa Champion (La Presy's first flamenco teacher) and the late El Curro, Texas' premier flamenco guitarist. "'Prisci' here was never recognized and that's a shame, because she touched a lot of lives here, too."

This is her story.

"LA PRISCI"

"She had a wooden platform under the bed, and she'd step on it and dance for hours in front of a big mirror," said older sister Gladys Donovan in her house in the Southwest side of SA, the same house where Priscilla grew up. From an early age, Priscilla — born April 1, 1952 — showed interest in dancing. As a child she studied tap dancing and acting, but in 1966 she discovered flamenco and her life changed forever.

She was part of the glorious generation of top-notch SA dancers that includes Timo Lozano (now teaching in Houston), Esmeralda and Carla Enrique (now in Toronto), Jesús Moreno, and Manolo Valente (both in San Antonio), who started with Teresa Champion and then went on to tour nationally and eventually spent time in Spain. But La Presy was special.

For Sylvia Castillo Davis, who met La Presy when they were both students at James Rusell Lowell Jr. High School, the memory of her talent is still vivid.

She had the confidence and the acting skills to walk anywhere and say I'M HERE," said Davis. "All she had to do was dance. That was enough for everyone to sit down and shut up."

Early dancing partner and eventual boyfriend Manolo Valente claims to have taught La Presy her first basic footwork (*zapateado*).

"I'm the one who didn't want to teach her, but she was very persistent and kept asking me," said Valente, who spent three years as a member of the company of legendary El Greco (José Greco, an influential Italian-American dancer and choreographer who died in 2000). Valente taught her some basic *zapateado* and asked her to practice for "two to four weeks." Two weeks later, La Presy called back.

"I went to see her and I was spellbound," said Valente. "Her feet were like machine guns, I couldn't believe it. She had learned everything. Those feet spoke to you. She had the unbelievable gift of a photographic memory."

But if Valente taught her the basics, it was Teresa Champion (El Curro's wife) who became La Presy's first full-time flamenco teacher. As was the case with every person interviewed for this story (both here and in Spain), Teresa Champion is still amazed by La Presy's capacity to absorb information.

"She was very good as a girl and incredibly talented as a dancer," Champion said. "It was as if she had a photo camera in her brain. We would teach her a step, and she'd never forget it."

Between the late '60s and early '70s, La Presy danced regularly in San Antonio at places like Six Flags, the Arneson Theater, and El Poco Loco on North Presa. In 1973, she joined the Ciro company in New Orleans' Chateau Flamenco (Ciro Diezhandino being a world-renowned U.S.-based Spanish dancer and choreographer). She began receiving offers to dance around the country; her career was on the rise. Then, tragedy struck.

The accident

On Easter Day in 1975, on the night she would replace dancer Morayma Muñoz at a show at New York's Chateau Madrid, the cab they were riding in was hit head-on and both Muñoz and La Presy flew out the back window. Muñoz died at the scene and La Presy was sent to Bellevue Hospital.

"[La Presy's] heart stopped at the emergency room a couple of times and she had to be revived," said sister Gladys Donovan. "She was told she could never dance or walk properly again," said Gladys.

But La Presy was tough and wouldn't take no for an answer. A year after the accident she was dancing again, and in 1979 she visited Granada, Spain. She fell in love with the place, returned briefly to the States, and then she was gone. Only this time, her look had changed.

"After the accident, she started wearing pants [to hide the scars from the accident]," said Josie Champion. "She never wore dresses or skirts again. A very powerful feminine/masculine look."

"Nobody wanted her to go and live there by herself, but she was headstrong and that's what she wanted to do," said Debra Archuleta, her niece.

In the early '80s, La Presy in Granada was like a fish in the water. Right from the start, she was able to blend in — she had the chops, and she had the looks. Her family confirmed the fact that she had some Comanche Indian blood in her, but not nearly as much as she claimed.

"She said she was a full-blooded Comanche Indian," said Nacho Martín, director of Granada's prestigious Carmen de las Cuevas academy, where La Presy taught from 1996 to 2000. "She had the blackest of hairs, the facial features. She had a very authentic racial look. Everyone thought she was a Gypsy."

Juan Pinilla, a well-known flamenco *cantaor* (singer), scholar, and journalist from Granada, shed further light on the significance of La Presy's acceptance among the Gypsies.

"In flamenco, the most difficult thing to achieve is the acceptance of Andalusian Gypsies," said Pinilla. Though flamenco has developed in Andalusia from a blend of cultures, including the Moors and other many peoples who have lived in Spain, it is widely accepted that it is a *gitano* thing. "The Gypsies think they own it and discriminate against Castilian artists. But La Presy was considered a Gypsy by the Gypsies, which is a badge of honor only reserved for high-quality [performers]."

Renowned *bailaor* Manolete met La Presy "about 30 years ago," when he spotted her dancing at a Granada hall named El Neptuno.

"Hey, what are you doing in Granada? You're dancing very well," Manolete told her. "I suggested she should stay in Granada." La Presy could not have agreed more.

But at that point La Presy wasn't the full-fledged flamenco powerhouse she would become later. Because she came from a classical and tap school, her body and arms were different, and she was overdoing her footwork.

"She had to adapt her body and understand that, if you do everything with your feet... well, you'll get too many calluses," Manolete said. "She was able to adapt and her transition was successful."

La Presy only took a handful of classes and workshops with Manolete, but she made them last.

"She was like a sponge," Manolete said. "She'd pick up the music and the steps quickly, store them in her little head, and practice on her own. She never forgot anything. And that's why her style always resembled mine. She could dance as well as anybody else and could've achieved more as a dancer. But she chose to stay [in Granada as a teacher] and was very strong at Sacromonte."

In 1985 she gave classes to 50 Gypsy children as part of an official minority campaign by the City of Granada, and in 1989 she presented her first choreography in Granada, a three-act ballet based on *One Thousand and One Nights*. She danced in France, Italy, Greece, and Switzerland, and in 1997 she taught at the Peña La Platería, the world's oldest flamenco association.

As her reputation grew, more and more dancers wanted to dance with her. She left Carmen de las Cuevas to open her own school in one of Sacromonte's *cuevas* (caves). While most flamenco stars made their career in Madrid and Seville, La Presy stayed in Granada.

"Only Mariquilla [María Guardia], La Presy, and a handful of others were able to establish themselves in Granada," said Nacho Martín, from Carmen de las Cuevas. "She was a key figure because she was a great teacher, especially when it came to classic flamenco basics. She came from the Ciro school, which is a very important one."

Her classes were grueling. La Presy had no time for those who wanted to have an "extracurricular activity." She wanted serious (and good) dancers. Many left, intimidated by her demanding nature and fierce personality. If you were her dancer, she had no problem telling you exactly how you were supposed to do that step.

"I don't see too many virgins in here," she used to tell her students during any of her legendary class interruptions. "*¡Tienes que mover las caderas* *como si te estuvieran comiendo el coño!*" ("You have to move your hips as if someone was eating your pussy!")

"She was wild, lethal, but she was also very funny," said singer-songwriter-dancer Lara Bello, who studied under her since the late '90s. "She would find things in you other schools couldn't find, because she was fearless. She didn't care about what people may have thought of her — all she cared about was for you to learn that step, and was willing to say anything to make you understand."

Home is where the heart is

In 1998, when her mother got very sick, La Presy returned to San Antonio for a few weeks. She did a few workshops at Teresa Champion's studio (then located on Flores St.) and then, in 2000, Josie Champion (El Curro's sister) brought her back to do workshops 18 hours a week for at least three months.

"She gave an extraordinary workshop," said Carmen Linares "La Chiqui," one of SA's top flamenco instructors. "When Josie brought her I sent about 20 of my students. It was very strong."

"As a teacher myself, I was flabbergasted when I saw that workshop," said Jesús Moreno, who toured with La Presy when they were with the Ciro company in the early-to-mid '70s. "She was amazing. One thing is to teach, but to go from dancer in SA to teacher, and then teach Spaniards, that's something else." And yes, Moreno also repeated the mantra glorifying La Presy's unique gift: "She had a photographic memory."

"I was giving her a way to make money before going back to Spain," Josie Champion said. "We fed her, we clothed her, put 15 pounds on her. She brought Spain to us and left me with enough flamenco material to last me for a lifetime."

Both Teresa and Josie Champion admit much of the choreographies they use to this day are La Presy's.

"Bringing her here was very special for me because she's one of my greatest influences," said Josie. "I learned flamenco with my family and my style reflects that. I love my family very much and Teresa means the world to me, but I do my own thing and my *compas*es [plural for *compás*, or the intricate time signatures of flamenco], are all La Presy's. She's the one I looked up to and the one I wanted to be like."

Once back in Spain, La Presy kept busy. She taught at Carmen de las Cuevas for four years before finally opening her own school in 2000.

Going down

When La Presy's family met with the *Current* for this story, an undated postcard was found among La Presy's memorabilia.

"Except for my visit home and other few outings, it's been a year to forget," wrote La Presy in the postcard. "There's a lot to confide but things are in limbo for me at this minute. I'm surviving and underweight… There are times I need yous [sic] and mom so much."

Gladys Donovan (La Presy's sister) and Debra Archuleta (niece) believe La Presy brought the postcard herself in either one of her two visits in 1998 and 2000.

"For some reason, she didn't mail it," said Debra. "But she left it here."

Whatever her problem was, La Presy kept on pushing with her classes until her body started to give in.

In 2008, in the middle of one of her classes, she experienced trouble breathing and asked one of her students to call an ambulance. She was admitted to the hospital with "chronic respiratory problems," according to Ángel Horcajadas, one of the doctors who saw her. "She took very little care of herself," said Horcajadas. "She smoked a lot and was in very bad shape. She only went to the doctor when it was too late. The impression that I got is that she lived in her own world and never listened to anyone else."

After that first visit to the hospital in 2008, she needed oxygen at all times. Nevertheless, she seemed in good spirits when Archuleta and Donovan visited her in Granada on separate occasions in 2009. For some reason, La Presy had asked Archuleta to call and she would come get them. "Don't just show up," she had told them. But Archuleta's husband, Bryan, insisted on "giving her a surprise."

When they arrived at La Presy's house, Archuleta froze.

"I just couldn't ring the bell," Archuleta said. "On the one hand I was happy to see her again, but on the other hand I was afraid she'd start yelling at me for showing up."

So she called her mother Gladys in the U.S., and Gladys called La Presy, who let them in. It was a happy encounter, but La Presy soon showed that taking care of herself wasn't one of her priorities.

"She was supposed to have her oxygen tank with her at all times, but never used it," said Archuleta. "She didn't want to be seen with that."

La Presy took Debra and her husband everywhere. Restaurant owners would show their respect for La Presy, but when it was time to come back to resume her classes, La Presy was exhausted.

"She'd say, 'Just give me a couple of hours to rest,'" Archuleta said. "All the walking, coupled with the classes, took everything she had."

In 2010 the doctors found an aneurysm, and she quickly deteriorated.

"She could be discharged in few days… Her problem is only a speech one," Dr. Horcajadas wrote the family on August 3, 2010. "She has a difficult aneurysm to operate on and unfortunately she suffered a vasospasm after surgery, affecting [the] left side. She hasn't motor deficits, so she can walk and take care of herself, but she has problems to communicate (not to understand)."

On October 2010, La Presy (who, when healthy, was "a wonderful writer," according to Archuleta) sent a somber letter that reflected the effects of her condition.

"I can feel very negative with my life and there has been many priceless errors," she wrote." (…) Right now I'm so afraid of my future. I traveled out of Texas and dreaming of all I could have. I've never [had] fear of dancing. To me it was something I felt very sure, and all the dreams and achievements have been glorious for all the doubts that I had. For my disdain for me, I can say my life has been so well for me."

"The last time we spoke on the phone she couldn't recognize me," said Alfredo Mesa Martínez, one of her guitarists. "All she could tell me is that she was very scared of what the doctors told her."

Unexpected help

Because she was a proud woman, few knew the real extent of her illness. Her health was quickly worsening and she had no one to take care of her.

No one, except Tony.

Antonio Rubio Delgado was La Presy's on-and-off lover for about 20 years. Some say he was an artist but, by all accounts, their relationship was highly dysfunctional.

"She told us that he had mistreated her and got her into drugs," one source said. "And we all believed her. I first saw her at the Peña [Flamenca de] la Platería [the world's oldest existing flamenco club, in Granada] in 2000 and she looked like someone you would say, 'Oh, she's a drug addict.' But after they broke up, she was her usual self."

It took therapy for her to finally end the relationship, but towards the end they started seeing each other again.

"He was never good to her, but he did somewhat help her when she got sick at the end," said Archuleta.

The family kept sending them money, but it was never enough.

"She would sometimes call and say there was no food, and we didn't understand," said Archuleta. "Her medical bills were paid [thanks to Spain's socialized health care], and she should've been well-stocked at home."

Tony, who reportedly is in poor health himself, couldn't be reached for comments, but La Presy's family told the *Current* that he often called to say that, whenever La Presy was discharged from the hospital, taking care of her was an overwhelming task for him.

"He'd say, 'I can't do this anymore,'" said sister Gladys Donovan, the only one who speaks a little Spanish in the family. "He'd go off and leave her there and sometimes he'd come back and find her on the floor. 'It's very frustrating, too much for me. I can't handle it.'"

Her last letter to Archuleta was sent in June or July of 2011. It was La Presy's way of simultaneously congratulating and chastising Debra for having kids. (Again, here's a partial unedited transcript of the letter:)

"Hi my niece *sobrina*. It's hard for me to write this copy for me. I lost my writing ease and reading is hard for me now. Because of my aneurysm are changing what I did well…

My mom and dad could see me short but I had all I needed with their approval. I have no approval now… Now I need brother and sister, but it's their life and they have kids on them."

For months, the family debated whether it was time to go see her. But their lack of money to travel, inability to speak Spanish, the fact that Archuleta was pregnant with twins, and the hope that La Presy would recover like her own mother (who had a stroke when she was 71 and survived another 10 years) delayed things. Plus, from a medical standpoint, she was in much better shape in Spain than in the States.

"She was old, indigent, had no Social Security and, if we'd brought her here, receiving Medicare would've taken months," Archuleta said. "She would have died sooner [in the States]."

When the family was finally convinced that someone should go to Granada and be with her, it was too late. La Presy died on December 25, 2011 at Hospital San Rafael in Granada. She was 59.

"It was very tough because, yes, she would've died sooner here, but that's what we did with my grandmother [La Presy's mother]," an emotional Archuleta said. "We didn't send her to a nursing home, we took care of her here. And we could have done that to [La Presy]."

"LA PRESY DIES: THE INDIAN BAILAORA THAT BECAME A GYPSY," read the headline of her obituary in *Granada Hoy*, the local daily. Patricia Guerrero, her student and first dancer at the Ballet Flamenco Andaluz, wrote a tribute to her on her Facebook page. Immediately after her death, her unclaimed body remained at the hospital for two days, with Tony unable to pay for funeral arrangements.

"She was in a situation of extreme poverty," said Martín, from Carmen de las Cuevas. "I had to take over because I saw that no one would or could take charge."

Martín paid about $3,000 Euros for the cremation and funeral, then organized a fundraiser to recover the costs. "Everyone contributed and I was able to recover everything, and more than 200 people showed up for the funeral. The whole flamenco world of Granada embraced her in a last goodbye."

"I'm the director of La Chumbera's school and I have to walk by her house every single day," said Manolete, choking. "I always remember her not just as an artist, but as a person. And I know people like Patricia Guerrero and her mother will also always remember the classes they took with La Presy. There is no discussion whatsoever about her legacy."

If anything, La Presy should've been pleased to know none of her efforts were in vain — in life and death, she earned the respect of her peers. She was more than just a well-respected teacher or a Tejano rarity in the ultra-competitive and sectarian world of flamenco: her teachings are bearing fruits, with Patricia Guerrero and Lara Bello as prime examples.

Guerrero is widely recognized as one of Spain's top young flamenco *bailaoras*, and Bello released a gorgeous, flamenco-flavored jazzy, self-penned album entirely dedicated to La Presy. Even without her students' success, La Presy had secured her own legacy as a genuine, well-respected and admired *maestra*. But seeing Lara and Patricia shine adds further vindication for a woman who gave everything she had to honor flamenco.

"She taught me everything a guitarist needs to know to accompany a *bailaora*," said Mesa Martínez, her guitarist. "But especially, she taught me how to understand flamenco in a special way."

That Andalusian thing

Flamenco is a tricky thing. Among its fans there's always the purist party-pooper who dismisses any foreign attempts as "not as good as those in Andalusia." As if only a Gypsy could truly have *duende* (the "it" necessary to truly feel and execute flamenco).

"People often think that maybe you have to have fingers swollen from picking potatoes to be able to play the guitar with feeling," once said Enrique Morente (1942-2010), one of the greatest *cantaores* ever. "Look, picking potatoes is every bit as worthy as playing a guitar. But I can tell you that a man with fine, sensitive fingers is not going to be able to make a go of picking potatoes. And I can also tell you that a man with fingers swollen from picking potatoes is not going to be able to play a guitar because he hasn't got the manual dexterity and he hasn't got the dedication. This is a profession like any other which you have to dedicate yourself to completely. It is an art of professionals."

La Presy was a professional, and she gave it all to earn the endorsement of people like Manolete himself, a man who will have none of that sectarian, exclusivistic take on the art.

"I've been in six national ballets and I know what I'm talking about," said Manolete. "We all have the same blood and the same heart. No matter where we are from. Anybody can dance flamenco, just like I can dance classical. What you do with it, it's up to you. If you just want to make money, you won't achieve anything. But if you take it seriously, you can be like La Presy. She was a good dancer and a very good teacher. She was loved by all because of her teachings and because, simply, she was a good, genuine person."

"We can't say she was one of Spain's best dancers, because she wasn't," said Juan Pinilla, who wrote the *Granada Hoy* obituary. "But, in Granada, she was one of the biggest dancers and definitely one of its greatest teachers. She was very, very important. As a flamenco critic I can tell you this — if she had taken her Granada momentum and gone to Madrid, she could've been as good as any other *bailaora*."

"She was well-respected by people like [*bailaor*] Mario Maya [1937-2008], Manolete, and [*cantaor*] Curro Albaicín," said Mesa Martínez, her guitarist. "She was known, but her artistic level and reputation were bigger than her popularity."

What La Presy learned in San Antonio was good enough to dance with Ciro and then impress Manolete in Granada. Then, she absorbed everything she could from the Gypsies and became an institution herself, single-handedly destroying the only-in-Andalusia myth. And that was the biggest eye-opening experience Bello had with La Presy.

"She had students from all over the world, and [us Spaniards] were a little bit prejudiced about it," said Bello. "Early on we didn't think foreigners could do it. But with La Presy I learned that that's a complete lie. At La Presy's classes I met wonderful dancers from many countries and, when I started traveling, I confirmed it. But it was La Presy who opened my eyes: art belongs to everyone."

La Presy knowingly made her dancers better and unknowingly made San Antonio flamenco proud. Teresa Campion considered La Presy one of her star students and credits her with returning encouragement at a bad time. When her son, 24-year-old Willie Champion Jr. died in a hit-and-run accident in 1983, Teresa was overcome by grief and stopped dancing for a year. When La Presy, already in Spain, found out, she called her *maestra*.

"Why are you retiring?" La Presy asked. "They know me in Spain because of you. If you retire, you won't give anyone else the opportunity you gave me." Teresa snapped out of her depression and resumed her career. "I'm dancing because of La Presy, because she asked me to."

Without even trying, she validated every effort ever made by our local schools — here was a woman who learned her basics in San Antonio, and went on to teach the genre's inventors.

All she asked in return was credit, and one last family request: "Let Tony live in my house until he dies."

La Presy's fruits

Lara Bello and Patricia Guerrero aren't the only ones La Presy inspired, but they are the most high-profile fruits of her teachings. On March 31, 2012, New York-based singer-dancer-songwriter Bello released *Primero amarillo, después malva* (First Yellow, Then Purple), a flamenco-flavored Latin jazz-pop/World Music album with the Ojo Música label. The album (especially the title song) is dedicated to La Presy, whom Bello studied under since the late 1990s.

Twenty-four-year-old Patricia Guerrero, first dancer with the Ballet Flamenco Andaluz, is one of Spain's top young flamenco dancers. She met La Presy when she was still a small child (go to sacurrent.com to see a video of La Presy and then-8-year-old Guerrero). They were both eager to talk about their friend and teacher.

Bello spoke from New York and Budapest, Hungary; Guerrero sent her answers via email from Seville, Spain.

LARA BELLO

"I went to her class and I started getting hooked," laughs Bello. "She was a great motivator and I stayed with her for years and years."

When she saw that La Presy had a serious, no-nonsense approach to the art, she knew she was at the right place. With time, she understood where La Presy's edge came from.

"I think her hard side started when she tried to enter the flamenco world," said Bello. "It's a tough, very private world, closed to strangers. She had to wear a mask as defense. But once she knew you were not an enemy, she would reveal a very, very sensitive person."

I ask her whether my fascination with La Presy is exaggerated, the product of a sentimental view on my part. How important, really, was La Presy in Granada?

"What she did was fantastic," Bello said. "It's not a common thing. Yes, you now see more people from other countries establishing themselves in Granada, but La Presy did it when it was much more difficult. And she went straight to dance at the *tablados* from the very beginning, among lifelong, well-established dancers and singers. She was part of that inner circle."

But La Presy taught Bello a lot more than just dancing — she taught her the dangers of a middle-of-the-road approach to life.

"I learned a lot from her, but perhaps the most important thing was to avoid doing things half-heartedly," said Bello. "She'd tell me, 'Every time you make a step, make it firm. If you have a misstep, at least have your foot firmly planted.' In other words: Whenever you do something, do it with all your heart and energy. Thanks to her, I apply that drive in everything I do."

The title of Bello's album refers to the way the flowers outside of La Presy's studio would change colors with the seasons. When she wasn't traveling, Bello would walk from her house to La Presy's *cueva* and take classes with her for two months.

"That image of the flowers stayed in my mind," said Bello. "This album is dedicated to La Presy and those roads we took to study with her in the last Spring. I cherish those happy moments inside of me, and they travel with me wherever I go."

PATRICIA GUERRERO

"Thank you Presy for being part of my dancing and my learning," wrote Patricia Guerrero days after La Presy's death. "Thanks for your knowledge and your advice. Even though I will never receive that phone call you always made, you will always be with me and I will always remember you. So long, my *maestra*."

"If you ask Patricia about La Presy, she'll start crying," said singer-scholar Juan Pinilla. "She's a phenomenal dancer who does everything well: clásico, flamenco... but always in an artful way," said Manolete.

Guerrero, now one of Spain's top young bailaoras, met La Presy at a key formative time in her life.

"With her I started to dance with *guitar* and *cante,* and to better understand flamenco in general," said Guerrero. "I was a young kid, ages 9 to 11, so it was a time of learning, learning, and learning."

When Guerrero, a precocious dancer, began to establish herself nationally, La Presy kept in touch with her.

"She always called me before an important show to wish me well," Guerrero said. "Unfortunately, I'll never receive those calls again."

The Ballet Flamenco Andaluz will be touring the U.S. in March, and "of course, I'd love to perform at La Presy's birthplace."

It would be a dream for La Presy's students, for Manolete (who also would like to perform in SA), and to the local flamenco scene — those who knew La Presy, and those who should discover her.

I was a child, but I never forgot her teachings and advice," said Guerrero. "In any career, all stages of learning are important, and what I learned with La Presy was so important. I'll always remember her."

Livin' La Vida Rosa: How Draco Beat Cancer and Topped the Latin Charts
(*San Antonio Current*, March 31, 2013)

It's hard to believe Draco Rosa (fka Robi Rosa, even though "you can call me anything you want, bro," he said) was once a contemporary of Ricky Martin in Puerto Rico's legendary (and insufferable) boy group Menudo.

But he's also the only Menudo member to enjoy critical respect in the music world. His solo albums, especially those between 1994 and 2009, established him as a tortured, bilingual, dark singer-songwriter who effortlessly mixed Latin rhythms, psychedelia, and classic and prog rock with an existential romanticism adept at taking chances and not giving a damn about what the industry expected of him. He danced to the beat of his own drum and, in 1999, his aversion for anything "commercial" took an unexpected turn: "Livin' la Vida Loca," the song he co-wrote and co-produced with Desmond Child (Luis Gómez Escolar is credited as the other writer), became Ricky Martin's first *Billboard* 100 number one hit.

The single sold more than eight million copies and the album, *Ricky Martin*, more than 50. For Draco, Ricky's success was a blessing: he could now, finally and more than ever, concentrate on his eclectic and uncompromising projects that go from music to film, and he went on releasing critically acclaimed albums in English and Spanish.

Then, in 2011, life stopped him on his tracks: he had cancer. He fought vigorously and, in the middle of his struggle, he recorded what could've been his last album. *Vida*, a collection of old songs in duets with many of today's biggest Latin music stars (including Marc Anthony, Rubén Blades, Enrique Bunbury, Calle 13, José Feliciano, Juan Luis Guerra, Juanes, Maná, Alejandro Sanz, Shakira and, of course, Ricky Martin, among others), was released on March 18, less than three months after being declared cancer-free. It is his most radio-friendly album, but also one of his best. Ironically, it is an album full of light and, unlike most duets albums, Rosa took the guests to his level, not the other way around. Even syrupy bachata superstar Romeo Santos sounds credible, as if Rosa's attitude and edge had brought the best out of all the guest singers, all of which received the release (and his recovery) enthusiastically in social media.

At the time of this writing, *Vida* was the number one Latin album in the USA and a well-deserved reward for an artist who spent most of his adult life studying the best music has to offer in the US, England, Argentina, the Caribbean and wherever serious artists try to make a difference with song and word.

Rosa spoke on the phone (in English and Spanish) with the *Current* from Puerto Rico.

Nice to have you back and strong, but what the hell happened?

In February of 2011 I was diagnosed with non-Hodgkin's lymphoma, diffused B-cell, lower abdomen cancer, of the blood as well. But I was misdiagnosed in late '09. I fell ill and, after a long period, it was agreed by many doctors that what I had was rheumatic fever. So they put me on Bicillin, which is a type of Penicillin. And then, to counter that — because that destroys your immune system — they put me on human growth shots. I ended up spiraling into another place, and a year later I got off of that and decided to seek out new doctors. This is when, finally, my endocrinologist said, "go see a hematologist." And that's when we discovered, in early February 2012, that in fact what I had was the non-Hodgkin's lymphoma. I felt ill in late '09, going into 2010. On December 31, 2012, I was finally cancer-free.

What a wonderful way to end the year and start a new one...

It was definitely great news, it was the best news ever. The idea of doing the stem cell transplant was definitely very, very good for me.

Did you ever think "this is it"? I mean, what kind of fighter were you? The "brave" type people love to talk about or the scared shitless one?

It was a little bit of everything. There were days that… I mean, I never said to myself, "Why me?" But I *did* say, "Why now?" I thought, "Hey, listen… I know the kind of life I've been living," my lifestyle since I was a teenager. I figured I wasn't going to make it to 27. When I passed 27 and was in my 30s I didn't understand what I was doing alive. I kind of kept living the way I was always living.

You mean...

You know, man... I just did what I did. I didn't think anything of it. That's just the reality. I was living my life as always. A charmed one, one of adventures, and my vices were my own, like many people and I was enjoying that. It was a lifestyle.

And when you thought you got away with everything, boom.

Life is what it is, it is a privilege to be alive, and especially if you are out and about with a certain zest about doing things and conquering and building [around] the magic that life is. I thought I appreciated it, but nowhere near as much as I do now. So, "Why now?" I thought if this was going to happen, I'd be much older.

So you set out to make *Vida* (Life), which is nothing but the album of your life, literally. I never felt so enthusiastic about a duets albums before. Were you hanging in there or you thought this would be your last?

It is tricky. The reality is, with a project like this, I didn't have a lot of time to analyze because I was in the middle of treatment, undergoing chemo, and not always *feeling*, not even 50 percent. And I think what was flowing through my veins was, you know, life and death, and when I came to the studio it was such a great moment to just work on music, that I had a lot of clarity. I had nothing else on my mind except working on the music. I didn't think about family, kids, money, work, or anything. I just was so excited that I could step out of the clinic and the fucking hospital so I could just really dive into a project the mattered to me, because I didn't know if it was my swan song, my swan project; it was that one last piece that I could work on, and I really wanted to do well, especially when I received a couple of them in particular that were huge challenges. There was Rubén Blades in "El tiempo va" that pushed me to sing like I'd never sung before. Or a track like the one with Tego Calderón ("Brujería"), which I had to sort of figure out, because he just sent me his voice on one recording, and I ended up rebuilding it to have him feel like he's right there in the room, throwing out his verse right there with the band, and I'm so satisfied with that. The same with the Calle 13 piece. They are special pieces that we worked hard to try to find a certain organic feel to it, and I thought we achieved that. I was very, very content with that. I've had to try and do my best so everybody and everyone sounded great. And I think everyone who participated actually put their all in a natural way, unlike a lot of these duet albums. I felt they were very passionate. I received these vocals and I felt the energy. I'm very blessed. And Marc Anthony... To hang with Marc was special. We hung out here at the studio and I felt like a kid with Marc because he's a Nuyorican like me, so we had some kind of connection that night. We did that piece and it was smoky, it was awesome. I love that piece.

Yes! I haven't felt so great about Marc since his first salsa album, when he was hardcore before going all poppy... You were able to capture the old Marc.

Makes me so happy you feel that way, I appreciate you listening to it. Thank you.

It is your most radio-friendly album, yet it retains enough darkness to be a Draco Rosa album. But I never expected it to be so uplifting. I mean, the King of Darkness was able to do his most optimistic album in the middle of the worst chaos. Not an easy thing to do.

I agree with you, I think that in the end it is exactly that. It does represent the light and it is uplifting, because it is uplifting for me. When I listen to the album — because I have listened to it, I have it in my car — it sprays enthusiasm and a zest for life. I don't know if I'm confusing what I'm feeling or what I'm receiving from the album. But I too feel the same.

It has a very special magic to it.

I agree with you 100 percent. And this is the best light these songs have ever been in, and I'm so excited that you see that. I think some of these songs have really come to where they needed to be. They're better sung, I had no idea I had to do this until I heard Rubén Blades' tracks. When I received his vocals I realized, "I have to re-sing this with my last breath," and I did that on that song, and you hear it. "Blanca mujer" [with Shakira], again, a very, very telling piece of my past that I sang with such life. I love that piece, and I feel this way throughout the record.

But how many of these songs did you re-record from scratch?

Some of them I used some bits and pieces from the past. It depended on the artist. For example, when I showed Enrique Bunbury his song, he told me, "I don't know if I can sing it, I don't know how I can do it." So I changed a few things. I went into the studio first, worked on the music, then I sent him the track. They sent me the vocal, and then I built the track. Every track was done depending on the artist.

What percentage of the songs were from scratch vs. rearranged?

Well, there are 16 songs, so I want to say it's a 50/50, 60/40 completely new vs. other songs where I've changed something on it. All of them have some kind of change, but some more than others, some are from scratch. Because of lack of time... I mean, I was at the edge, we got everything done, we're getting it mixed, and then I go into stem cell replacement, and that took a couple of months. So that was it, it was done. They were like, "Let's mix, this is the way we're going," so that was that. There was no going back, even though I could have stayed another four months working on it. I wanted to do more things, but that's just the reality. It's like, "OK, this is it. Fuck it, we can't go any further."

Will you take *Vida* on tour?

In June I'm going back to Phantom Vox, my studio, to record new songs. Then I plan on doing some one-offs, a couple of gigs with The Holy Phantom Vox Orchestra, to present some of the duets without actually having the different artists. Maybe one or two will show up, we don't know, but in the meantime, it'll be just the Holy Phantom Vox Orchestra.

Metric's Emily Haines: What You See Is What You Get
(*San Antonio Current*, April 23, 2013)

"I really want our art guy to win," Metric singer-keyboardist-songwriter Emily Haines told the *Current* on April 16 from the Honolulu airport on her way to Sacramento. She was talking about Sunday's Juno Awards (the Canadian Music Awards), where Metric won two of five nominations, including Best Alternative Album for *Synthetica*.

And that's all you need to know about Metric: there they were, days before the Canadian version of the Grammys (a trophy they had won twice already), and all Haines could think of is hoping Justin Broadbent, the guy who designed the package of the band's terrific fifth album, wins his own Juno. And she knew damn well the award would go to him, not the band.

But that's Metric. Utopian stars who still think rock and roll can be fun and success is good and all that crap, but who also clearly understand what's real and what's temporary, what's worth saying, hearing and grooving to, and what's disposable.

Haines didn't have to talk to the *Current* or anyone; the band wasn't doing interviews and the *Synthetica* press rounds have been long over. But hey, the band's making a rare San Antonio appearance and she agreed to a quick chat on very short notice, minutes before taking a plane.

That's Metric: what you see is what you get.

Thanks for coming to San Antonio. Sometimes we think no one loves us...

We like to go everywhere in the world. The rhythm section (bassist Joshua Winstead and drummer Joules Scott-Key) are both Texas boys, so I'm sure they have some history in San Antonio.

Is the US a hard nut to crack? You're having great success, but you should be much bigger.

I don't know if it has to do with the territory, but we've made choices as a band that's made our path more of a slow-and-steady approach. We really said no to a lot of things and tried to maintain control of our career. It's really about us and the people who want to hear our music. A lot of times you see things shoot into the stratosphere and it's exciting, it's amazing, but they often come right back down. That's not a good destiny for us, though. We'd like to be out there for people for many years to come.

***Synthetica* doesn't sugarcoat things: things are bad, there's a lot of b.s. going on, yet your albums (and especially your shows) are full of light. How do you achieve that balance?**

First of all, thank you very much for telling me that, because we're pretty nose to the grindstone. We do it and hope that it is translating, so it makes me very happy that you're getting the point. For all the things that we are trying to address, as human beings we're very grateful to be alive at all, playing music and expressing ourselves. Ultimately, rock and roll is something uplifting that allows you to have a good time and be connected to your friends. It shouldn't be a downer to be aware of where you are and what's going on. Be engaged in life, you know? In music nowadays… Well, *always*, but especially now, music is approached as total escapism, you know? [laughs] Lyrically and sonically it's all like… "Wow! All right…" I have my moments of that too, but we're trying to balance things a bit. We need to pay attention, especially the younger ones. Pay attention and be involved. Life is for living; don't make it a total downer. Shouldn't be a downer to be aware… or awake.

On one of the episodes of *The Making of Synthetica* on YouTube you said you once wanted to be a rock star, but now you just want to become "a totally androgynous badass writer." Can you elaborate?

[Laughs] It was my good fortune that I grew up in a different time. There was no *American Idol* or *The Voice* and all that stuff, putting all these kids in front of people and making a kind of a mockery of their genuine ambition and emotion. There was nothing like that for me. I was in a small town and was obsessed with Michael Jackson, writing letters to him, sending him songs, being sure that he would want me to be in his band. As my career evolved, I never saw myself in any special category. I just really liked to play music with my friends, in no special genre category. But then this new genre emerged, the super-manufactured pop star, and whatever part of me that found that entertaining, I now feel it draining away from me. I feel maybe it is about time to make it clear that what I really like to do is writing. I love to perform in front of 10,000 people, but my most important role for my generation and for my time is to be a songwriter. It's kind of a recent revelation.

So, what should we expect from you and the band as performers in San Antonio? Last I saw you was at Austin City Limits last year, and it was wonderful. But is this Jack Daniel's gig one of those "short set" deals?

Not at all. We'll give you a full set, hour and a half. New songs? I don't know. There's been a lot of writing going on, but we'll see. Our set has really evolved since *Synthetica* came out in June. We're always integrating elements from our past and ideas for the future, and we improvise a lot. It'll be a great night. Can't wait.

Nina Díaz's Spiritual Makeover
(*San Antonio Current*, June 18, 2013)

"What's up with Nina?" I asked Faith Radle, Girl in a Coma's manager, looking at the band's lead singer, Nina Díaz. It was pouring rain that afternoon in late May, but we were safely sheltered at the ballroom of the Omni Hotel, minutes after Judge Nelson Wolff gave his State of the County address and seconds before I lamely asked, "Is she going to the gym, or something?"

Before Radle could answer, the judge asked her a question, so I moved to the side and took another look at Díaz — even though the band had performed only one song in front of an unusual crowd (corporate big wigs, political donors, city authorities), Díaz sang and played as I had never seen her before. In addition to her usual fierceness, this time she was joyful, and her skin was shining with the effulgence someone sports after coming back from a pilgrimage in India.

At one point, Díaz came up to me, smiling.

"Hi! I haven't seen you at the temple lately." She meant the little San Antonio Hare Krishna temple, a special place for both of us. I'm passionate about Indian philosophy and became formally initiated into devotional yoga in 1986, but am now what any old-school Hare Krishna would call someone in very poor standard who "blooped," or "fell down into the material ocean." But the devotees Díaz met at the temple are the second generation of Hare Krishna followers, who have a much more mellow, tolerant approach than that of their respective gurus who, in the late 1960s and early '70s turned Hare Krishna into a household name via chanting, book distribution, temple building, and a good deal of embarrassing scandals.

Whatever my reservations about the Hare Krishna movement, the devotees are my brothers and sisters. They literally saved my life in 1998, when I visited India for the first time. It's a long, boring story, but Díaz' face and energy reminded me of those days. Still, I wasn't prepared for what she told me.

"Guess what!" she exclaimed. "I have a spiritual name now!"

What? Nina Díaz, the singer for Girl in a Coma, became a Hare Krishna? Not quite.

Her spiritual name is Neela Megha Shyama; in Sanskrit it means "big blue body resembling a black cloud." When initiated, devotees take up Krishna names followed by "Dasa" for men and "Dasi" for women, meaning "servant," as in "servant of God." But Díaz isn't formally initiated, a long process that would require her to choose a guru and make vows of chastity, vegetarianism, and refusal to partake in drugs or gambling. Instead, the devotees gave her a name as a sign of affection; no strings attached.

"She was already heading down the spiritual path and I could see her definitely wanting a change," said Jeff Palacios, guitarist for Sugar Skulls and a regular temple-goer. He's one of several local artists and musicians who have been attracted to the Hare Krishna life — others include filmmaker Laura Varela, artist Adriana García, and two local musicians who live as celibate monks: electronic recording artist Bryan Hamilton, who became formally initiated as Bhagavan Narada Dasa, and Karma's Michael Evans.

Though not initiated, Díaz does, however, carry her bead bag everywhere, which is the life and soul of a devotee. Inside the bag, there is a rosary of 108 beads, and devotees chant the Hare Krishna mantra on each bead. Initiated devotees chant a minimum of 16 rounds (108 mantras being one round) a day; Nina chants two rounds a day. She attributes chanting on the beads as the reason behind her giving up drugs, alcohol, and cigarettes.

"When I got my japa [meditation] beads I was still smoking, and I just told myself, 'I don't want to smoke with my bead bag,'" she said. "It's like having your child in your arms and smoking in its face. So since then, I haven't been smoking, and I had been smoking a lot, like a pack a day."

"I took her to get her *japa* beads and bag as a gift for her birthday," said Palacios, who along with other devotees visited Díaz and her family for some time to give them *prasadam*, or vegetarian food that's cooked by the devotees, offered to Krishna at an altar, and then distributed. Sometimes self-described as "the kitchen religion," cooking and distributing food is another key component of Krishna consciousness. Strict devotees won't eat anything unless cooked and "offered" to Krishna by other devotees, then distributed to temple visitors or friends at their homes. *Prasadam* is a Sanskrit word meaning "the mercy of God," as if one was eating the remnants from God's plate.

"I felt she was ready to start chanting and start focusing on bigger things. She knew it too! When we did *kirtan*," said Palacios, mentioning congregational chanting integral to the Hare Krishna experience, "[Díaz had] the biggest smile I've seen!"

At first, Díaz took a cautious approach. She had been struggling with drugs and alcohol, and Palacios took her to the temple a couple of times, starting in 2011.

"At first I was like, 'OK'..." Díaz said. "I was going through a lot of different changes as far as substance and alcohol abuse, which I'm not afraid to admit, so early this year I went back and this time it stuck."

When she went back, she experienced first-hand another key belief of Krishna consciousness: that sound, hearing transcendental vibration, is a powerful purifying tool. Díaz was deeply moved.

"Tears came down because I was ready to give in and [tell God] 'I'm here,'" she said. "I was rock bottom, in a way. There were a lot of things going on in my life, but at that point I said, 'I'm ready for you to love me, and I'm ready to love you. I'm ready to accept I'm not in control — You're in control.'"

It sounds like typical 12-step work, but for Díaz the music, vegetarian food, the incense, and philosophy had a special magic she hadn't found elsewhere. In addition, the basic tenet of Krishna consciousness (the soul, the real self, is eternal, while the body is temporary) took her back to her pre-GIAC days.

"My [biological] father is a mortician, so I grew up thinking this body is temporary," said Díaz, who was mostly raised by her mother and stepfather. "[My biological father] would literally pick us up sometimes and there would be a dead body in a bag [in the car]."

In spite of her early awareness of the fleeting nature of the body, the fact that she grew up under the spotlight took a heavy toll on her mind.

"I was a preteen thrown into adult situations," she said. "The [SA] scene has seen me grow up from 13 to 25. You can tell by my music how much I've progressed, how I've changed. But I had demons, everybody has demons. And the only reason why these demons would keep coming back is because I never asked for help. I never said, 'I'm tired.' I never said I couldn't understand this. I never communicated with anyone. It's the whole concept of, 'nobody can help you unless you're willing to help yourself.'"

Opening herself up to a spiritual way out of chaos was "reality's slap in the face," Díaz said, and she now strongly believes she has no need for drugs and alcohol in order to be creative. While she's telling me this, I remember what Steve Earle wrote in the liner notes of his recent box set *The Warner Bros. Years*: "I made four records before *Train a Comin'* and I'm putting out my 15th as I write this," wrote Earle. "I've been nominated for 14 Grammys and I've won three. I've done way more shit sober than I did fucked up."

"Exactly!" Díaz said enthusiastically. "But you know what? Not drinking, not doing drugs, not smoking, isn't because I want to say, 'Look at me, I'm this much sober or look how many days I've been sober,' or 'look at what I'm doing.' It's because I want to live to see you tomorrow, because I want to sing to you. It's not because I want to show that I'm better than you."

Regardless of motivations, a fellow musician approves of whatever is going through Díaz' head and heart right now.

"I have my fucking best friend back," said singer-songwriter Carly Garza, who's known Díaz since high school. "I really don't know a lot about all of that [Krishna philosophy], but it has changed her in a really good way … I'm just happy that she is healthy and doing positive stuff, because it helps me become a better person too. It makes me want to be healthy and productive."

While devoted to Krishna, Díaz's approach to spirituality is non-sectarian and open-minded, not easy to do whenever you join any religious organization.

"It's OK to be an atheist, I think it's totally fine," she said. "I will not judge you. It's not going to be like, 'Oh, I can't talk to you because you don't believe in Krishna.' I want to hear your views and I want to understand why. I want to understand everything. The transition that I've been through is wonderful. And if I could share that with anyone, I will. If you want to share your opinions with me, I'll listen. I'm not going to disregard you or say that you're wrong because nobody is fully wrong and nobody is fully right."

Is Díaz just going through a phase and, sooner or later, will she either go back to her former habits or simply snap out of it and put Krishna in a drawer? She doesn't think so.

"It's not a phase," she said, calmly. "Why would you go back to a bad place after figuring something out?"

But even if it was a phase, Hare Krishna scripture tells her that would be an irrelevant fact.

"In this endeavor there is no loss or diminution, and a little advancement on this path can protect one from the most dangerous type of fear," says Krishna in the *Bhagavad-gita*, the main book followed by Hindus and Vaishnavas (devotees of Vishnu or Krishna).

"Yeah, that's very nice," she said, "but I've spent too many years going back to those drugs, that alcohol, or that guy… I would be a fool to do that again."

No matter what happens on Neela's spiritual path, Nina, the rock singer, is not going anywhere, and her big test post-Krishna took place in May, when Girl in a Coma opened for Smashing Pumpkins in Houston, Dallas, and Corpus Christi. In a normal situation, she would've been thrilled to be there.

Instead, at first she was hesitant and nervous. Then, it clicked.

"I realized [that] I'm doing this for [God] right now, I'm doing what [God] gave me," she said. "And when I played, my heart opened up in a way I never felt before. It was like when you're a child and you finally learn how to whistle or how to snap your fingers, and you're like, 'Oh this is what it sounds like.'"

Her newly sober life has influenced the way she writes too.

"There is a new Girl in a Coma song that's like a [mantra]," she said, "and I'm anxious to see where it goes from now on. My newfound creativity is like a door that has always been there but I've been too afraid to actually open and walk into."

Their SA show Saturday at Josabi's comes after a successful mini-tour on the West Coast with Piñata Protest and a solo gig by Díaz in L.A. But wait… Did I say "successful?"

"Some people may think I'm successful because of the things I've done and the places I've been to," Díaz told me. "I know what I've done and I'm really happy that I've done it and I'm really grateful. But the things I'm doing now and the things I'm doing today… Waking up, talking to you, being able to say the things I really feel and really mean them, that, to me, is more successful than playing any big stadium, doing any tour, or any dollar bill. And when it comes to music, the songs I'm writing and the way I feel when I perform now, it is the happiest I have been in my whole career. That, to me, is real success."

Jeremy Scahill's *Dirty Wars*
(*San Antonio Current*, July 2, 2013)

Jeremy Scahill (investigative reporter for *The Nation* and the author of *Blackwater: The Rise of the World's Most Powerful Mercenary Army* and *Dirty Wars: The World is a Battlefield*) views former Vice-President Dick Cheney as a "cartoonish villain."

"But I don't see President Obama that way at all," he told *Huffington Post*. "I think he's a sincere, deliberative guy who believes that what he's doing is the best way available to him as the commander-in-chief to keep the country safe. I disagree that that's what he's doing, but I don't question his sincerity."

Which doesn't mean Scahill is easy on the president. On Rick Rowley's powerful documentary *Dirty Wars*, based on Scahill's book, the journalist goes deep into remote areas in Afghanistan, Yemen, and Somalia trying to answer the question the Obama Administration won't: who is being killed by the U.S. in secret drone attacks worldwide? How many? Why? Why what was once scandalous is now the norm when it comes to foreign policy? Why are we attacking countries we're not at war with?

Dirty Wars, which won Best Cinematography (Documentary) at Sundance, opens in San Antonio at Santikos Bijou on July 5. Scahill spoke with the *Current* in mid-June on the phone from New York.

Dirty Wars is a very disturbing film. You wrote extensively about these topics, but making a movie about it is a whole different ball game — you were at the center of it all.

When I started this story, we were looking at this new president, President Obama, who many people believed was really going to change things and was going to push back against the excesses of the Bush/Cheney machine. And what we were noticing a bit early in the administration is that he was intensifying the war in Afghanistan and expanding US. drone strikes. It was very clear that Guantanamo wasn't going to be closed anytime soon, so we set out to make a movie that was going to look at war under President Obama. We started in Afghanistan by looking at these night raids that were expanding. The idea was that there was a covert war buried within the bigger conventional war. And after we realized that the force doing this was these elite commandos that had this incredible secret history, then it became a journey that took us around the world. We didn't expect to be in Yemen or Somalia when we started this story. But to answer your question directly, I don't write articles about myself, so for me being the character in this film was something I resisted very much. But after doing it I felt very gutted and shattered as a person. You meet all these people that share these horrifying things that happened to them in their lives, and it changes you as a person. You see things in a more raw and intense way.

Just for the sake of argument, what's wrong with US soldiers apologizing for killing the wrong people? Isn't that the right thing to do?

What you're referring to is the time we went to this village outside the city of Gardez [Afghanistan] and investigated the night raid where three women were killed by US forces — two of them were pregnant — and they also killed a guy who was a senior Afghan police commander [trained by the US]. And these people were all at a party celebrating the birth of a new child. So these commandos come in and they kill them because they believed that they were Taliban people. And instead of realizing that they made a mistake, they actually dig the bullets out of the women's bodies and they try to cover it up and blame it on their family members, saying that it was an honor killing. And then there was an investigation that happened in England. I was investigating it and my colleague from *The Times* of London, Jerome Starkey, was investigating it. And then we learned, only because of these extraordinary events you're talking about, that [the killings were done by] JSOC, the Joint Specials Operation Command. Weeks after the killings of these people, this convoy shows up to their village with all these Afghan and American military soldiers and they have these two sheep, and they offload the sheep and offer them to the family. It's an ancient forgiveness ritual in Afghanistan, they were sort of mimicking this ritual that people would use if they had killed a loved one. Only because of the photographs we know that the man who brought those sheep was Admiral William H. McRaven, who was the commander of this ultra-secretive elite military unit. And the reason they were apologizing there was because there were going to be riots against the Americans in that province, so they were trying to tamper that down. But in most cases where American forces kill civilians, they don't pay them anything or say any apology. They just move on because they know that no one is going to go in and investigate it.

Why one of your inside sources in these secret operations could give you plenty of information except the number of deaths?

Because it's classified. They are not allowed to tell the American people how many people around the area are killed. It's a secret. And it's also a secret how you get on the kill list. And it's a secret how you get *off* the kill list. The whole process is done in secret. What he was saying is, "I know the answer to that question, but I'm not allowed to tell you because it's classified."

What's the status of Yemeni journalist Abdulelah Haider Shaye? Why would President Obama personally intervene to keep him detained?

[Haider Shaye] was one of the main reporters revealing that the US was bombing Yemen and engaging in a new covert war in Yemen. He was arrested a number of times and threatened in Yemen. And then he was eventually thrown in prison [in 2011] and accused of being an Al-Qaeda facilitator, which is a completely ridiculous charge against him. There were big protests in Yemen after he was sentenced to five years in prison. And the dictator in Yemen was going to issue a pardon of him. That day, President Obama found out that this was going to happen, so he called the Yemeni dictator [Ali Abdullah Saleh] and said the US wanted him to be kept in prison, and then they ripped up the pardon. He remains in prison to this day and he has been in prison for almost three years. [On May 27] he smuggled a message out of the prison. And he said, "There is only one person responsible for me being in prison today, and it's President Obama." [The actual translated letter, originally published on the *Yemen Times* website, read: "It's inaccurate to say the Americans imprisoned me because some of them defended and supported me and opposed my detention. Actually, the only person responsible for kidnapping and detaining me is Obama."] When I spoke to the White House and the US State Department, they said that he was involved with Al-Qaeda and that they wanted him to be kept in prison. And when I asked where their evidence was that he was affiliated with Al-Qaeda they said, "We won't answer any more questions about it." They won't give any evidence to back up their claim. They're just keeping this Yemeni journalist in prison.

A handful of progressives are denouncing this, but for the most part we're like, numb, so used to this type of activities. What do these secret drone attacks say about ourselves?

At the beginning of it, I thought that I could just harden myself and just tell these stories as if they weren't affecting me. And you're hearing these awful, tragic stories from everyone that you meet. And in the course of reporting on it, I realized how deeply it affected me as a person. And I feel like I learned a lesson — that if American people stopped using the term "collateral damage" and started viewing the people in Yemen or Pakistan or Somalia and Iraq as human beings, not just as "the enemy" or a "terrorist," but actually saw their humanity, then I think these policies would change. War is sanitized right now. We have drones being used to bomb countries and they're being piloted by people sitting in the Southwest of the United States, sitting in a trailer. And when we sanitize war and dehumanize people in other countries, it makes it easier to say, "Oh this is a smart policy," or "This is a clean war." This is *not* a clean war, that's why we call it the "dirty war." Not because we believe that there is no such thing as a clean war, but because those in power are trying to make it seem like it's a clean war. And it's not.

It wouldn't be the first time the US government does that. What's different this time?

I think we're looking at something that is starting to look like Latin America in the '80s where the US was backing the *contras* and death squads in Nicaragua or supporting right wing military dictatorships [in the '70s]. And you have the CIA and the US military engaging in all sorts of covert actions. To me, it seems like we're in the dawn of an era where we are sort of returning to that mentality: that covert actions should be the main policy of the US. So it's not that it's happening on a larger scale, it's that we have a popular, democratically elected president who is trying to legitimize this and saying that this is acceptable. The incidents that we talked about in Latin America, they're viewed as scandalous, but [what the U.S. is doing] now [is] being viewed as "the policy." And that's what I think is the real issue that we need to confront.

Sixteen-year-old Abdulrahman al-Awlaki, an American citizen, was killed by a drone attack shortly after another drone killed his father, also an American. Was the teenager's death a targeted killing?

We don't know, and that's part of the reason we're raising this question. Anwar al-Awlaki was saying all of these atrocious things about the United States. In his case [the government] never presented any evidence that he was an operational member of Al-Qaeda. But they killed him anyway in September of 2011. Then, two weeks later, his son Abdulrahman al-Awlaki, who had just turned 16, an American citizen born in Denver, Colorado, is sitting outside, having dinner with his teenage cousin and some friends. And a drone appears above them and blows them up. The White House has never explained why they killed this kid. All that we know is what they have sent through links to the media, that, "Oh, he was at a meeting with an Al-Qaeda leader," but then a man said that, "He was at a meeting and he was still alive," then they said, "Oh, he was collateral damage. We were trying to kill someone else, but he was killed." But they made no explanation as to who they were trying to kill. Then, the Attorney General of the United States, Eric Holder, said he was not specifically targeted. What does that mean? They're not saying that he *wasn't* targeted. So, for me, I want to know why he was killed because it would say a lot about who we are as a society. Maybe he was killed in what they call a "signature strike," where they are killing people that are military-aged males and they later say that, "Oh, they were terrorists," even though they don't know their identities. But maybe there was bad intelligence about him and they killed him intentionally. I don't know the answer. One of the reasons we made this film is because we feel like they should answer that question.

You've done the talk shows. Is the media in general getting the point?

I think we have this weird, polarized media culture where, on the one hand, Fox News is kind of our cartoonish version of the media outlet, very right-wing. And on the other hand, you have MSNBC, which at times is like a state media for the Democratic party. I think we have an opportunity to have a real discussion right now in this country. But time will tell, I don't know. We have a pretty bankrupt media culture in this country. And there's not a lot of acting on important questions. I'll be hopeful but it wouldn't surprise me if it all just goes away quickly.

It all comes down to the government (and way too many citizens) believing lying, deceit, and illegal activities sometimes are necessary if that's going to "save one American life," doesn't it?

You just used the word "illegal." No, I don't think that our forces are operating on behalf of the US. I don't think our government should be engaged in any illegal activity. Look, the basic principle for me is this: I believe that nations have a right to defend themselves. I do not believe that nations have a right to wage preemptive war or offensive wars. And the United States has been waging, for the most part, an offensive, preemptive war. So, if there is a case where there is an action taken in defense of the country or in defense of our citizenship, then we [must] have a debate about what is the most effective way to respond to those threats. But that is not what we have been doing, not even close. We are engaged in pre-crime, like *Minority Report*, in our actions around the world. That has got to stop. And I believe that everything that we do should be legal and I also think that we should be rethinking our foreign policy and should only use military force if it's an actual action of self-defense.

Hilburn on Cash
(*San Antonio Current*, October 22, 2013)

As the *Los Angeles Times*' pop music critic for more than three decades (1970-2005), Robert Hilburn was the type of editor that would edit with the writer sitting right next to him, going line by line, and celebrating an improved sentence with effusive high fives. He applied that same passion to his *Johnny Cash: The Life*, arguably the ultimate biography of The Man in Black.

I was a freelancer in Los Angeles for almost five years in the early '90s, and I had the good fortune of working directly under the supervision of "Bob," as we all called him. And he was every bit as Bono would describe him years later in the introduction of Hilburn's memoir *Corn Flakes with John Lennon and Other Tales from a Rock 'n' Roll Life* — Hilburn wasn't interested in "scenes," but in sounds, and was able to see something in young, flawed bands that gave him fuel, while the bands themselves got inspired by the wisdom of the ever-youthful veteran writer.

"Bob's role as critic was to encourage suspension of disbelief in the audience, but in the artist as well," wrote Bono. "That is an environment in which music grows. He made us better. ... Without ever being pious or elitist, he has the Levitical/Jesuitical energy of a keeper of the flame."

Hilburn, who recently turned 74, spoke to the *Current* on the phone from his home in Sherman Oaks, an L.A. suburb.

Why another book on Johnny Cash?

I don't want to sound pretentious, but I wanted to treat Cash like a president, almost. What I found missing from a lot of biographies of celebrities, music or actors, is that they talk about the person's life, but they don't really talk about the artistry of the person, why the person is important in any way. They'll say whether the film is a hit or not, but they don't say why he or she wanted to make the film. Was it good or bad? I wanted to say why he was important, so that 50 years from now — and I think Cash will be remembered 50 years from now — a person will read the book and will get the sense of why he was important during these times.

One of the things I liked the most about your book is how, early on, you tell the story of rock 'n' roll from Cash's perspective, as a link between country and rock 'n' roll.

That was one of my favorite moments. I loved Sun Records. This [book] combined all my interests in music: I loved country music, I loved blues, I loved rock 'n' roll, and I was a fan of Johnny Cash as a teenager. The difference is that I loved Elvis, and Chuck Berry, and Little Richard, and Buddy Holly and all of those guys, but they were speaking to me as a teenager, teddy bears, and hound dogs... Cash was only a couple of years older than Elvis, but when I heard "Folsom Prison Blues" he had an adult voice and adult themes, so it really struck me. "I shot a man in Reno just to watch him die..." I was shocked when I heard that. I didn't know you could say that on the radio!

I was used to people saying, "One, Two, Three O'clock, Four O'clock rock!" "I want to be your teddy bear" or "Whole Lotta Shakin' Goin' On." There was a lot of sexual terms but not a lot of adult darkness stuff. There was something serious about Cash. I heard a lot of country music, but he wasn't like other country stars. That's one of the main things I tried to answer with the book: why was he different? Why did he have a sense of artistry? Coming from a cotton patch in Arkansas and entering a country field where no one else before him, no matter how big the star, had no more ambition than another hit in the jukebox, why was Johnny Cash different? In all my years as a journalist with the *Los Angeles Times* I pretty much knew everything. I interviewed Lennon, and Dylan, Springsteen, Bono, Stevie Wonder, Michael Jackson... And I thought I could get a pretty good read on people. I thought that, if you talked to somebody, you had the final answer, that they were the final authority. But when I started writing the book, I realized how little we know about celebrities and how much I didn't know about Johnny Cash, even though I was around him over and over and over again in his life, doing stories about him.

Celebrities choose to tell us what they want us to hear. I don't really know what Bob Dylan is really like, even though I've interviewed him a dozen times. But when writing this book, I would find out that things [Cash] said were just not true, and I don't think he was trying to lie, but make the story a little bit more interesting, so he would embellish upon it. And the people around him, everyone sees something different. And there would be little things, like the first time he flew into Memphis, after being in the Air Force; [someone] says he came to Memphis on the Greyhound bus, [San Antonio's] Vivian [Liberto, Cash's first wife] says he flew into the airport; Cash said he flew but Vivian wasn't at the airport. So, you have to talk to so many different people to figure out what likely happened. At one point you have to be sort of like a judge to the whole thing. Those are the simple things, but the hard part is when there are significant things and you're trying to piece together what the truth is. I wasn't within 50 miles of what Johnny Cash's life was really like. His personal life turned out much darker than I thought it was. He had burdens, and guilt, and drugs, things that weren't quite honorable, and I was really surprised. But at the end of the book he comes off as a hero, because he keeps fighting through all that stuff to make music that inspires somebody. I kept telling myself, "Oh my gosh... Should I tell people about this? Is this too private or not?" Some members of the family didn't want you to say things that might hurt their dad's image, but [daughter] Rosanne Cash was very good about this. She said, "I don't care how uncomfortable it makes me feel; if it's the truth, tell the truth." That was very helpful. It was a difficult journey, but I just loved every minute of it.

You're the one who taught me about ethics in journalism, not going backstage, keeping a distance from the people you write about. Yet you once "confessed" to me that with John Lennon it was difficult not to get too close because he was such a special person, so you, John and Yoko developed a close friendship, yet you never stopped being critical of him when you had to. In comparison, what was your relationship with Cash like?

I first met Cash in 1966, or '67. I had just started writing about country music for the [*Los Angeles Times*] as a freelancer. I wanted to do rock 'n' roll but there was already somebody writing about it. I did a review of Cash at the Long Beach Auditorium, I think. In those days there wasn't a publicist there, you had to go backstage and knock on the door, and hopefully they'll answer and talk to you. I remember knocking on the door and, "What??!!" His voice came out, he was in really bad shape at the time, he looked awful, his voice was raspy. I walked in the dressing room. He was alone, he was wiping his hair, jittery motions. I thought he was just hyperactive; I didn't realize it was the drugs that were talking.

After that we met at Folsom; there was a graciousness, a warmth about Cash, especially by '68 or '69, when he was getting off the drugs. He was a relatively shy person, he would kind of retreat in the dressing room or at a social function, he'd let June take over. But he always made me feel comfortable, he'd sit down and talk to me. We both came from small towns, so I think that helped. And secondly, I was somebody from a big newspaper who was paying attention to him, and that really impressed him. He'd always talk to DJs who'd tell him,

"Oh, we love your music," but here was someone from "the Los Angeles newspaper." The guy in the Air Force who taught him how to play guitar came from my same town. I spent a weekend with him and June at the Carter Family cabin in Virginia, just six months before their death, and that was a really important moment, because I wasn't planning to do a book, but he talked a long, long time about regrets in his life, and it helped me understand a lot of things about him.

I loved John Lennon because he'd make you feel comfortable right away; he'd sit down, have fun, you could talk about Elvis, and Johnny Cash, and things he loved. Johnny Cash [wasn't] as outgoing as John Lennon but he'd make you feel comfortable in the same way, he made you feel you were talking to a real person.

In all the years I interviewed people, I think I took my mother to two or three shows, and I never took her backstage because I didn't want to go backstage. But one day I told myself, "I think she'd really like to meet Johnny Cash." She loved Johnny Cash, and everybody loved Johnny Cash back in that day. It was amazing he'd get such a wide following. So I took my mom because I knew he would understand I wasn't trying to be a groupie and he'd be gracious to her. And he was, and that was a great snapshot of him. He wasn't the kind of people that would go out of his way to meet people, he was kind of shy. But he came over to her, shook her hand and said, "Anything I can do for you? I hope you enjoyed the show." I wouldn't have taken that chance with most entertainers because I think most would've brushed her off.

What's the story of the famous Folsom Prison photo?

I was just there trying to write a story and I was looking for angles. He was standing there trying to sense the audience. He was nervous, this was an important step in his career, and I was just looking around for things I could use in the story. I thought it was going to be an exciting moment, but who knew it would be a landmark album?

He spent relatively a small amount of time in San Antonio, yet those were key years in his life.

That was *so* important, because he came out of Dyess, Arkansas, which was like 50 miles from Memphis, and he had been out of Dyess four or five times in his life, a small town of 2,500, and he didn't have a lot of self-confidence. His father never really thought he'd amount to anything. He'd gone to Detroit to try to work at an auto factory and had suffered a lot of anti-Southern bias, and he didn't know if he'd suffer the same bias in [SA]. He was very nervous going to the Air Force, but it turned out he did very well and passed all these tests at Lackland. He was a star, other [soldiers] would come up to him and ask for his help. That did great for his confidence, and the second time he came to [SA] he had no experience with women, he barely had girlfriends in high school, and he meets Vivian at this roller rink. He knew how to roller skate because he worked at a rink in Dyess, but he pretended not to know so she could help him stand up and so forth. He was looking for a girlfriend so he could tell the guys at the barrack "I got a girlfriend," he could write her letters, and he felt very deeply in love very quickly. It did great for his confidence that someone from outside of Dyess could be interested in him. When he went to the Air Force, he would write her a letter once or twice a day, every day for three years, more than 1,000 letters. She was hoping they could live in [SA], because her family was there and had strong roots in SA, but he wanted to go to Memphis because it was closer to Dyess and his brother was already there, and that's how he ended up in Memphis. And in SA would've been harder to start a music career. But he didn't go to Memphis to start a music career, but because his brother found him a job.

Despite all the drama in his life, he was a lucky guy, being in the right place at the right time throughout his life...

He sure was. I even thought of giving speeches on "Johnny Cash's luck." There are so many instances... Can you think of a specific one?

Well, when he happened to unknowingly be driving around Sun Studios at such an important time in music's history...

Oh, yes... Well, the first lucky incident is just him going to Memphis. He goes to Memphis because he wants to get a job there. But the truth is that, for a young, unschooled Johnny Cash, there isn't a better place he could've picked than Memphis. Sam Phillips is just starting Sun Records, and the first day [Cash] arrives back from Germany Elvis cut his first record there. Johnny Cash loved that record. He saw Elvis appear at a drugstore opening singing the song, and he asked him, "How do I get a job at Sun Records?" And he called Sun Records and they kept putting him off day after day after day. After work he would go home and drive by Sun Records not knowing it was there, until the day he finally went to see Sam Phillips and [Phillips] said, "OK, sing some stuff, maybe we can make some music together." Had he moved to a different place, he would've probably not made it because [Cash and the Tennessee Two] weren't that great, not at all like other stars of the time. And the other important thing is that, by recording with Sun Records, he always had a rock 'n' roll audience interested in him. Had he gone to Nashville and made those same records he would have never made it. He'd be considered a country star like Marty Robbins or somebody like that. By going to Sun, he was always part of that Elvis Presley/Jerry Lee Lewis world. So, when he goes back to Folsom Prison in 1968, *Rolling Stone* is all excited, because here's a rock and roller doing that kind of stuff. If Marty Robbins had done the same thing, [*RS*] would not have cared.

OK, so that was the first stroke of luck, and the last one was meeting Rick Rubin.

That sure was. But the biggest one of all, probably, is when he's in Germany and in his first week he sees a movie called *Inside the Walls of Folsom Prison*. Had he gone to Germany a week later, he would have never heard of Folsom Prison and wouldn't have written the song. But even then, he gives up on writing the song, and one day he's walking down the barracks and a guy was listening to a song he had bought on a whim the night before, "Crescent City Blues." Cash hears that, goes over to the guy and says, "Could you play that again?" And he pretty much copied, or stole, or however you want to put it, but so much of "Folsom Prison Blues" is from "Crescent City Blues." So, if that guy hadn't bought that record, [Cash] would not have heard that song.

But by 1993 he had been dropped by Columbia Records, he was doing terrible in Mercury Records, he had no more faith that people even cared about him, he thought his career was over and his legacy forgotten, and this rock 'n' roll/rap producer walks into a show at the Rhythm Café in Santa Ana… He had been playing arenas in his life and now he's playing these little cafes. June Carter said, "This is ridiculous, John. You can't work with this guy, a rock/rap producer." But [Cash] had no alternative. When I talked to Rick that is the thing that struck him the most about Cash's reaction — the fact that Cash was curious. "Why would anybody be interested in me? My career is over with." So Rick's biggest challenge was rebuilding Cash's confidence in himself. And that's a really inspiring story, to see how these two guys became so close and how Rick struggled, and struggled, and struggled to get Cash to believe in himself again. And once John started to believe in himself, he was able to do some of the best work of his life, at the age of 65.

Recently, some young local bands here did a Johnny Cash tribute…

Really? Where was that?

Here in San Antonio!

That's great! I think Rick Rubin brought him into a new generation of people. If it hadn't been for the Rick Rubin years, he would not have had the same stature and the impact on people as he has today. The old people are gone and their influence has gone away, but it is the young people that got turned on by the Rick Rubin era that are still here. He appealed to so many different people. Rockers and punksters, and the reggae crowd are attracted to him because there was an essential truth in what he was saying. People *believed* Johnny Cash. He was very good at empathizing with people, especially with the underdogs, because he was an underdog himself. He had been in trouble with the law, so he could relate to people in prison whenever he sang in prison. He knew how to design shows in order to communicate directly to his audience, either in prison or at the White House. June didn't want him to release the "Hurt" video. "John, your fans are going to think you're destitute," and all that, but he thought it was a piece of art. He was so brave to put that out.

Reading the book, it's obvious that you really loved and admire Cash but, as usual in your work, you had no problem being critical of him, and it is clear that Cash *did* make some awful albums…

Oh yes, he had bad albums. After the superstardom of the '70s, the prison album and the TV show, he's got a son now, he wants to enjoy that part of his life that was a blur in the '60s. He was on drugs and felt guilt every day of his life about leaving his daughters. If you look at the picture in the cover of the book, those sad eyes… He always seemed to have those sad eyes. The sadness over leaving his family and his brother dying… There was a lot of sadness in his life. So, in the '70s, he wants to devote his life to his family, invites the girls to come back to Nashville to be with him, he has a son, meets Billy Graham, goes out with him in crusades…

In the '60s, music was his only comfort, he devoted night and day in writing better songs and recording concept albums. By the '70s he had started to relax, paying attention to all the things he neglected in the '60s, but he now started neglecting his music. And slowly the albums kept getting weaker and weaker. By the time he realizes this and tries to correct it, country music had left Cash behind. You get all these Kenny Rogers, and country radio won't play Cash anymore. So, he goes down and down and down. Once in a while he'd come up with a good album, but his confidence was gone and Columbia drops him. So, the period from '75 to '90 or even 1993 was a very uneven period for Johnny Cash. When he wanted to think of the music again, it was too late. There were good tracks here and there, but for the most part those albums were poor.

But another very important thing happened just a month before he met Rick Rubin. U2 invited him to the studio to sing the lead in "The Wanderer." Written by Bono, it's a gospel song. Cash was very intimidated because he had no confidence and here was the world's biggest group asking him to sing with them. And he did it and got all this acclaim, and the album was a big hit, and *Rolling Stone* gave it a good review. That really helped him get his spirits up a little bit before Rick Rubin came in.

Cumbia: How Colombia Made Selena a Star
(*San Antonio Current*, November 5, 2013)

When I heard someone on NPR say cumbia was "the musical backbone of Latin America," I almost crashed my car into a light post.

"You wish!" I thought. Then, after veering out of trouble and cooling off, I realized the host was absolutely right. No other musical genre has taken stronger root in every single corner of the three Americas. There's cumbia in its birthplace, Colombia, but there's also cumbia everywhere else, and I'm not just talking about the "influence" of cumbia — I mean solidly established scenes that rearranged their regional musical landscapes, each version with its own distinctive local flavors added to it.

To name all the genres and subgenres of cumbia would take half of the magazine, but you can't talk about cumbia without mentioning original cumbia, the 2/4 rhythm born on Colombia's Atlantic coast during slavery with its mix of African, Spanish and indigenous roots; Mexican cumbia (and that includes alternative mixes with rock, led by accordionist Celso Piña in Monterrey); Peruvian cumbia (both its own style and psychedelic *chicha* from the '60s); Panamanian cumbia; cumbia-rock; Argentina's cumbia villera (shantytown cumbia, a now-mainstream rudimentary style born in the '90s with lyrics mainly dealing with sex, crime, drugs and the occasional political commentary); Heck, even Charles Mingus experimented with cumbia. And, of course, there is *cumbia tejana*.

For beginners, Friday's Échale Series show at the Pearl featuring Austin-based Master Blaster Sound System and Mexico's Los Master Plus will be a fun introduction to the electrocumbia/hip-hop style, but also a good excuse to figure out how the genre came to Texas and developed into cumbia *tejana*.

"Everybody calls Selena *La Reina del Tex-Mex*, or *La Reina del Tejano*, but what did Selena do?" asks A.B. Quintanilla III, Selena's brother, bassist for Los Dinos and leader of Kumbia King All Starz. "She did mostly cumbias and some norteño and mariachi, and pop in English. My father is one of the first ones who would say, 'Tejano is what made your sister!' and I'm like, 'Dad, 'Como la Flor' is not Tejano, it's cumbia!'"

Cumbia *tejana* is a reality, and an easily identifiable one at that: those keyboards, that sentimental singing, the romantic lyrics. From a commercial standpoint, cumbia tejana (which was a key, if not *the* key, component of the Tejano boom of the '90s) indirectly started with Mexico's Rigo Tovar, whose *Matamoros Querido* (1972), recorded in Houston, launched a style that influenced the generation of musicians that would form La Mafia, Tejano's biggest act until the Selena explosion. Even though conjunto musicians like Valerio Longoria and Santiago Jiménez Sr. were among those who recorded cumbias in the past, La Mafia's *Estás tocando fuego* (1991) was the album that launched the cumbia tejana trend.

"Before that, [Tejano musicians] would add maybe one cumbia as a filler, but we felt very strongly about the pop element," said La Mafia's Armando Lichtenberger Jr. After recording "No lo haré" on 1990's *Con tanto amor*, for the next album La Mafia went all out. "In *Estás tocando fuego* we had six polkas and four cumbias, which was something unheard of. Look at Selena's albums after *Fuego*, and there's plenty of cumbias. But before *Fuego*, you won't find a Tejano album with more than one cumbia."

Selena opened for La Mafia between the mid-to-late '80s and 1991, but after that it was the other way around — Los Dinos' renewed international sound turned Selena into a superstar, and tragedy turned her into a legend in 1995.

"I asked myself, 'How can Cubans and Puerto Ricans understand Selena's music?'" said Quintanilla. "And you know how I got them to do that? With one simple thing: the *cencerro* [cowbell]. If you listen to 'Amor Prohibido' you can hear the 'too-KEEN, too-KEEN.' I played it salsa-style, it wasn't coincidental. After that, Selena went from selling 25,000-50,000 to more than 500,000."

Simply put, cumbia is popular because it's an infectious, malleable rhythm that grabs you whether you like it or not.

"It's an incredible groove, a universal beat we can all adapt to our own styles, and easy to play," said Lichtenberger. "It's not too fast, not too slow, like reggae. Any UB40 song could be turned into a cumbia."

Gabriel Zavala, Best New Male Artist winner at the 2013 Tejano Music Awards, is "the only guy [in Tejano] trying to do something different," according to Quintanilla.

"The thing that makes cumbia so loved worldwide is its ability to be danced [to] with little or no dancing experience," said Zavala. "I've seen people just walk to the rhythm and that's acceptable on the dance floor, whereas salsa or merengue's moves are much more advanced. You don't even need a partner to dance cumbia!"

Full of enthusiasm, Zavala even gives cumbia an esoteric twist.

"There are also some numerology patterns that I have found in the rhythm of the cumbia that might have an illuminati or extra-terrestrial origin," he said, dead serious, "but that's a topic for another article!"

Steve Vai: Strat Abuse
(*San Antonio Current*, November 19, 2013)

Legendary guitarist Steve Vai will perform at Backstage Live on Wednesday, November 20. He spoke with the *Current* on the phone from his home in Los Angeles.

First of all, as I tell everyone who comes to San Antonio, thanks for stopping by instead of ignoring us, like most do, in favor of Austin or Houston.

It's been a long time since I've played there and I can't figure out why, 'cause I have a great audience there. I'm really looking forward to [going] back.

You couldn't just make a simple album, could you? You had to start a trilogy and make us wait years for each chapter to come out... Tell me about *The Story of Light*.

Yes, I'm always looking for less conventional stories and I'm always challenging myself to do something that's different. The way I laid it out was... different. I didn't want it to be so obvious, like a conventional concept record, so I thought of doing the music in three installments. The first was [*Real Illusions: Reflection*, 2005], the second *The Story of Light* [2012], and the third will come out sometime in the future, and at one point I'd like to get all the songs and put them in the right order and add a fourth record with new narratives, and change the melodies and the vocals. In the meantime, it's just music that can be enjoyed by those who like that kind of stuff.

So... Will we have to wait several years before chapter 3?

Yeah.

One thing is to be able to transcribe music, but quite another to be able to transcribe music for Frank Zappa at age 18. What was that like and why can't some people "get" Zappa?

Frank's music was more challenging than anybody else's. I could've tried to do atonal music, which I did, but I liked Frank's music for the same reasons you like it. It just resonates with you. Some people like blue and some people like red. I don't care to really understand why some people like certain things, and some don't. In the future, people will discover Frank's music and it will change the quality of their whole life. Frank's music changed a lot of people's lives. I've always been close to his music and that's why I chose to transcribe it. I was one of those fortunate people that kind of followed the thread all the way to L.A., and Frank found something in me that was valuable.

When I listen to *The Story of Light*, at times I feel I hear Zappa, and then I think: "Who influenced who?" Do you feel you influenced him in any way?

You'd have to ask him that… [Zappa died in 1993] (laughs) Every time you work with somebody you find things that inspire you, but I can't say I influenced Frank at all. Maybe there were some things going on at the time in the way of guitar technology that I introduced him to that I don't think he knew well, but it was just stupid little things like that, you know…

What's your favorite moment from, say, *You Are What You Is* [1981, an album in which Vai is credited as "Strat Abuse"]?

There's a piece called "Persona Non Grata" that turned into the "Theme from the 3rd Movement of Sinister Footwear," and there's a guitar solo that Frank did and I transcribed and doubled, so when you listen to the song, you hear me on one side and Frank on the other. It's pretty extraordinary how closely I doubled his performance. That was quite a feat.

Punk started as a direct response to flashy, technical guitarists like you. What's your take on DIY music? How do you view technically limited musicians who are trying to do their thing?

I have two ways of looking at other people's playing. One is a very critical view, which listens with the same ears that listen to Jeff Beck, Jimi Hendrix… I look at any guitar player and there's a particular way that I might criticize them in my mind, like, "Well, the intonation is not very good, the vibrato is nice, they don't really play fast…" That's just one way of kind of sizing them up. But it's a very small part of what I do when I'm watching somebody. The larger part, and it's getting larger and larger as I go through life, is a very non-critical, non-judgmental view of somebody doing anything. Because what you discover eventually is that, anytime you meet anybody or see anybody doing anything, you've really already created in your own mind an identity for them and a critique for them. You don't really know the person but you criticize them in your head. So, what I do when I'm watching a guitar player, if they have no technique or maybe too much technique? I don't judge it at all. And what happens is that you see this person is being animated by something else. You see that what they're doing is expressing themselves the best way they can at that particular time. And that's all that anybody can do — to do their best at any particular moment. You can't say, "They should be like this" or "they should be like that". They're incapable, and I'm incapable of being anything besides what I am at this particular moment. As you go through life, you go through experiences that change you and educate you. But ultimately, what is, is. When I see somebody playing, I see the universe expressing itself through people. You asked about Frank [Zappa], and I saw that with him. Frank was completely in the moment when he created music. He didn't make any excuses and whatever he did he was completely invested in it. It was his way of expressing himself. And if somebody picks up an instrument and tries to express himself even though he can't even play it very well, I see it as something very beautiful, there's something absolutely beautiful about it. You're listening to God, in a sense, expressing yourself in a multitude of ways. So that's what I prefer to do nowadays, instead of saying, "Wow, they can't play as fast as me."

Your new music is challenging but also accessible, song-based.

I just go by ideas. Whatever idea comes up, that's what I follow. Sometimes it goes towards convention, sometimes it makes sense and sometimes it doesn't. The song is very important, but sometimes I do something unexpected because that's what the vision was and I'm not thinking about the price I have to pay later. You just go with what you're feeling and then the song takes shape. There are many different kinds of musicians and each one has a different set of tools. Some have a tremendous amount of technique and technical musical information, and some are completely emotional, that just create out of the way they feel and don't use the intellectual mind at all. Well, anybody on either end will be at a deficit. Because you need a balance. If you're only emotional and don't have any way of really expressing your visions, because you're done away all with technical ability, then you'll destroy your potential to get your ideas really across. And if all you do is intellectual or technical, then your music will have no soul to it.

What are you going to play in San Antonio?

I like to build a show that's entertaining on many different levels. I like people to feel that they're seeing great musicianship, a show with great dynamics, very intense sometimes and at times very delicate. The songs are selected by the event flow. Usually, we play about five or six songs from the new record, a handful of songs people were expecting and then a handful of songs that I have either never played or haven't played in a long time. This show has a lot of that. Everybody gets a little moment to shine, and we have an acoustic set. One of the things that we do that's been going on really well is that I invite people up from the audience to build a song with us onstage. For example, I have someone come up and I have him or her sing a drum beat, Jeremy [Colson] plays the drum beat, then I have him sing a bass part, and then they sing a melody for me to play. It's great, you'll be so surprised to see some of the results. It's really amazing.

A lot has been said about the importance of "practicing" for mortal musicians. But how does someone at your level "practice"?

My level is relative, because your level is how you see yourself. To this day, the thing that's most interesting and exciting to me is the same thing that was most interesting and exciting when I was very young, and that's to pick up the guitar and have an idea of playing something, and work on it and suddenly being able to play it. That never goes away, you never run out. If you run out it means the universe is limited. Every day is an opportunity to find something that's different. Now, do I sit and practice? Well, no. I mean, sometimes I do certain mindless things to warm up, but for the most part, no matter what I have to do, even if it's just play the guitar or record, I usually take about an hour at the end of the day and I just sit for an hour and shut the door and just play the guitar. That's my favorite moment.

I don't remember if it was Pete Townsend telling Clapton, or the other way around, but when they saw Hendrix in concert for the first time, one told the other (I'm paraphrasing), "Man, I just saw someone who's going to put us all out of work." Who's the guy you feel could put you "out of work"? Is there anyone you look up to?

Yes: Allan Holdsworth. When I look at any guitarist in the world, the analytical head of mine kicks in and I know in my head what they're doing. Is not that I wish I could do that, or I would even try it; I'm perfectly happy with *them* doing it. But when I listen to Allan Holdsworth play, I'm stunned. I can't believe how amazing, and beautiful, and musical and melodic he is. It's almost as if he's undiscovered. He's way ahead of his time and I just don't think he's understood.

Are you eating? I hope it's veggie stuff.

[Laughs loudly] I apologize for eating doing the interview!

No problem, as long it has no meat.

I just finished and no, it's no meat at all. It's an eggplant sandwich.

Good. Unlike you, I'm the finger-pointing, militant, pain-in-the-ass type of vegetarian. Are you a veggie for ethical or health reasons?

Well, I've been a vegetarian for 32 years now. I haven't talked much about it. You'd tell people you were a vegetarian back then and they'd think you're weird. But it just works for me. When I started I wasn't very healthy, I didn't feel good, I was going through a lot of mental depressions. Being a vegetarian was one of the things I did to change my whole life. It works for me on a health level and on a moral level. I just feel better, but I don't criticize anybody, nor do I care at all what anybody eats.

Anything else?

I'm really excited to be [in San Antonio]. Look at the [tour] reviews on ticketmaster.com to see what to expect. It's really hard for me to convince people to come to the show. When an artist says, "Come to my show!" What does it mean? It doesn't mean anything.

Really? You have trouble convincing people to come? I find that hard to believe.

It's more effective if they hear it from somebody else. [The show has] gone as long as three hours, but it's usually two and a half. Is that long? It doesn't feel long when you're watching it, but you'll have to be the judge of that.

Augie Meyers: Kissing Death Goodbye and the Eternal Hustle

(*San Antonio Current*, November 26, 2013)

Every time I get together with Augie Meyers, I want him to lead with a joke. Yeah, yeah, we'll talk about your new album, whatever, but make me laugh first.

"I don't know, man," he tells me at García's Mexican restaurant on Fredericksburg Rd., his favorite diner for the last 40 years. "My jokes are kind of risqué."

"No problem," I reassure him. "This is the *Current* — anything goes."

"OK, then…"

Thus we enter Augie Meyers' world, one where there's always time for a silly joke or a crazy story. His eyes open wide, and he relishes the opportunity as if he had been practicing for this precise moment all his life.

"This lady is walking down the street, she faints, she sees the good Lord and says, 'I'm only 30 years old! I don't wanna die!'" Meyers begins.

"'Honey,' says God. 'You're OK. You have another 55 years, 10 days and 11 minutes to live.'"

Meyers is winding up, now.

"'Thank you,' she says. So she went to the hospital across the street, had her tummy tucked, veins taken out of her legs, dyed her hair blonde, had her tits fixed, butt moved a little bit… For seven months she was in the hospital, got out, crossed the street… and boom! A truck hit her and killed her. When she sees the Lord, she says, 'I thought you said I had 55 years, 10 days and 11 minutes to live!'"

Meyers pauses for effect.

"'I did, sweetheart, but I'm sorry!' says God. 'I didn't recognize you!'"

OK, granted — it's old, and much funnier in person but, comic merits aside, the fact that Meyers doesn't find it hard to joke about death tells you a good deal about the guy. The keyboardist for Sir Douglas Quintet ("She's About a Mover" wouldn't be the same without his Vox Continental organ) and the Texas Tornados himself had a brush with death four years ago. A person who heard on the radio about his need for a kidney gave him a second life, and in 2010 he got the much-needed transplant. "I call him my angel," he said of Jimmy Lucas, the Dallas computer technician who saved his life.

If you thought this would slow down Meyers, you don't know Augie: this September he came back with his best music in recent memory. *Loves Lost and Found* is the country album he always wanted to make (he released *Country* in 2009, but "this one's better," he says, and I agree). He's back on the hustle, having already written what he calls a "mariachi" album (two fiddles, *guitarrón* and no drums), a handful of blues numbers and a pocket book of "Augiesms" (more on that later), high-profile TV appearances (as part of Tom Waits' band on *Late Show with David Letterman* in 2012), and traveling, lots of traveling.

Touring was something hard to predict in 2009, when he started feeling ill while gigging with Little Joe y La Familia in New Mexico, the same state that took our Doug Sahm, Meyers' Quintet and Tornados buddy, 10 years prior when Sahm died of a heart attack in Taos in 1999. Meyers' wife Sarah had been urging her husband to see the doctor, but he kept telling her, "I'll go when I'm back in San Antonio." When he couldn't even walk, it was time to go to the hospital for what Meyers thought was a problem with his lungs.

"No, it's your kidneys," the doctor told him. "Either you go on dialysis today or we're going to kiss you goodbye." Shortly thereafter, the doctor took Sarah aside.

"Look, if [he's] alive in the morning, we're going to take care of [him]."

"He didn't tell *me*, he told my wife," repeats Meyers. "If your potassium level is four, you're sick. If you're six, you have a heart problem. Eight, you're dead. Mine was 8.25. It was *that* bad."

Meyers was on dialysis for 13 months, nine hours a day, connected to his stomach. But he didn't stop — he took it on the plane, to Los Angeles, New York, Chicago, anywhere he went. He would write or read, always with Sarah by his side, whether it was at the hospital or home in SA. Twenty-eight potential donors had been tested and discarded. It was April 2010, and in May he would have been taken off the transplant list. But at that particular moment, unbeknownst to him, Jimmy Lucas was driving on a Dallas freeway listening to a radio interview with drummer Clay Meyers, Augie's son.

When asked about his dad, Clay said, "He needs a kidney." Lucas felt something.

"I don't know, I just felt compelled to do it," Lucas told the *Current* on the phone from Dallas. "I thought it was the right thing to do, I felt pretty strong emotion." He laughs nervously when he says, "It must have been a God thing…"

Everyone else thought he might be crazy, including the doctors. So much so that Lucas almost bailed at the last minute.

"[The doctors] took me to a three-hour psychiatric evaluation," Lucas said. "I told them, 'I'm just trying to do something nice, and you're making me feel like I'm crazy.'"

Meyers explained, "He figured if he did something good, it would come back to him, and two weeks [after the transplant], he got the job he always wanted."

The transplant took place on April 22, 2010. "Am I still here? Am I still here?" Meyers asked Clay upon waking up, according to the *Express-News*. Meyers and Lucas met in San Antonio three months after the transplant.

"He told me I was his guardian angel," said Lucas, now a regular at Meyers' shows in Dallas. Lucas has since married (his new wife coincidentally lost a kidney to disease), and in October, he received Meyers' new album as a birthday present.

In typical Meyers fashion, he closes this chapter of his story drolly. "I figured Heaven wasn't ready for me and Hell was afraid I'd take over," said Meyers.

Now Meyers is back in the saddle, with a vengeance. He's still looking for a place to show his stand-up comedy, even though his favorite venue no longer exists.

"I wanted to do it at Casbeers [at the Church]," said Meyers. "I was on tour and, when I came back, it was closed. I liked that place. The audience was right there in front of you and the acoustics were really nice, so I'm looking for another place. I got all my jokes written down."

Written down, and ready to be deployed in any situation. When the topic changes to his new habits (he says he no longer gets high, he hasn't had a drink in six years and now only drinks coffee, without brandy, when he sits at the piano), he encourages me to quit smoking.

"If you want to quit and you have your mind to it, you quit," he said. "If you want to quit smoking you use a patch, and if you're a sex addict you need a patch on your balls." Then, the punchline: "They call it 'Dickotine.'"

He plans to continue touring on the strength of *Loves Lost and Found*, but he's already actively pursuing the mariachi album (for which he'll shoot a video in the next few weeks). He's also written a few blues songs.

"I write in spurts," he said. "My last two albums were country, but now I'm doing mariachi and blues, and I finally finished a song for Sarah."

Don't tell me you finished it…

"Yes, I did."

The song is called "You Used To Be On My Mind But Now You Just Get On My Nerves," a track he once told me he'd write for his wife. "She heard it and she likes it."

It goes a little something like this: *"You used to be on my mind but now you just get on my nerves/ you used to look so fine/ but now you're running out of curves."*

Sarah is game, but I told Meyers I strongly disagree: she hasn't run out of anything, with all due respect.

He smiled. "I just did it for the record."

Then there's the book, tentatively titled *Augiesms: Thoughts to Think About*.

"I'm trying to get it finished before the end of the year," he said. "One-liners, sometimes two-liners, just things I write."

He offered a few examples. "One of my mottos in life is, 'I want the most, I expect the least, I appreciate what I get, and I run like hell with it,'" Meyers recited. "You know… My grandfather used to tell me years ago: 'If you don't have time to get it right the first time, when are you going to find time to do it over?' Stuff like that. 'How come it always breaks when you're broke?'"

"The Sound"

Someone once said that the problem with the world is that the intelligent (or talented) are full of doubts, while the idiots are full of certainties. This applies to Meyers: he still can't pinpoint "Augie's sound."

"I just played in Louisiana [in October] and some girl and her cousin drove all the way from North Carolina," he said. "They told me they listen to everything, the Dylan albums, the ones with Doug Sahm, Tom Waits… 'But we want to see you, in person, play your sound.'"

And what is "your sound"?

"I don't know!" he said. "We were in Italy last week; this cat tells me 'I want you to play on my album.' I said, 'What do you want to hear?' He goes, 'I want to hear *you*.' And that's what I did. I don't know. It amazes me when people say things like that and talk about 'my sound.'"

You could explain "the Augie Meyers sound" as that percussive, cutting Vox Continental sound that joins the rhythm section on tracks like "She's About a Mover," "Mendocino" and "Love Sick," the opening track of *Time Out of Mind* (1997), the first on a string of superb late-career recordings by Bob Dylan. But why try to explain the "Augie sound" when he's much more than just a sound? And why even try, when The Man himself already did?

"What makes [Augie Meyers] so great is that internally speaking, he's the master of syncopation and timing," Dylan once said, "and this is something that cannot be taught. If you need someone to get you through the shipping lanes and there's no detours, Augie will get you right straight through. Augie's your man."

"I never got burned out," said Meyers. "I love what I do. I thank the good Lord... for being able to do what I want to do."

The Hustler

Sometimes you don't have to get burned out to stop playing. People change. Or maybe they're not burned out but they just can't find work. Throw a rock anywhere in SA and you'll find a legendary conjunto musician who finds it hard to make ends meet. Meyers must've done something right, besides good playing. Is it drive? PR? Sarah? Clay? Why can't other talented musicians of his age find work?

"I don't wait for the phone to ring," Meyers says. "I go out there and make it ring. I'm always looking, hustling. I talk to some of my friends and ask them, 'You've been playing?' 'No, man... The phone ain't ringing.' 'Then go out there and see what's going on!' 'There's nothing going on!' That's why there's nothing going on with you. There's something going on, but you have to look for it. It's like when a girl comes up to you and says, 'Hey, I want to go to bed with you,' and you go, 'OK,' and she says, 'Your place or mine?' and you go, 'Well, if you're going to argue about it, forget it!'"

He closes with another Augiesm.

"I learned a long time ago that if your in-flow is less than your outgo, then your upkeep is going to be your downfall," he said. "I live by that rule. I travel all over the world and still get up early in the morning, and my friends tell me, 'Augie, you're too old to do that, you're 73,' and I go, 'So what? You say I'm too old because you can't do it, but I'm going to do it for as long as I can.' And when I can't do it no more, I'm not going to be sorry. I'll just say, 'That's it.'"

Las Marthas: The Weirdest Fiesta Ever
(*San Antonio Current*, January 14, 2014)

"Laredo is mostly Mexican-American, and here we are celebrating George Washington's birthday. It's kind of crazy. Why do we do this?"
— **Laura Garza Hovel**

At the end of the Mexican American War in 1848, Texas and several other full or partial territories became part of the USA. When Mexico's Nuevo Laredo was founded on May 15 of that year by 17 Mexican families who had been living in Laredo, they disinterred their dead, crossed the border and buried them in Mexican territory. Fast-forward 166 years later, and Laredoans from both sides of the border celebrate George Washington's birthday with a lavish, surreal and frivolous colonial ballroom dance in which families "present" girls to America's first president.

"It's the same families," said Josefina Saldaña, Director of Latino Studies at New York University, in Cristina Ibarra's *Las Marthas*, a fascinating ITVS/PBS documentary screening Thursday at Santikos Embassy as part of KLRN's free Community Cinema Series. Saldaña asked, "Why would a Mexican community celebrate an Anglo oppressor?"

That and many other questions are skillfully raised by Ibarra. Instead of taking sides, she was smart enough to simply let the camera show the three main aspects of this story: the dominating conservativism of the mostly well-to-do organizers (dress designer Linda Leyendecker Gutiérrez proudly remembers the time when the Society of Martha Washington committee "was invited to the White House by our lovely president George W. Bush, who we all love in Texas"), skeptical academics who question the spirit behind the celebration (most notably Saldaña and former University of Texas — San Antonio professor Norma Cantú), and the one thing everyone agrees on — the fact that, whatever reservations one may have, the celebration has turned into a unique Mexican and American hybrid.

"It always seemed like high border surrealism to me, carnivalesque, performing Yankee hegemony in such an over-the-top manner it becomes popular satire," author and professor John Phillip Santos told the *Current*.

The first George Washington Celebration took place in Laredo in 1898 as a sort of minstrel show by Anglo migrants who staged battles in which the Indians beat the Mexicans. In time, the celebration became Mexicanized, partly due to the fact that Mexicans had to find a way to establish their "whiteness" in the midst of a wave of killings, lynchings and land theft.

"But [the Anglos looked] at these Mexicans dressed like George and Martha Washington and [they went], 'Oh, they're OK,'" said Saldaña.

"I can understand how some folks might be horrified [by *Las Marthas*]," Cantú told the *Current*. Now with the University of Missouri — Kansas City, she's one of the talking heads featured in *Las Marthas*. "Perhaps studying *fiestas* has given me a different lens and I can understand a community's needs for celebrations. San Antonio has Fiesta — to honor the defeat of the Mexicans! And who celebrates? Mexicans! And on and on."

The girls portraying "Las Marthas" — named after the original First Lady — take part in the exclusive celebration by invitation only and go through a rigorous, grueling preparation for many months. In the movie they're represented by cocky Laura Garza-Hovel and shy Rosario Reyes, now a student at Trinity University. The elaborate gowns they wear cost between $15,000 and $30,000 and just being able to curtsey in them is a superhuman task. The dresses are so heavy that "you can't breathe and your back and knees hurt," said Garza-Hovel, who seemed to relish when Reyes broke down in tears during one of the rehearsals. "You should know what you're getting into."

To answer Garza-Hovel's above question ("Why do we do this?"), Reyes cites tradition and the fact that "this presentation really gives you the sense of belonging to Laredo."

Whatever your personal feelings on the celebration, *Las Marthas* is so expertly told that at the end of the movie you're at the edge of your seat, wondering whether any of the debutantes (especially Rosario Reyes, the one you're rooting for) will perform well or fall down the steps when they're introduced at the ball.

"From the moment I first saw a Mexican-American debutante dressed as a Colonial heroine, I was immediately captivated," Ibarra told the *Current* via email. "Growing up along the border myself, I am always looking for ways to explore the contradictions of border life. From the outside, this might look like 'just pretty girls in pretty dresses,' but when we look at the bicultural ways this event is celebrated, we uncover multiple layers of meaning that deepen our views of the Latino experience in the United States."

The discussion following the screening is worth staying for and will feature all the movie's major players: Garza-Hovel and Reyes, dressmaker Linda Leyendecker Gutiérrez, director Ibarra and producer Erin Ploss-Campoamor.

KLRN Community Cinema screening: Las Marthas
Free
7pm Thu, Jan 16
Santikos Embassy 14
13707 Embassy Row

Phil Anselmo: Music, Horror and KOs
(*San Antonio Current*, January 21, 2014)

Phil Anselmo has survived it all — Pantera's success and tragedy, the bitter ending of Superjoint Ritual, drug abuse, and back and knee surgery. Now, he's a practical man.

"I just felt inspired," he told the *Current* from his home in New Orleans, explaining why he decided to embark on his first-ever solo tour behind 2013's *Walk Through Exits Only*, the album he released as Phillip H. Anselmo & The Illegals. "If I feel inspired, I'm going to act on it. So, I felt inspired, I did a record, and now we play shows. Nothing too scientific there."

Neither pure death nor black metal, *Walk Through Exits Only* is Anselmo's straightforward attempt to disassociate himself from the average metal band out there.

"I sing about real things that happen to me and I carry no fucking invisible ideology around on my shoulders at all," he said. "I see a million bands copying black metal over and over, and even some death bands do the same thing to some degree, so I wanted to do something different. I didn't want to record speed for the sake of speed or double-kick for the sake of fucking double-kick."

One of the things he sings about is the media, as exemplified by opening track "Music Media is My Whore." Or is it?

"Look, in this album I was going very absurd with a lot of my lyrical content and titles," he said. "The absurd thing about it is that, if you look at the lyrics, it's nothing about the media. It was just something to grab attention. I have a great relationship with a lot of the press, but some are only interested in grabbing a juicy headline and write about fictional things or things that are controversial. So that's my little kick back to the press, so to speak. It's all a joke, really..." When I move on to the next question, I can hear him say, "...but not really."

On Monday at Backstage Live, Anselmo and his Illegals (Superjoint Ritual's Marzi Montazeri on guitar, 16 Horsepower's Steve Taylor on bass and Warbeast's Joey "Blue" González on drums) will show us Anselmo in apparently his best shape in years. During the interview, his mind is sharp and his body, he says, is ready to roll.

"I've been through a lot," said Anselmo, who underwent back surgery in 2005 and knee surgery in 2009, and who, in 1996, was clinically dead for "four to five minutes," after overdosing on heroin following a Dallas concert. "But physically, besides the obvious pains and aches of getting older, I'm fine and good to go," said the 45-year-old.

Drugs are not a problem this time around either.

"It's been 11 years [and] I haven't used any hard drugs at all," he said. "Honestly, the hardest thing I use these days is probably beer. Fucking beer is enough, man. I probably can't finish a six-pack without having a fucking hangover."

Despite his past physical and addiction problems, nothing was harder to overcome than the death of former Pantera guitarist "Dimebag" Darrell Abbott, who was killed onstage by an imbecile named [fuck him] during a Columbus, Ohio, Damageplan concert (Abbott's band). [The imbecile I refuse to name in this book] was killed by police at the scene.

Abbott and Anselmo had a public feud ever since Anselmo was blamed for the breakup of Pantera (Anselmo claims the band never contacted him to return); *Metal Hammer* magazine quoted Anselmo stating, "Dimebag deserves to be beaten severely" in 2004 (the same year of Abbott's death), and that was just too much for some fans and Abbott's family. Even though Anselmo claimed his comments were tongue-in-cheek and that he was furious the "goddamn magazine" put his quotes on the cover, Abbott's family requested that Anselmo not attend the funeral. Some even speculated that Abbott's death was related to his fights with Anselmo, but the connection was emphatically denied by police.

"There is no evidence leading detectives to believe [imbecile] was communicating with Phil Anselmo or any other individual ... in an effort to hurt Dimebag Darrell Abbott," said a police detective report cited by the *Columbus Dispatch* in 2004.

After Abbott's funeral, Anselmo posted a teary video on YouTube in which he repeatedly says "I'm sorry" to Abbott's family, band members, fans and friends.

"Bless his family and all of his close friends," a visibly moved Anselmo said in the video. "I never got to say goodbye in the right way, and it kills me."

Last September, Anselmo seemed finally ready to make amends with his former Pantera bandmates.

"For me, really, I think it would mean a lot for [bassist] Rex [Brown] and [drummer] Vince [Abbott, Dimebag's brother] and myself to sit down and, I guess, bury the hatchet where we can be on more friendly terms," he told Fuse TV. "And, you know, I think it would mean a lot to the fans. Without Vince, there's not any Pantera reunion at all; it's useless. But he damn well knows my door's wide open. He needs to bust out the keys and unlock his, man. I'm waiting, but I'm not holding my breath."

When asked by the *Current*, all Anselmo said is that he lamented the fact that Pantera "will never happen again."

In any case, Phil Anselmo in 2004 looked and sounded completely different than Phil Anselmo in 2014 — now, he's *on*. After a New York show in September, *The New York Times* described Anselmo's set as "remarkable."

"The Illegals make a much more complicated, splintered-groove, quick-change kind of metal than his other bands of the last decade," wrote Ben Ratliff. "Lots of breaks, sequential or alternating riffs and strains and rhythms powered by double bass drums."

The man behind the drums, Fort Worth's "Blue" González, met Anselmo when he was 18.

"He just turned 22, 23 recently," Anselmo said (González will be 24 in July). "He's a baby, and I had to teach him, or re-teach him, the structure of extreme music the way I saw it, because there [are] a lot of time signatures changes within the music that are not concurrent with everyday black metal."

The second leg of the tour started in Houston on January 10 and, depending on his mood, SA fans may have a chance to listen to a handful of Pantera and Down classics.

"I think every night should be different," Anselmo said. "We're definitely going to play most of our stuff but, as far as blasts from the past, I'm going to leave it up to how I feel that night. Anything is possible, really."

Playing in SA means he'll be returning to a place he knows well.

"I tour all over the world and in SA there's always, always, always a gigantic Hispanic, Mexican presence, and they're always some of the greatest heavy metal fans ever, anywhere," he said. "Don't ever think I don't remember SA. I love SA and it's going to be great to come back."

Technicians of Distortion Tour feat. Phil Anselmo & the Illegals
$21
8pm Mon, Jan 27
Backstage Live
1305 E Houston

The horror, the horror…
In addition to his passion for metal, Anselmo is a lifelong fan of horror movies and boxing.

"Impossible, impossible," he told the *Current* when asked about his favorite horror film of all time. "I love horror films from every era and I love many, many different styles." Can he at least choose three? "No." I pressed him and asked for his take on *The Exorcist*, and that ignited a brief talk on some of his favorite horror films from all time. Warning: this ain't *Cahiers du Cinéma* talking.

The Exorcist (1972)
"Excellent film, but overdone at this point. I mean, *The Exorcist* itself is great, but all the other possession films are bullshit, not very scary for me at all. The original is a great stylistic movie and you have to think that, for 1972, it was a very cutting edge fucking movie, very unforgiving. Most horror freaks have a special spot in their heart for it. It's a classic."

Nekromantik (1988)
"Both original and sequel are cutting edge and hideous. They should be X-rated, to a certain degree."

I Bury the Living (1958)
"Old black-and-white films like that are so fucking great and so well done. They're atmospheric, fantastic."

The Thing (1982)
"The John Carpenter version [based on 1951's *The Thing From Another World*] is fantastic."

Evil Dead (2013)
"I hated [it], it's terrible. All fucking mishmash bullshit."

Night of the Eagle (Renamed as *Burn, Witch, Burn* for US release, 1962)
"Great fucking movie."

Curse of the Demon (1957)
"Excellent movie with special effects way before its time. I like so many horror movies it's fucking ridiculous, man."

Anselmo On The State Of Boxing

Did you see Maidana-Broner?

I did. I loved it. I thought it was fantastic. Not an Adrian Broner fan at all. I loved seeing Marcos coming so determined and making a statement early in that fucking fight and putting that big-mouthed motherfucker on his ass and continuing to apply pressure. I was very proud of Maidana. The only thing better he could've done was stop him cold.

What's your take on Sergio "Maravilla" Martínez?

He's such a great, great talent and also a good guy, great for the sport. I just wonder about the toll the injuries have taken on his body. And I know about that kind of stuff. When you can't come in at 100 percent, especially in the sport of boxing, it's tough. In boxing, throwing punches comes from the hips and the legs, there's a lot of leverage needed. As great a balance as Martínez has, if his injuries don't let him [throw his] punches as he used to, it'll be tough for him against great opponents. I wonder if his days are numbered.

Two words: Gennady Golovkin.

Golovkin, Golovkin… A lot of people are betting high on Golovkin, but I need to see him fight *somebody*. He's definitely a great body puncher and a very sound technician, but I've seen better prospects before. Golovkin is good, but I'm not totally sold on him.

Is Manny Pacquiao shot?

He's such an excellent boxer. If he had been 100 percent he would have knocked out [Brandon] Ríos. He beat him bad in that fight, but he should have put the nail on the coffin and stop him. I'm not accusing anybody of anything, but have you noticed his body doesn't look quite as ripped as it used to? You wonder about the use of physical enhancement drugs, and the same could be said about Juan Manuel Márquez. He has the steroid look in his head, the veins on his head and body, the build on his body… It does not look real. Anyway, I didn't want to go in this direction, but having said this, Manny Pacquiao is still an excellent boxer, incredible hand speed, he makes it all look easy. His timing is still there, but is he still a destroyer in that weight division? I'm not sure.

Whatever happened to American heavyweights?

First and foremost, I'm not "pro-American boxers." Boxing is an international sport and I want the best man to win; I don't care where they come from. The Klitschkos are the best heavyweights, period. Vitaly left to go into politics, and that's fair enough. As far as American prospects, Deontay Wilder has the body type, the size, and the punch in the right hand that may carry him through. The only thing I'm not sure about is how we would do if he's extended in fights. If he's properly conditioned, he'll come through and the questions will be answered. If they keep lining him up against shot former champions, of course he'll keep his knockout streak alive, and people love to see KOs. But once he's put in with the Tyson Furys or the Klitschko brothers, it'll be a different game for him. Whether he makes it out or not remains to be seen."

Anselmo on his top bands

Superjoint Ritual
All the intentions were really good, but I wasn't in the best frame of mind as a person. Certain band members, I think, took advantage of the situation with myself being in a bad place, which eventually turned me off to the whole thing. Fun while it lasted, with a bitter ending.

Pantera
Great musicians and the tightest band I've ever been in. Some of the best times in my life. The loss of [guitarist] Dimebag [Darrell Abbott, assassinated in 2004] marked a sad ending because it means [Pantera] will never happen again. But there's more great memories than bad memories.

Down
We are wrapping up our new EP and the guys [came over in December] to [record] lead guitars. The EP should be ready to go out within the first quarter of 2014. We're going strong and it's a good atmosphere.

The Illegals
I always envisioned these were the guys I wanted to play with [as a solo artist]. I felt there was room in metal for different expressions and time signatures within extreme music, different parts that go together and flow together, and I'm very pleased with the album we made.

Belinda Sallin, director of *H.R. Giger's World*
(enriquelopetegui.com, May 13, 2015)

Dark Star: H.R. Giger's World opens in select cities nationwide on May 15. "H.R. who?" is something the average moviegoer would ask, but when informed Giger (pronounced GHEEgair) is the Oscar-winning man whose inspiration gave birth to the *Alien* monster, things change.

What doesn't change is the fact that San Antonio remains a sort of movie dumpster, a so-called "secondary market" that always has to wait to see the best films while our powerful neighbors enjoy the party. The movie will be shown in Dallas (May 22-28, Texas Theatre), Austin (May 23-26, Alamo Drafthouse), Houston (May 23-28), and Fort Worth (May 28-31, modern Art Museum).

A couple of weeks ago I spoke on the phone with director Belinda Sallin, who was in her home in Switzerland.

Right off the bat, your movie (especially the intro) has a chilling effect on the viewer, similar to the one we have when looking at a Giger painting. Was it a conscious effort on your part to make such an un-Hollywood doc?

Thank you very much! I'm happy you feel that way. And yes, absolutely, it was clear in my head that I didn't want to make a conventional biography, I didn't want to start with a photograph and go, "H.R. Giger was born in…" You can read all that, it's been done already, you can find it on the internet or in books. I was so surprised when I met him for the first time, or when I entered his house, I was completely overwhelmed. I thought it was extraordinary how he lived, in his own world, with his art and all of its consequences.

It seems the metalheads and other bands got Giger more than, say, the established art world.

These are the people buying his books, his publications, his posters. [Giger] got the acknowledgments from his fans, but he didn't get it from the well-established galleries or art institutions. So, he was very glad about his fans and he appreciated them a lot. But he was also a shy person, he didn't like to leave his home. And to interact with his fans was quite difficult for him, but he did it. That heavy metal connection is funny, because that was *not* his kind of music, not at all, but he was a very open-minded man. He knew when something was special, as in the case of Celtic Frost and Triptycon, and his relationship with Tom Warrior, which is really extreme metal. He loved working with Tom, but it wasn't his kind of music. His music was jazz; he really liked Oscar Peterson and Miles Davis, things like that.

Did he have a chance to watch the movie, or parts of it, before he passed away?

No, unfortunately. He did see a sort of teaser I did. I wanted to show him what I wanted to do, what my concept and intentions were. And he liked it a lot. It was a short teaser. He said, "Yeah, that's good, you don't have to explain everything, I don't want you to explain everything. It has to be a little bit mysterious... It's OK if things stay enigmatic." For me, it was very important that, after his death, Carmen Giger supported us, and she continues to do so. She told me, "Yes, go on, finish the movie." She saw it before it was released here in Switzerland. She was the first person to see it, and she was really moved. She told me he would've liked the movie, because "it's a very deep portrayal of him and it's true." This meant a lot to me.

He passed away shortly after you finished shooting, but it was obvious that he was very frail. How difficult it was to shoot his scenes?

It was a challenge to shoot with him. He was only available for very short periods of time, so I had to carefully consider what I wanted from him, what scenes I needed to do with him. And he didn't like to talk anymore. For much of the film he is silent, but he never liked speaking about his art. This is important to know. It was a relief for him when I showed him the teaser and told him we didn't have to do hours and hours of interviews.

When did you feel it was time to make the movie?

I've known his art since my youth; I saw *Alien* and I was shocked... (laughs) I saw pictures, posters, books... I was always intrigued and fascinated by his art. But I lost it a little bit out of my sight over the years, until one evening I met a former life partner of his, Sandra Beretta. This was really a special moment for me because she started to tell me about him and I was immediately interested, and all these images I had in my head returned, I had never forgotten them. I think this is the quality and power of H.R. Giger's art: Once you see his work, you don't forget it.

Tell me about the museum and bar. Only Giger could've come up with something like that...

Yes! The museum was built because Giger didn't get the acknowledgment of the established galleries and institutions in Switzerland. He said to me, "They won't show my work here, so I had to build my own museum." He realized all his dreams as a child, and he built his museum in an old castle. It's an amazing place, in the mountains, a little village, and the bar is next to the castle.

Was that always the case or they stopped showing his art as soon as he became famous because of *Alien*?

There are several reasons. I think Giger was difficult to categorize. Even when he was categorized under realism or fantastic realism, he also had a strong relationship with pop culture. He had many tools and outlets. He made films, comics, music videos, design… In the 1970s this was quite unusual. Then in 1980 he won the Oscar, and this was quite a scandal. He was taken less seriously by the art world than he deserved. But it's hard to say whether winning the Oscar was a damage for him, because he became world famous. He was not interested anymore in this discussion, at least in the last two years of his life, when I met him. "They don't show my art in these institutions, so what?" Maybe his composure came from the fact that he knew he didn't need the establishment to enjoy worldwide success. Who needs institutional approval when you already reach countless people all over the world? The thing that impressed me the most about him is that he followed his dreams regardless of what people thought or said. He did what he wanted to do; he took his own path.

Rob Trujillo on Jaco and *Jaco*
(enriquelopetegui.com, May 25, 2015)

A phone conversation with Metallica's bassist about his movie on Jaco Pastorius, arguably the greatest bassist who ever lived.

I've always wanted to see a movie about Jaco Pastorius, and you've been involved with this project for about five years now. How did the project evolve?

Basically, I've been involved as the main financier, executive producer, for over five years. but it all sort of started long before five years. It goes back to about 19 years ago when I became friends with Johnny Pastorius, Jaco's eldest son. We had a mutual friend in Florida, in Fort Lauderdale, who was a bartender, and Johnny Pastorius came in with a credit card to buy some drinks. My friend, who is a surfer in the East Coast (I live in Los Angeles), said, "Hey, that name's familiar, this name Pastorius…! Is that name related to a bass player?" And Jaco's son said, "Yeah, Jaco." "Right, Jaco!" And he was like, "My friend Robert Trujillo, he has a photograph of your father at his house in Venice Beach!" And then right there the connection was made. Soon afterwards I came through town with Ozzy [Osbourne], this is in 1996, and I met Johnny and one of the first things I said was, "You know, some day you gotta make a film about your father," not thinking that *I* would be involved in the film. I was like, "You should share the story because it's important. There's a lot of people, not just jazz musicians, fans, rock fans, punk rockers, funksters, who are fans, and you have to share that story with the world." That's when it all started.

Over the years he checked with me, "Hey, Robert, we're going to work on this documentary film, we want to interview you." And then two years later the same thing. Every couple of years I'd get a phone call or we would see each other, and I didn't see progress, and this part is really important: Johnny and another guy called Bob Bobbing came to [a Metallica] concert in Fort Lauderdale. Now all of a sudden, five years ago, Metallica is playing in Ft. Lauderdale and Bob was sort of navigating the project at that time, and he saw and was impressed by Metallica. He didn't know anything about Metallica, and he wondered, "This band is so big, and this bass player loves Jaco." That night I spoke to Bob and said, "You know, look, for this movie you really have to check in with Flea from the Chili Peppers, Geddy Lee [Rush], so many other rock musicians, because you have to bring excitement, some fire to the party, because Jaco was not just one-dimensional, he's not just a jazz guy, but he's also a funk guy, the attitude of a punk rocker, he's rock 'n' roll, he's really well-rounded." I said, "Even young people are going to love Jaco." He got very excited and then they asked me to be a part of the team. So I did join, and basically kind of adopted the film. I realized there's no way this film is going to be finished and completed unless somebody puts the money and makes it a reality. Documentary films take time. They're passion-driven, but they also take money. If you can't fly to Florida, New York, California or wherever, what are you going to do? It has been a very expensive journey for me.

Can I ask you what the budget has been so far?

Over $800,000. Insane!

Is that a combination of your money and money from other sources?

All my money. We had to raise money at the end because I ran out of money. We had to raise money for post-production so we could mix the sound and obtain clearances.

Oh, clearances… I've been working on a doc for 10 years, and the clearances are killing me!

Oh, that's very complicated stuff. Clearances for film… I learned a lot in the last two months. I learned *so* much. Five years ago I didn't know anything, and that's why I was just, "Yeah, let's make this film, yeah, I'll pay for this!" and all that. But the reality is that most people don't finance their own movies. Most people who make films have investors, and there is a reason for that. Films are very expensive.

Did you have to hire somebody to deal exclusively with clearances? For me it has been a nightmare.

I'm glad you can understand what I'm going through. I needed to hire a professional, and the only reason I got a professional that was wonderful, is that, luckily for me… Where do you live, by the way?

San Antonio. But I was in L.A. for 19 years. Including five in Culver City, where you grew up…

Right, right… Luckily, because I live in Los Angeles and know a lot of people in the film industry, I was able to get help. One of my friends work for Oliver Stone, he writes music for Oliver's movies, and he knew I needed help. So he connected me to a music supervisor he knew, someone who does great work with documentary music. She really loved the film and she cared, and she represented me as the music supervisor. So it was her job to reach out to Joni Mitchell's people, to Sony Music, Warner Brothers… That's what she does for a living, and it costs money. What she does is work out the deals with each of the publishing companies and the musicians, so it's a very long process and a lot of it has to do with making deals. The important thing to understand is, when you're making a documentary film, the people that are allowing you to make the music need to understand that this is not a blockbuster, *Transformers*, or an Angelina Jolie movie. This is a passion piece, this is art. This is charitable in a lot of ways, because if you're sharing someone's story with the world, and you're bringing it to light on the screen and you're trying to celebrate somebody, you're doing something charitable. And you're spending the money and you and your team are investing the time to bring something to life for the world. All of a sudden you have to pay for these songs and they want top dollars. Some of these people want crazy money. "I want $40,000 a song," "My artist deserves $50,000" or whatever… A lot of it is deals, you know? There has to be deals worked out because, if you don't have somebody working for you to get you a good deal, a lot of times you can't use the song. That's the reality. The same thing goes for footage. When you see Jaco playing live at Montreux Jazz Festival or in any other rare footage, my film producer has to track those down, to find out who owns the rights to the high-res photographs that are taken. All these things I didn't know about, and all of a sudden it's like, "Oh my God, it's so much money!"

OK, but one thing is myself going through hell trying to obtain these rights. But you're Rob Fucking Trujillo, bassist for Metallica! Even *you* have to suffer?

Yeah, but I have two kids, and my wife, and I got payments, you know… I lead a normal life as far as… I have to pay bills, I have to feed my family… I recorded *one* album with Metallica in 12 years, really… I didn't write songs on the "Black Album," you know? I think people have the wrong perception of me. They think, "Oh, you're rich!" It's like, you know... I have to make ends meet too, you know what I mean? It's like... Anyway, so for me to take on a project like this I have to be very passionate about this. And this was how the project came to be. It has been difficult to get it together. We did a PledgeMusic campaign to help raise money for clearances and other expenses.

But did you raise the money once you knew how much these clearances would cost?

No, no, no... I had to figure out roughly an idea of how much I would need and then I had to put a budget together.

But how can you figure that out if each rights owner makes a different deal?

Well, I have a team. Professionals know how to figure that out. That's why I've been so fortunate to be surrounded by people that care and who are professionals. And it's never dead-on, you know? Sometimes it's not enough. I think when you're doing something like this you have to do the best you can. If you come up short, you need to figure out a way to complete the journey. And that's just reality. When you're making art, or music, or anything, usually, at least in my universe every time I've done anything creative (and I'm not talking about Metallica, I'm talking about Infectious Grooves or any project I've done outside Metallica), these opportunities to be creative are great, but they also cost money, especially film. Too many people think, "Oh, why does he need money to finish the movie?" Well, somebody's got to pay for the movies people want to see, you know? I wanted to see a movie about Jaco, for a long time. I was looking around on the internet, hoping that someone was going to make a documentary about Jaco, because I care, until I realized, "it's not going to happen unless I do something about it." And hopefully this is the first step for more to happen in the future. His music and story should be heard and he should be recognized as an important composer. The bass is one thing, but there's also the composition and the story.

When I read Charlotte Chandler's *I, Fellini*, a first-person account of Federico Fellini's life, I was amazed to see how difficult it was even for a genius like him to obtain financing for his movies. Jaco, who was a recognized genius in his own right, went through something similar towards the

end of his life: he couldn't get gigs. How was that possible? Did that happen because of the drugs or he couldn't work even before he deteriorated?

I know you know the story. At certain times in his career, Jaco had a lot of things he was dealing with. Jaco, as you know, was bipolar, had a very serious mental condition. It started to cause problems for him later on in his career. So here's this talent, this incredible musician, but at the same time he was dealing with other things in his life. The mental condition fueled by whether it was alcohol consumption or anything, drugs, alcohol, makes existing very difficult for people with a bipolar condition. And you're also talking about a time when a lot of people didn't understand what [bipolar disorder was], how to deal with it, how to, you know, medication or whatever. If it had happened today, it would probably be different because there are ways to maintain a healthy existence with this condition, but back at the time when Jaco was doing what he did there weren't these options. It was difficult for him to get a gig because he had problems.

I'm from Uruguay, but I saw Weather Report in Buenos Aires in 1980, I think, and Jaco blew us away. I was 16, and we were digging all the great jazz-rock bands, Return to Forever, Mahavishnu Orchestra, etc., and for a long time we had considered Stanley Clarke to be *the* man on bass. Then this guy Jaco comes out of the blue and pulverized everybody. Do you have a similar recollection, that Stanley Clarke (or anybody) was the man and all of a sudden Jaco changed everything for everybody?

I had a similar experience. I'm 50.

There you go. I'm 51.

I saw Jaco play in 1979 for the first time and then I saw him I think in 1980, at the Playboy Jazz Festival, I saw him with the Word of Mouth big band, and I also saw him with the smaller version of the big band. So I saw him on four different times and I even had an encounter with him in 1985. When I first started hearing about him, I didn't even know what he looked like. They didn't have the internet, so you always heard these rumors, "Oh, there's this bass player, he's incredible!" I was a fan of bass because I loved Sly & The Family Stone, a lot of the funk bands from the '70s, you know? And when I started listening to jazz-rock and fusion, like Return to Forever and Stanley Clarke, I was really excited to the point I didn't even really cared to hear vocals that much for a while.

It was short-lived, but there was a time when all I wanted to hear was ripping bass solos. When I saw Jaco for the first time it changed my world the same way it had the effect on you guys in Buenos Aires. There was this performer who was like a rock star, shirt off, long hair, a crazy, unique sound. A really dynamic style, his tone, his presence, his energy. And also I was impressed with the crowd. It was very mixed, diverse, there were rock musicians, heavy metal musicians, jazz people, skateboarders, surfers, wow! The truth of the matter was, most people there went to see Jaco. I have nothing but respect for the other members of Weather Report, but a lot of these people were there to see Jaco. And that's when I realized, "Hey, this guy's really, really cool."

Was it you in the movie who said Jaco was "the coolest cat who ever lived," or something like that?

No, that was [the Red Hot Chili Peppers'] Flea. This experience you and I talk about was shared by a lot of people. Then you take the influence he had as a writer and as a player in terms of his feel for funk, or the way he could create with harmonics, you know… I started to try to do that with my writing, and that's how Infectious Grooves came to be. It was a band that I created music for that was really inspired by Jaco, and also by Cameo, and Black Sabbath, but Jaco was the main influence of my writing in the late '80s and early '90s. That's why I wanted to make the movie. I had young people come up to me and say, "Hey, because of you I really like Weather Report." "I bought *Heavy Weather* on vinyl!" 'Cause a lot of young people are listening to vinyl again, you know? The same with [Joni Mitchell's] *Hejira*, you know? My goal is just to bring awareness to his story and his music, but also to *all* that music! I hope everybody embraces music from that time period, like Return to Forever and all those bands.

What was the reception like at South by Southwest? Were you able to make any deals?

We're real grassroots. For me, the most important thing about SXSW is that we were accepted. With all the films out there, for them to honor and care about Jaco and the movie was huge. I don't have a marketing team, I don't have a publicist, I don't have all the forces that you need to go into a high-powered festival. I can count on one hand the people that I have. It's a very small family and we do the best we can. The screenings went well, everybody loved the film, and it continues, you know?

But you do want to have a theatrical release, right?

Yes, yes… If there is a demand to show it in theaters and a demand to do everything you need to do, I want it to have a chance like any other movie. I want it to be seen. I didn't make a movie not to be seen. Right now, we're talking to various companies and we're going to do the festivals this year. We'll do Buenos Aires, Asbury Park [already happened] on April 10, and also Chicago [it happened on April 18 for Record Store Day], and Washington DC also around those days. Also, there will be a Jaco celebration at Hollywood Bowl on August 11, I think, on a Wednesday [that'd be August 13]. And also Monterey Jazz Festival is doing something for Jaco. It's working, there is awareness, there is excitement.

I liked the way the movie handled everything related to his death. You didn't even name the murderer (I call it the murderer because that's what he is) and concentrated on Jaco's legacy. What was your original approach? Did you at any point try to talk to the guy who beat Jaco to death?

As you know as a filmmaker, it's very difficult to find a balance. Jaco's story is very intense. You have dark times, there are times of huge success and beauty and glory, there were times of fun, funny, Jaco had a sense of humor, was a funny guy who always had a positive spirit even when things were bad. You know, like in the scene you talk about, he laughs and he says to Jerry Jemmott, "give me a gig!" Jaco's life was balanced between his passion for music and his love for his family. Family was important to him. But there was also the illness, and the way he was killed… It was a very dramatic arc. What's important in making a film like this is, how do you balance it? How do you balance the bad with the good, and the beautiful with the not-so-beautiful? It's a very delicate balance, and that's been the hardest thing. In the last five years, every year we thought we were finished, and all of a sudden we realized we were not finished because the balance wasn't right, or a treasure came in, like in the last year Joni Mitchell came on board. And that was *really* huge and important for the film. A lot of miracles have happened. How did that happen? I mean, for four years she was unreachable and, all of a sudden, I ran into her at a party, and we're friends now. But for four years she was like an enigma. And also Jerry Jemmott himself, Jaco's favorite electric bass player. He's a legend. Jerry Jemmott was living in Alabama two years ago, you know what I mean? Nobody really knew where he was. He was sort of low-profile, and now Jerry moved to Los Angeles. I met him through mutual friends and he's an important part of this film. But two years ago he wasn't even in the movie. We got a lot of treasures, and each time we had to re-edit the whole film. Editing is a long process. It takes time and energy. And time is money, but it was important to be done. Photos that Sony had in the vault, concert footage from Havana, all stuff that we were able to use.

One thing that left me a little confused: when Jaco was in Argentina, he had a reputation as a health nut, and he would drink these mixes of pure lemon juice and pure garlic. But according to the film, reality wasn't so… wholesome. I mean, I was surprised when I first heard about Jaco's problems with drugs.

This is a touchy subject. Very, very touchy. There were influences in Weather Report that started to cause him to party. And that's when things started to change, when he joined Weather Report. There was a good chance that, around the time you saw him [in Argentina] that he started to drink more. And in those situations there was also a lot of pressure because not only are you getting the pressure to drink, which was the common thing to do with musicians around you, but this was the '80s, and there was also cocaine. This was all part of being a musician at that time. You're onstage in front of thousands of people praising you, "You're the greatest bassist who ever lived!" The pressure of always having to be The Greatest and having a personality that, in a lot of ways, allowed you to be the life of the party… The alpha male. Joe Zawinul and Jaco were the alpha males, the brothers that were fighting and had that creative tension with each other. But there was also mutual respect and love for each other. But there was a lot of pressure on Jaco to be great, and a lot of that happened during the Weather Report years. The years you're talking about were the years when things started to change.

Have you seen his son Felix play?

Oh, yes. I know Felix very well. I've known the family for a long time and know them very well.

I mean, seeing him with a bass on his back is such an amazing image.

And he's an amazing player. Honestly, he's the closest thing to… Even the way his hands are on the bass… It's like, the bloodline, you know? [laughs]

He plays a fretless too?

He plays everything. I think he mostly plays a six-string Fodera. He's not really a fretless player, but he can play a fretless as good as anybody.

Talk about carrying a weight, being a bassist with that last name…

Yeah. I would imagine, because you want to be your own musician and wear your own hat, and have the pressure of having a dad who was one of the greatest bass players who ever lived. People probably expects him to always play his dad's music, "Hey! Play 'Teen Town'!" "Play 'Continuum'!" I'm sure it must be difficult to always have that demand around him. But he's an amazing player and a really, really good person.

Jaco, as you show in the movie, grew up listening to Cuban music on a transistor radio from an early age, which explains lots about his love and understanding of Latin music. I always felt that Anglo musicians had better technique, but that Latin, say, guitarists, are musically richer because we listen to all kinds of stuff besides rock, lots of local, regional influences. But Adrian Belew, who had produced a superb album by Mexico's Caifanes, once told me that he disagreed. I'm paraphrasing: "Latin guitarists are technically better, because they can play anything from rock, to blues, to flamenco, to rancheras, you name it," he told me in the '90s at the then-called Universal Amphitheatre. Anyway, what I really want to ask you is, in what way did Jaco's Latin side influenced you as a player?

He was from Florida and I'm from Los Angeles, and we were both influenced by Hispanic contingency, lots of *mexicanos*. I can go outside right now, I'm at the studio, and I can walk outside and I can guarantee you in the next couple of hours there's going to be ranchera music coming out of a truck. But I also was exposed to the Beatles, Beach Boys, Santana and Beethoven and flamenco. My father played flamenco guitar. The first music I heard as a kid was flamenco music, flamenco guitar. That was the first time I saw a guitar being played with fingers, not a pick. And that's why, when I started playing bass, I started playing with my fingers right away. The beauty of the Latinos is that, I believe, there's a special ingredient in a Latino musician. Take Dave Lombardo, from Slayer, the drummer. The ingredient in Slayer is special because classic, early Slayer has a spice to it, and the spice is coming from the rhythm, and the rhythm is coming from the swing, and the swing of the drums, as heavy as it is because we're talking metal here, is an invisible feeling coming from the groove of the drumming. That Cuban thing is very rhythmic and very funky, and that's what's so special about Slayer's music. And that comes from our Cuban friend Dave Lombardo. The first album I bought as a kid was Santana's *Abraxas*, and that's because I was moved by bass lines, and the percussion, the energy of it all. That's why I was excited about the bass, because I loved the feel of the rhythm section. That said, I was talking to Geezer Butler, from Black Sabbath, a few months ago, and he told me he's more excited about rhythm & blues bass, you know? And he's known to be one of the greatest rock, metal bassists. But what makes him happy is funky bass. The Latinos have a lot of funk, man. If you take that funk and apply it to heavy metal music or dance music or whatever, well… I think that's something Latin musicians have. There's a bass player called Armand Sabal-Lecco. He played with Stanley Clarke a lot, he's with Al Di Meola right now. He's from Cameroon and played with Paul Simon. Armand is a phenomenal musician, but why is he phenomenal? He understands rock music, he understands punk music. Jaco felt Armand was incredible. And Armand also understands pygmy music, and music from Cameroon where he was born.

Yeah! That brings me to something I overheard Santana saying in one of the first Latin Grammy Awards. He was talking to somebody during rehearsals, and he was saying, "We should invite Nelson Mandela. All we [Latinos] do is African music." There's no way around it: you always go back to Africa.

Exactly! It's important to understand that, and it's important to recognize and appreciate all styles of music. I believe music is much more exciting when it is grooving and funky. And funky doesn't always mean it is disco, or dance or whatever. I strongly believe the reason Metallica is so special is that James Hetfield is funky! James was a drummer first, and his ability as a drummer has transitioned into his ability as a rhythm guitar player and singer. And the fact that he can play really heavy, funky, metal riffs and he can sing rhythmically on top of that, to me that's funky. And that comes from indigenous… [laughs] you know, rhythms! It comes from the earth, it's what makes our heads move! And Jaco had that.

Speaking of which, what's up with Metallica? Are they all there at the studio now?

Kirk [Hammett] just left. We're writing, working on new songs.

Yeah, your assistant had told me you were "rocking it out" in the studio, but you have so many projects I didn't know what project you were in at the studio.

No, right now I have the movie and Metallica. Like you said, making a movie is a very involved thing, distribution deals...

Yeah! After this film, making an album is a piece of cake!

[laughs] Totally! You know what I'm talking about, man! That's why this is a good interview, because you understand what it means to be a musician, to make music, and you also understand what it means to make a film, a documentary film specifically. So many people looove documentary films, docs are popular right now, but people don't understand they're passion-driven, they cost money and time, and someone's gotta pay for it.

Well, it was well worth the effort. As a longtime fan, I loved it. And I think those who didn't know about Jaco will be blown away.

I agree. This creative, passionate journey doesn't have to do with a style of music. This is for everyone. Jaco says it in the movie when asked about what advice he could give people out there: "Hey, listen to everything. I'll play in a country band and I'll love it, as long as it is good." That's the bottom line here. Some people say, "Hey, what's a heavy metal bassist doing a film about Jaco?" And it's like, number one, they don't know anything about me; number two, as I said already, with Infectious Grooves I did three albums completely influenced by Jaco. Take what Jaco delivered and create with it. Be creative, be open-minded. When you hear a Jaco album you're not hearing... "Come On, Come Over" is a great song, super funky, R&B at its best. He could've made a whole album of it, like a Tower of Power record or something. Which is really cool, but he didn't do that. He gave you that, he gave you some classical, some jazz, some World Music, he really made very diverse recordings, and that's how he shared his music.

Sandra Cisneros: My Apology
(*San Antonio Current*, August 31, 2016)

Sandra Cisneros' nearly 30-year, on-and-off relationship with San Antonio is a dysfunctional one. Here she found enough love to move from her native Chicago in 1984 and establish her Macondo Writers' Workshop, but also enough people "throwing rocks at you" that, in 2013, she packed her things and moved out quicker than you can say *Caramelo*. Even the *Current* took part in the rock-throwing via an infamous 1998 cover story (subtitled "¿Santa? ¿Puta? ¿Heroine? ¿Spin Artist?") and another in 2012 ("So Long, La Sandra") shortly after the ever-nomad departed for San Miguel de Allende, where she appears to have finally found her roots.

After much hustling, I was only able to secure a 10-minute phone interview with Cisneros — but she opened up and spoke for almost half an hour in English and Spanish about everything, from José Rubén De León's take on *The House on Mango Street* to her upcoming visit to San Antonio and San Marcos in October, when she'll officially present her literary papers recently acquired by Texas State University's Wittliff Collections. Paperback and Spanish-language editions of her nonfictional 2015 collection *A House of My Own: Stories from My Life* are due out in September. She's already working on her next book, but "can't talk about it now."

What was your first reaction when De León approached you to direct *Mango Street*?

I've been following his work for a long, long time. He's very professional in everything he does. There were different productions of *Mango Street*, some better than others, and when José approached me, I have to say that knowing the caliber of work that he does, the [Federico García] Lorca production [*The House of Bernarda Alba*], his music, everything, I felt I could trust him. I have a lot of *confianza* in him. I said yes, but told him the production I loved the most was the one Amy Ludwig created, which is pretty faithful to the book. He had a lot of great questions and suggestions about the characters. I don't know exactly what he's going to do, but I'm very excited because I know I'm going to see something that [has] never been done before, even though the Jump-Start production [21 years ago] was great.

Did you do anything on your end to make the play happen? José told me that, at one point, he felt he wasn't going to be able to put the show together. Something to do with permits...

I don't know what my agent told him, but we hold a very tight control of my stuff. I don't want the wrong people to do something dreadful; we always want to keep the integrity of the piece. *Permisos? No sé, la verdad no sé.*

I don't know how you feel about it, but I still feel sorry and embarrassed by the way you left San Antonio. I think some people didn't understand we were lucky to have you here. You deserved better treatment.

As soon as I got there and for as long as I lived there, I felt I never was embraced. There was a lot of conflict, mainly in the artistic community, not the community at large. The artistic community is a small one and there's a lot of insecurities that people have. And I understand why people would act like that. I came from outside and there is a history in Texas of people coming from outside and taking what was theirs. I do understand and have a lot of compassion for that. But I also think San Antonio has very little money and opportunities for the arts. A lot of times, a lot of people are fighting for the same scrap or job, so there's a lot of rivalries when there shouldn't be. I tried to do the best I could, but... *Hay mucha infelicidad* [There is a lot of unhappiness] in the arts. I tried to do what I could to create more opportunities for artists when I got there. There's tons of good artists in San Antonio, visual arts, but it's not necessarily a great town in terms of opportunities for writers. We made some change through Macondo, creating a coalition of writers, but that kind of change requires a great deal of effort and cooperation from the artists themselves, and that's hard to do without sacrificing their own writing. For me it was hard, because many people opened doors for me and helped me, many people helped my success, and you have to give back; that's just the truth, you have to do that. In retrospect, I see there was a lot of *envidia*. I see I was the target of some people's unhappiness, but I don't think I was the source of it. I just think it was a reflection of how little there is for writers, especially in San Antonio.

Did it make you sad, frustrated, angry?

Yes, it was frustrating, and yes, all of the above, of course. You're in the trenches and there's people throwing rocks at you, you can't help but take it personally. People say, "Oh, Sandra, don't take it personally," but still, you do.

At the time, it was very distracting for the work I was supposed to be doing. But now, in retrospect, I understand how difficult it is to be a writer in the Southwest, especially a writer of color, especially now, it's very difficult. But the little Macondo seed worked, because there are several writers who are publishing. I'm a connector, that's what I do. I help people nourish each other.

That damn "Puta" cover… I hate it when gringos use Spanish words without understanding their meaning.

That was a reflection of the writer's own unhappiness. I hope she found her own fulfillment as a writer. It was totally disrespectful, but I forgive that writer. I hope she finds a lot of success. I think she had an agenda before she even began talking to me. *Pero que le vaya bonito*. I wish her a lot of success, because once a writer finds success they don't have to be so angry and attack others. That violence says more about her own state of being.

Are you finally established in San Miguel, Guanajuato, land of beautiful churches?

Desde mi ventana veo cuatro iglesias. [I can see four churches from my window.]

Will you be able to stay there and control your nomad spirit?

In Texas, I never felt embraced. I received a lot of support, but I felt more a parent than a daughter. If I never felt embraced in Texas after so many years, I will not find it anywhere else in the Southwest. So I came here, where I have roots. My ancestors lived here during the Mexican Revolution. At last, I feel that I finally came to the land of my ancestors. I feel a very strong connection, as if my ancestors had guided me here. But I always come back to San Antonio — which is very close — and Chicago, where I have a lot of friends … Norma Cantú, John Phillip Santos, Lionel and Kathy Sosa, Arturo and Antonia Madrid and lots of other people who helped me a lot. I don't feel I "left" any place. You can never do things by yourself, there's always a *colectivo* that helps you. And I'd rather talk about those people who helped me, instead of a few mosquitoes. I don't have to give them any more importance. The number of people who support me is much greater than those who bother me, so I just want to send a lot of light to those unhappy *mosquitos*.

Nina Díaz's latest incarnation
(*San Antonio Current,* October 18, 2016)

It's mid-September at the 4,000-seat Sandia Amphitheater in Albuquerque, New Mexico, and Nina Díaz and her solo band are a few hours away from opening for Cyndi Lauper. Nina had just stepped out to the parking lot to retrieve something she needed for her simple show wardrobe, when someone knocked on her dressing room door. Nina's drummer —and, for the last two years, boyfriend — Jorge González answered the knock at the dressing room door. It was Lauper, asking if Nina would sing "Girls Just Want to Have Fun" with her on stage that night. Jorge relayed the message when Nina got back. He says she responded in an unimpressed, matter-of-fact way, "OK, let's go," even though she couldn't remember all the lyrics.

"Oh, no problem… If I had to sing one of your songs I'd need the lyrics too," Nina recalled Lauper telling her. She stumbled a couple of times during soundcheck, but it went well.

After her own opening set, Nina was determined to memorize the song. She practiced Lauper's 1983 hit for an hour, listening to the song countless times. She missed most of Lauper's set, but when the time came to join her onstage, she was ready. Or sort of.

Lauper decided on a slowed-down version that night, and she wanted Nina to sing the intro. Nina thought to herself, *Just get that first verse right.* She sang the first line, and the crowd thundered. "I felt it all through my body, and I hadn't felt that in a *long* time. At the end I had this natural high."

"Nina had no idea she'd sing with Cyndi, who just threw her in the water," Jorge said. "And Nina kept her head up, like she always does."

Well, not always. Three years ago, Nina was a mess. She drank too much and was using meth, like on the night of January 9, 2013. Nina was recording a demo for "January 9th," a song that would become one of the many highlights from her debut solo album, *The Beat is Dead,* when her drug-induced paranoia hit bottom.

Nina thought someone was outside, watching her through the window. Something finally spooked her (she says she "felt this big, like, push"), dropped her guitar and ran to her mother's room, screaming, "I think there's someone outside my window!"

Of course, nobody was there. Looking back on it later, she thinks maybe it was the spirit of her dead grandparents trying to warn her, "telling me to take care of myself and take care of my music, or I would die."

Or get caught.

One night, an acquaintance casually told Nina's sister Phanie (the drummer for both Girl in A Coma and Fea, a GIAC spinoff) that Nina was looking to score drugs from her. "As if Phanie wouldn't flip!" Nina says. Phanie confronted her. At first, Nina denied it, but change was inevitable once Phanie found out. She did her detox mostly alone, at home, for four days, then tried an AA meeting for the second time in her life, all after a failed attempt to get clean years earlier.

"March 25, 2013, is my sober date," Nina says, which seems to be true — she looks healthy and her mind is as sharp as ever. Soon after joining AA, she broke the news to her manager, Faith Radle, and then to her bandmates: she wanted to go solo.

Nina told them she felt she had the songs in her, and that they were better suited for a new project, independent of GIAC. If anyone had any doubts she could pull it off, Nina's NPR Tiny Desk concert in late August quashed them when she and her band offered a memorable, naked version of three key album tracks ("January 9th," "Dig" and "For You"). Even in stripped-down form, the songs proved Nina to be a genuine songwriting force.

"I would love to do an acoustic show with *The Beat is Dead*," Nina says, thinking back on it. "I see that happening after the first tour of the album itself, maybe before going back to the studio with GIAC."

Besides her own resiliency, the fact that Nina is surrounded by love at home and on tour didn't hurt in her recovery. Entering her North Side house, where she lives with her mother María, adoptive father (Margo Gonzales, whom she calls "my real dad") and brother Nick, is almost like entering a Chicano pop culture museum. There are the dolls hanging from a carport, a basketball double-shot arcade and a pool table in the living room, pictures of Selena, Girl in a Coma, family, an old piano, and old concert flyers everywhere. The house includes two separate rehearsal rooms: one for GIAC/Fea and one for Nina. The voice of Michael Hutchence regularly rings through the house.

"I start my day watching INXS videos. Or Queen," Nina says. "It calms me. There's something about [Hutchence] that makes me want to get out of bed and do my stuff."

Underneath the little TV blasting INXS videos, there's a little altar featuring a picture of Radha-Krishna, incense and candles. They're the remnants of her time hanging out at the local Hare Krishna temple, which she attended during her early stages of sobriety. She says she "got spiritually lost for a moment," so she's been trying to get back into chanting her Krishna mantras.

"I just kind of got beat up mentally, going through a lot of different emotions and I got stuck and lost."

Taped on one side of the altar are three handwritten pages beginning with "Dearest Daughter" and ending with a heartfelt request that makes a reference to Girl in a Coma's latest album: "While I realize this is a lot to ask, just keep me with you for all your days… and do your best to trust me on this one last thing… I'll always be with you to make sure you are always happy and safe… that's all 'the rest.' I'll take care of the 'Exits' part. Love XO."

The letter was given to her by Stuart Lederer, an Austin-based guitarist with the 1992-93 lineup of the Flesh Eaters, who passed away in 2015. "He was my rock 'n' roll dad, in a way," Nina says. When Lederer died, he left her guitars, amps, and this letter.

Nina walks around the house wearing gray sweatpants, yellow socks, no shoes, and a David Bowie T-shirt. She adores the man, and even her little long-haired Chihuahua mix is named Ziggy (the other two four-legged members of the family are a friendly poodle named Ralph and the intimidating Nash, a massive outdoor beast that looks like he could eat your feet). Father Margo and Nina's boyfriend Jorge are in the house and, as usual, you can feel the good vibes. Yes, Nina had plenty of love and support at home, but she credits her bandmates (Jenn Alva and sister Phanie from GIAC, and bassist Austin Valentine, guitarist Travis Vela, keyboardist Johnny Shrink and drummer Jorge González with her solo band) with keeping her down-to-earth on the road and in the studio.

In public, everyone talked about how supportive Jenn and Phanie were upon finding out Nina wanted to go solo. Truth is, things didn't go so smoothly at first.

"It's hard to explain the relationship with the [GIAC] girls," Nina says. "People think, 'Oh, they're sisters, they love each other.' That's true, but it's also true that in any relationship, family or business — and in GIAC we have both — a lot of stuff may come up."

As the youngest in the trio (28, and they've been together since Nina was 13), she had to get used to Jenn and Phanie constantly trying to look out for her. "They do it because they love you, but sometimes you just need a little bit of space to figure things out." So, she broke the news to them and there was no way back — Nina was going solo.

"The girls were afraid," said Nina. "'Oh, is she going to leave GIAC now'?" There were some arguments, but within the first year Jenn and Phanie had started Fea, which Nina says "relieved a lot of pressure." She didn't feel any need to hurry up and rush her own album. As she puts it, they were now all "learning a lot of stuff doing [our own thing]."

Jenn, who plays bass for Girl in a Coma and Fea, says that, at first, she and Phanie "weren't into the idea" of taking a break. They loved playing together, and felt they still had so much more to do. "It took a little bit of time for us to understand it all, but it also gave us the opportunity to do Fea, a project we always wanted to do," Jenn says. "All in all, it turned into this mega-positive thing."

With Fea shining in its own right (forget about "punk," "riot grrrl" and all that nonsense — Fea is a full-fledged rock 'n' roll band, plain and simple, and a very good one at that) and a new album by Girl in a Coma on the horizon, the question is: How will the band sound now that all its members have evolved as separate artists? Clearly the enthusiasm is still there.

"We've already been writing new GIAC songs, and each one of them is just ridiculous," Jenn says. "Nina's grown tremendously as a writer. Before that, she was into abstract stories but now she's much more direct, and whereas in the past, we only allowed our energies to be as one GIAC unit, now each one of us have our own little attitude and confidence."

Nina has a similar view. While she's proud of Girl in a Coma's past work, she says, "I haven't felt for them what I feel for my solo album." More solo work will probably come in the future, she says, but these first songs are special. "This is the one where I'm really letting it out."

"Maybe it's because I wasn't really *there* before," she says. Now that she *is* there, she says she envisions the new Girl in a Coma having a renewed, striking edge — or "that extra alt vibe," as she puts it, "like Stone Temple Pilot's *Tiny Music* or the Breeders' *Last Splash*. Or the Pixies." Being outside the band made her realize its strengths and full potential, she says. "I see a very strong future for GIAC."

Jenn agrees that Nina's fight for sobriety saved not only herself but the band they grew up with.

"The whole thing could've gone sour so easily," Jenn says. "Luckily, we're sisters and always watching out for each other."

NINA DÍAZ IN CONCERT, $15 (all ages), 8pm Fri, Oct 28, Carlos Alvarez Studio Theater at the Tobin Center, 100 Auditorium Circle.

How the Last Bandoleros Reinvented Tex-Mex and Blew Sting Away
(*San Antonio Current*, December 17, 2016)

"Hello Cleveland!" yells someone, somewhere within the bowels of the Tobin Center, and it ain't Spinal Tap's Derek Smalls. His name is Emilio Navaira IV, the drummer for the band that, at least for the 15 minutes it took us to find their freaking dressing room, became known as The *Lost* Bandoleros.

"When it's time to play, can someone take us to the stage? How are we going to get there?" asks bassist/vocalist/brother Diego Navaira, who is growing impatient while the others (guitarists/singers/Brooklyn roommates Jerry Fuentes and Derek James) keep on laughing at the absurdity of the situation.

"Have you ever gone through anything like this before?" James asks, smiling at the others. After going up and down stairs and elevators for what felt like 10 miles, they finally reached their destination. Diego crashed on the dressing room's sofa as if he had just finished a grueling stage of the Tour de France, but the mood is great: It's November 12, and they were there to perform at the 36th annual Tejano Music Awards, where hours later they offered a two-song tribute to their father, Tejano legend Emilio Navaira III (scratch that — it's Emilio, *period*), who died unexpectedly earlier this year at age 53.

"I wanted to make sure people remembered he was also a country music star," says Diego about their decision to perform "Even If I Tried" (from Emilio's 1995 *Life is Good* album, which peaked at #13 on the Top Country Albums chart and #82 on the overall *Billboard* 200 chart). The other song in the tribute was a heartfelt rendition of "Mundo perfecto" (from Emilio's 1996 *Quédate* album), with Diego on vocals and Emilio IV on acoustic guitar. "We toured with dad for the last six or seven years of his life, and after the shows we'd do an acoustic jam for ourselves," Diego recalls. His father would sing Eagles or Beatles tunes, not his own — except for "Mundo perfecto," which he never really played live. "He really loved that tune," Diego says.

The tribute to their father came after an incredible 2016 for the band: TV appearances (including *Jimmy Kimmel Live!* and the NBA All-Star game in Toronto with Sting), a recording contract with Warner Music Nashville, and jams and recording sessions with the former Police frontman, who they will open for during his 2017 U.S. and European tour (and, possibly, some South American dates).

Their infectious, hook-laden, early Beatles-meets-Tex-Mex brand of country rock-pop (all wrapped in perfect three and four-part harmonies) was officially launched with *The Last Bandoleros*, the six-song EP digitally released in October (a physical version comes out in January, with a full-length release following later in 2017). At the time of this writing, the first single, "Where Do You Go?" (released on July 23) peaked at #49 in *Billboard*'s Country charts, slowly climbing after a no. 52 position the previous week.

Reviews have overall been positive. Nashville music writer Bev Miskus said the song had her "checking the station and the decade." "The strong, unusual instrumental opening gives way to a wall of harmonies that never let up," she wrote on *NashvilleThreeSixty.com*, complimenting the prominent accordion, '60s Brit-pop groove, and the band's ascending, harmonic vocals. Back in May, *Rolling Stone* called the then-trio (Emilio IV started as a touring drummer but is now a full-time member) one of the "10 New Country Artists You Need to Know," describing them as "the next generation of Tex-Mex renegades."

The Bandoleros — including touring accordionist Percy Cardona — are often compared to the Texas Tornados (the Tex-Mex/conjunto elements), Los Lobos (strong singing and songwriting, a killer Latin fusion and the ability to rock hard) and The Mavericks (great singing and all that rock/country flirting). They're all reasonable comparisons — but the Bandoleros are a more natural, contemporary, updated version of the Tornados, fueled with the energy of youth.

At least that's the assessment of Augie Meyers, one of the two remaining original members of the Tornados. "There's a bunch of bands that imitate the Tornados, but they sound horrible," Meyers told the *Current*. "But [the Bandoleros] were great, I loved their harmonies."

Really, the Bandoleros are first and foremost a rock band — one that even jokes about how much they look the part. When someone mentions Emilio's *MTV Unplugged*-era hairdo, calling him "Emilio Cobain," he corrects them: "It's Kurt Navaira. That last name is too strong to be left out."

It's hard to disagree. During the heyday of Tejano in the '90s, only Selena was a bigger Tejano solo act than Emilio Navaira. And not only did he cross over to country music, but he loved the Beatles, Eagles, ZZ Top, Nirvana and all the great music from the '60s and '70s, instilling that passion and musical open-mindedness to his kids from an early age.

"Emilio knew how good they were, he was very proud of them," said Joe Reyes (of Buttercup and Demitasse), who has known and played with the brothers and Fuentes since they were young teenagers (Diego, Emilio IV and Reyes covered the Beatles on several gigs, and the brothers are featured on Buttercup's upcoming Spring album). "[Emilio] told me the story of how he took them out of school to take them to see *A Hard Day's Night* at the Bijou, and that's when everything changed for them. When they left the theater, they were stunned, just like me after I saw *Help!* on TV."

Dad's inspiration helped, but the Navaira brothers were born with a special talent: It seems they truly can hear, write, sing and play better than most kids their age.

"They stole my job from Studio M!" jokes Reyes, who learned how to produce records from Studio M's Mike and Ronnie Morales in the late '80s. "As I became busier with my own stuff, [Fuentes and the Navairas] took over all the guitar production I was doing, and they were great."

So the Navairas kept playing and playing until they formed Ready Revolution, a pop-rock band. Enter Jerry Fuentes, an SA native who released his first album while still a young teen and, like Reyes and the Navairas, was a protégé of Mike Morales. Eventually, Fuentes moved to Brooklyn and met Derek James, and the two became friends and roommates. They set up a studio in their basement and Fuentes would regularly come back to SA and continue writing. It was Ron Morales who suggested Fuentes meet the brothers.

"They were all like, 'You have to meet these two brothers, they came in after you left and they're amazing!'" Fuentes remembered. He and the Navairas met and clicked immediately, both personally and musically. They wrote feverishly for months, until they realized they had songs for a whole album.

"We didn't want to give the tunes to no one else," said Diego. "When we got together and wrote those songs, it was just magic. We soon realized we had to take it as far as we could take it."

Fuentes had met Sting manager Martin Kierszenbaum (who wrote one of the Texas Tornados' early bios when he was at Warner) through a mutual acquaintance and did some studio work for the former Police frontman. The sessions went so well Sting invited Fuentes and Diego to play with him at the NBA All-Star game in Toronto in February. They sang backup vocals on Sting's new album, *57th & 9th*, and the Sting/Bandoleros live version of the Police's "Next To You" is featured on *57th & 9th*'s deluxe version.

"I've worked with [Sting] for 26 years, and he works on musical impulse," Kierszenbaum told the *Current*. "He had great vibes with those guys."

"It was very surreal," said Emilio IV. "Three or four times in the studio I thought, 'Wow... That's Sting over there...' but after a while we got to know him and he's such a nice guy."

"He allows you to feel comfortable around him," added Diego.

Preparing for the upcoming Sting tour, the band had a handful of terrific SA performances, including a free show at the Havana Hotel during the Música en la Calle fest on November 4 (with Blackbird Sing and Los Texmaniacs) and a Sam's Burger Joint gig where they joined headliner Marc Broussard onstage on November 18. On both occasions, they soared and earned scores of new fans, many of whom had no idea who they were. The best part: the full-length, which was produced by Fuentes, will reflect how they sound live, and vice versa.

"What you hear on the record, you're going to hear live, and we were very conscious of that when we were recording it," said Diego. "Sometimes we had three-part guitars, but we decided not to do anything we won't be able to pull off live."

Rock, country, Tex-Mex, fusion… Call them whatever you want. They seem like the kind of band that could play *pasodobles* or Polynesian chants if they wanted; their precision, swing and, as Reyes rightfully says, "good taste" to come up with disarming hooks would remain.

"Let me tell you something they won't tell you," said Michael Morales, the Grammy-winning head of Studio M. "This is a young supergroup. More often than not, when you put together the best musicians in the world, they make terrible records. But in this case, these guys were all groomed learning not only to be the great musicians that they are, but the *right* musicians. The *right* musicians play great but also write *the right songs*, and this is what happens with the Bandoleros."

"They basically play by ear, and their ears are pretty good," said Reyes. "Those guys have the ability to detect what the song needs, and they master so many different styles. Even though they're so young, they've been playing forever, that's all they've ever done, and it shows. They do their thing but can also hang and play with Sting. That's how good they are."

The Sting, Joe Sumner (Sting's son) and The Last Bandoleros tour starts February 1 in Vancouver, Canada, and ends May 4 in Buenos Aires, Argentina.

Barbershop singing in San Antonio: Loudest Shade of White
(*San Antonio Current*, October 5, 2017)

barbershop: unaccompanied group singing of popular songs usually marked by highly conventionalized close harmony. From the old custom of men in barbershops forming quartets for impromptu singing of sentimental songs. (Merriam-Webster dictionary)

"Are these people 92 or something?" my 8-year-old daughter whispers in my ear. We're at the chorus hall of the University United Methodist Church on De Zavala, in front of the mammoth Friends in Harmony chorus. Ages range from 7 to over 90, but the average age seems to be 54+. Due to hurricane season, this is a slow day at the office — only about 80 singers show up.

"We're the fastest growing chorus in the whole of the [Barbershop Harmony] Society," says Artie Dolt, who is not 92. "I'll be 75 this year, and I have tuxedos older than you." He's the dean of San Antonio barbershoppers, and a powerhouse with the enthusiasm and energy of a 16-year-old. He's been directing and singing in choruses for 57 years, winning a quartet Mid-Atlantic district championship in 1966 with the New York/New Jersey's Hallmarks. He formed Friends in Harmony in 2013, starting with a group of 19 singers who, like Dolt, had left barbershop because "it stopped being fun."

"When I was singing with other organizations, we'd get through a line in the whole three hours practice," said Ed Garland, the president of Friends in Harmony. "It was all about perfection, and it wasn't fun anymore."

Still, Friends in Harmony manage to stop me in my tracks with a thunderous, chilling rendition of "If the Lord Be Willin' and the Creek Don't Rise" and an equally powerful rendition of the Star Spangled Banner, which they will sing (as they've done before) in two upcoming Spurs games: November 7 against the Los Angeles Clippers and a televised game against the Lakers on March 3. They've already booked the 2500-seat Laurie Auditorium for a Spring Spectacular on May 19, featuring Instant Classic (2015 International Quartet Champions, from Indianapolis) and GQ, a popular Sweet Adeline (female) quartet from Baltimore. "They do some eight-part numbers together that are just incredible," said Dolt. "We've already been told busloads of barbershoppers from Houston (both men and women) are coming for this."

Even though Friends in Harmony have participated in some regional competitions ("just to have fun and hear the other quartets and choruses"), the words "contest" and competition" are not part of the group's vocabulary.

"You come [to Friends in Harmony] because you enjoy singing and camaraderie," said Dolt. "For some, this is their life. They literally live for this chorus."

One of them is 68-year-old Larry Schaef, who was diagnosed with pancreatic cancer last December.

"Ninety-five percent of the people are dead in the first six months," said Schaef, who is now at stage 3. "But there is a five percent that aren't, and that's me. This chorus keeps me alive. I didn't feel good today, but as soon as I heard that first chord, that put life in me."

The Marcsmen are the antithesis of Friends in Harmony. Last year, they came in second in the Southwestern District competition, only beaten by Dallas' 12-time International Champions Vocal Majority, widely regarded as the heavyweight barbershop chorus in the world. Marcsmen won the district in 2012 and, a year later, came in 13th in the world at the International contest, the best finish by a group of less than 29 men on stage in the history of the Barbershop Harmony Society. This time, with Vocal Majority on the horizon, Marcsmen will try to put between 30 and 40 singers onstage, but their expectations change.

"We're hoping for a wild card," said Marcsmen co-founder Manny López. "If we score 80 or more points, which we usually do, we can be one of the 10 wild cards to join the 30 district winners."

"Marcsmen are what we call a state-of-the-art barbershop chorus," said Brian Lynch, PR man for the Barbershop Harmony Society. "Just reaching the Internationals is like being in the NCAA finals. Their achievements are huge. They're in a pretty elite group."

The key element of barbershop is that the melody (the lead) is carried by the second highest voice. Unlike the standard chorus, gospel or hymnal church music (SATB, or soprano, alto, tenor and bass), where the soprano carries the melody, in barbershop the melody is carried by the second highest voice (the second tenor). But before singing, Marcsmen spend close to 30 minutes preparing physically and mentally for the three hours of practice ahead. In what they call "focus sessions," they get the body warmed up, loosening neck and torso, and then concentrating on melody, intervals, sound production, alignment, breathing and other exercises meant to help each singer find his best voice… before the actual singing.

"A lot of people think singing doesn't involve the body, but it really does," said López, one of the former Texas State San Marcos students who formed the group in 2007 and also the director of San Antonio Chordsmen, another barbershop chorus. Three members of Marcsmen (bass Wallace Stanley, lead Peter Cunningham and baritone López) joined Stanley's wife Diane (a soprano in Opera San Antonio) to form Southern Stride, a mixed quartet that, at the time of this writing, ranks number one in the country and is expecting an invitation to Germany's BinG! (Barbershop in Germany) Festival in April.

"We don't want to get too excited, but we're crossing our fingers," said Stanley. Both choruses and quartets compete in district and international competitions, the men governed by the Barbershop Harmony Society and the women by Sweet Adelines International, the latter formed in 1945.

However, besides their love for four-part harmonies, both independent organizations share a tumultuous racial past that's evident anytime one stands in front of a barbershop quartet or chorus: the whiteness of it all, an irrelevant fact (no one would demand "diversity" out of a mariachi orchestra or a hip-hop band) if we didn't know the African American origins of barbershop.

"We are owning our heritage, trying to rectify those errors and making sure [racial bans] will not happen in the future," said Lynch.

In a 1992 essay called "Play that Barber Shop Chord: A Case for the African-American Origin of Barbershop," historian Lynn Abbott wrote that "the contemporary image of barbershop harmony is couched in a romanticized perception of the 'Gay Nineties,' with dapper, white, middle-American barbers and their patrons posed next to barber poles in attitudes of harmonizing," explaining that the period's mainstream literature seldom reinforces that image, while early African-American literature was "shot through with references to barbershop singing."

"Not many years ago, singing as an amusement prevailed above all others," the Black publication *New York Age* wrote on November 24, 1888. "At these meetings of friends, as soon as the small games were exhausted, the proposition to sing was gladly accepted and nature's musical instrument filled the place with pleasing harmonies ... the gentlemen would unite and for hours make the night melodious with their tuneful voices."

Vaudevillian Billy McClain once said that, in the late 1880s, "about every four dark faces you met was a quartet." But African Americans were barred from theaters and concert halls, so those meetings took place on the street, barbershops or on people's homes. Gradually, white barbershoppers adopted (and adapted) the sound to what is known today as barbershop singing, and white historians often offered a whitewashed version of the music's history. By the time the Barbershop Harmony Society was established in 1938 (originally, and impractically, titled Society for the Preservation and Encouragement of Barber Shop Quartet Singing in America, or, believe it or not, SPEBSQSA), the membership was all white. How did it happen?

"Two words: Jim Crow," Valerie Clowes told the *Current*, speaking from Toronto. She's the daughter of Lana Clowes, the Canadian singer of Afro descent who, in 1963, had to leave the Sweet Adelines and join the rival Harmony Incorporated, which had been formed in 1958 as a protest to Sweet Adeline's whites-only policy.

When the all-black, all-male, Harlem-based Grand Central Red Caps quartet won the New York district competition in 1941, they were denied participation in the International finals. "Relative colored quartets competing St. Louis," wrote SPEBSQSA (from now on BHS for clarity) founder O. C. Cash in a telegram sent to the New York chapter, "Board of Directors decided some time ago such procedure would be embarrassing and ruled it out. None has competed in the South and West. Best regards."

The civil rights movement helped correct the wrongs in Barbershop, and in 1962 the BHS lifted the ban on African-American membership (Sweet Adelines would do the same in 1966) and, in 1970, banned the use of minstrel performances (white singers with black painted faces).

The BHS' "Everyone in Harmony" plan of today lists amongst its goals the sharing of the barbershop gift "with young and old, with people of every color and every background," and plans a posthumous recognition to the Grand Central Red Caps.

Most notably, in 2016, the all-female Sweet Adelines International did what was unthinkable not too many years ago: to give a lifetime membership to Lana Clowes (the black Canadian singer who, in 1962, faced expulsion from SAI due to her race) and to celebrate the Adelines' establishment of a Diversity Task Force, meant to "build bridges with potential singers, regardless of race, religion, nationality, sexual orientation, gender expression or physical abilities."

"While we cannot change the past, today we dedicate ourselves to being an example of real change and hope in our world," Sweet Adelines president Paula Davis said in the ceremony, fighting back tears. "Today, we will begin to be a living example of what it means to harmonize the world."

"That messy, painful past, is here to teach us, not haunt us," said Valerie Clowes in accepting the award on behalf of her mother. It was a moving, heartfelt moment, and even the rival Harmony Incorporated acknowledged it.

"We held our heads high knowing that we stood on the right side of this issue for many, many decades," said Christina Llewellen, International President of Harmony Incorporated. "But we were mostly glad and proud of Sweet Adelines for taking a really brave step, which probably opened them up to quite a bit of criticism."

In San Antonio, it's obvious to me that doors are wide open for anyone who wants to sing barbershop, but to see a reflection of the city demographics on the risers will take some time.

"In my chorus of 120-130 men I have one black man," said Friends in Harmony's Dolt in early October. "However, within the last 30 days I've gone to visit some of the black churches on the Eastside with the idea to get them to hear us so we're more inclusive and we embrace more people into the hobby." When asked about which African American churches he's been talking with, Dolt hesitated. "We're in the VERY early stages of trying to establish a relationship with these folks. My first goal is to get the opportunity to sing at one of their Sunday services. We need exposure first, then we can try to embrace those interested in our organization."

One of such services showed a willingness to give it a try.

"Our guys love to sing, and I think a small minority of them would like to sing [with a mostly white barbershop chorus]," Hugh Hawkins, director of the men's chorus at the Macedonia Baptist Church, told the *Current*. "But as of today, we haven't been offered that invitation."

Lack of exposure is another key reason why we don't see more black faces on the risers.

"I hadn't heard anything about barbershopping in SA until I got invited [by a co-worker] two years ago," Tim Davenport, the sole African American member of Friends in Harmony, told the *Current*. "And most black churches I know sing with instruments, not a capella." Hawkins agrees.

"It's their version of our singing and we don't hear anything about it, they keep it quiet," said Hawkins. "The only time I hear from [barbershop singers] is on TV or something, we're not at all exposed to it. But even though what we do is gospel, I could put together a [barbershop] group like that in a second. We can diversify."

There is no doubt both the BHS and SAI have made tremendous progress in terms of race, and I have no suspicion whatsoever about barbershop's openness to all; these men and women are all about the music. But no matter how many good intentions and real achievements, there is still one aspect of barbershop that brings us back to its checkered past — a good chunk of its repertoire.

"That desire to change and rectify mistakes of the past is true for the majority of leadership and a lot of the membership," said Valerie Clowes about the Sweet Adelines, speaking from her home in Toronto, "until one has to face the fact that their favorite song is obscenely racist. A lot of those songs from that era talk about how great the South was, which was true only if you were white and had money."

One of the early barbershop "hits" was "Way Down Yonder in the Cornfield," a slave song which included lyrics like "O some tell me that a nigger won't steal/But I've seen a nigger in my cornfield" (later changed to "Some folks say that a rebel can't steal/But I found twenty in my cornfield"). Another example is "Mississippi Mud," which was recorded, among others, by Ray Charles, even though the "When the people beat their feet on the Mississippi Mud" line was changed from the now-politically incorrect "When the 'darkies' beat their feet on the Mississippi Mud" original. I asked Lynch whether BHS competitors still sing these songs, even if the song versions are sanitized.

"It's a great question, and one that doesn't have a direct, simple answer to it either," said Lynch. "As you can well imagine, there is sensitivity involved in singing songs from an era in which people did not enjoy equal rights. It's a fine line between celebrating the music for its own purpose and acknowledging the culture in which it grew up. Even now, as we're looking at our expanded efforts towards inclusion and diversity in our organization, these debates are going on every day in both our leadership and membership." I press him: is the BHS still using these songs in competition? Lynch pauses and thinks.

"I understand and trust that you're not trying to trap me in a statement, but I would say for the most part no, [those songs are no longer used]. We have sufficient awareness of those cases, so no, we would not do that."

I ask Valerie Clowes if these discussions on whether or not to continue singing offensive (even if sanitized) Dixie songs are the equivalent of the Confederate monument/flag debate.

"Yeah… Exactly," she says.

For their district competition in Dallas on October 6-7, SA's Marcsmen won't have to deal with that problem. They will sing Robert Rund's "Tomorrow is Promised to No One" and Bob Dylan's "To Make You Feel My Love," while Friends in Harmony will stay home doing what they do best: harmonizing and having fun.

"For those who want perfection, there's the Marcsmen; for those who want to have fun, there's us," said Dolt. "Don't get me wrong, [the Marcsmen] are phenomenal, but it's not what we do. If every note isn't perfect, if everything isn't in perfect balance, that's not going to affect world peace. What will affect world peace is my relationship with each member of the chorus. That's why we're called Friends in Harmony, and that's why I'm aggressively trying to embrace a very inclusive element in our chorus, and the chorus is supporting me 100 percent. That's what we want and that's what we are going to do."

Manumanía
(*San Antonio Current*, March 6, 2018)

"MANU-20, TAIWAN-SA, 1,265 KM, I'M HERE FOR U," read the sign 22-year-old Wen Yu Lin held with her father. It was about an hour before the San Antonio Spurs faced the Philadelphia 76ers at the AT&T Center on January 26. "I've been following [Manu Ginóbili] since I was 12," said Lin, who played for Taiwan's national team at a high school level. "He's the best."

Manu Ginóbili was born in basketball-crazy Bahía Blanca, Argentina (he'll be 41 on July 28), but he was far from NBA material. Though always fierce and capable of scoring, he wasn't tall or strong enough to amount to anything more than a stand-out on a local or regional team. Nevertheless, his now-legendary discipline and hard work led him to great success in Europe and on Argentina's national team. Ginóbili was a 57th overall draft pick for the Spurs in 1999, but instead of joining the NBA, he went back to Italy's Kinder Bologna where he won it all in the Italian league and the EuroLeague, for which he was named MVP. He finally joined the Spurs for the 2002-03 season, which was impressive enough, but winning his first of four NBA rings in his first season here took him over the top.

"Manu is a student of the game who knows his rivals very well," said Carlos Maffrand, the "Manu historian" at @InfoManu, a Twitter account devoted to all things Ginóbili. "In the NBA, he was never the tallest, the strongest, the fastest or the one who jumped the most, but oftentimes he has been the most intelligent player inside the court."

Though a still-injured Ginóbili didn't play against the Sixers that night back in January and the Spurs experienced a crushing loss, Lin, the former Taiwanese high school player, got a chance to take a photo with her idol, as did dozens of fans near courtside.

Most of them were from Argentina. The overseas Manuheads who come to San Antonio just to see Ginóbili include those who plan their own trips, and those who take advantage of tours organized by online travel agencies like Kit Viajes and Sportmagic to capitalize on Ginóbili devotion, which increased significantly around the All-Star Game in Los Angeles on February 18. That devotion continues to explode thanks to Ginóbili's killer form.

Under the hashtag #ElPibede40Tour (roughly translated as #The40yoKidTour), the Twitter account @InfoManu is arguably the best way to stay on top of the Argentina-San Antonio tours — and practically anything related to Ginóbili. With Twitter and Facebook accounts launched in December 2011 with Ginóbili's blessings, @InfoManu is managed by Manuheads in Texas, Argentina and Brazil who met through a now-defunct forum on manuginobili.com. The agency-organized "Spurs Tours" include game tickets, hotel stays and chances to see and interact with Ginóbili up close before games. Building on the success of tours in November and February, the next tours arrive in San Antonio this month.

"I'm sure you realize that Manu is not really into self-promotion — he only posts a few photos and articles on his personal Twitter and Facebook accounts," said Jane Ann Craig, an Austin-based Ginóbili fan who drives to San Antonio for every home game and often interacts with Argentine fans near courtside. "So [Ginóbili] was more than happy to have someone else take over the task. He also had enough 'history' with us, and he trusted us."

The growing @InfoManu community now boasts more than 45,000 Twitter followers and more than 33,000 Facebook followers. The latter, according to Craig, comprises fans in 40 countries, with 25,000 from Argentina and 1,200 from the U.S. About 30 percent are women.

"Needless to say, the Warriors game [on March 19] will be spectacular," said Ariel Sonnet, an Argentine living in Brazil. One of the key members of @InfoManu, Sonnet met Ginóbili in November during a tour organized by Kit Viajes. "The groups are always around 20 people per trip, which we think is the exact quantity so that we can all enjoy more."

While Kit Viajes' tour covered the Sixers, the Sacramento Kings and Denver Nuggets games, their March tour will include games against the New Orleans Pelicans (March 15, with access to a courtside warm-up), the Minnesota Timberwolves (March 17, with a court visit during half-time) and the Golden State Warriors (March 19, with on-court shooting after the game). Starting at $1,735, the package includes seats near courtside and a six-night hotel stay. Sportmagic, on the other hand, is selling packages that include the Timberwolves and Warriors games along with a four-night hotel stay for $1,550 per person (roundtrip airfare from Argentina to San Antonio starts around $1,500).

To experience Manumanía firsthand, I attended the Sixers, Kings and Nuggets games in February. Approaching the AT&T Center's main entrance, one could hear Ginóbili fans adapting soccer chants while waiting in line for the security check. "*Oléee-olé-olé, cada día te quiero más / Soooooy, soy de Manu ... Es un sentimientooo ... no puedo parar*" ("Each day I love you more / I root for Manu / It is a feeling / I can't stop." As those fans filed through the VIP entrance, I spotted Jane, @InfoManu's Austin contact. Just as I was about to follow her to the Spurs' warm-up area, Dan, one of the stadium's ushers, asked Vicente Trabal, a 13-year-old kid from Uruguay, "Would you like some autographs?" The kid's face lit up, eyes open wide. Gonzalo, Vicente's dad, became a Spurs fan during a work visit in 1997, two years before the Spurs' first NBA ring. "I immediately fell in love with Duncan and Robinson," Gonzalo said. "They were different."

One by one, the Spurs who were warming up for the Sixers game stopped by the assembled fans to take photos and sign autographs. Ginóbili stayed on the court, looking strong.

"If I can have a photo [with Ginóbili] and an autograph, I'll leave happy," said Argentine Alejandro Albamonte, who came with his son. "We came two years ago with the whole family, but this time…" Ginóbili suddenly appeared and Albamonte forgot all about me. "Manu!! Manuuuu!!!!" After taking a photo of his son with Ginóbili, Albamonte disappeared into the crowd.

While Ginóbili signed autographs, I asked him for his take on @InfoManu.

"They're doing a terrific job," Ginóbili replied in Spanish. "They're followers from all over the world. I love what they do."

Mónica Rubio and Pablo Carbó came all the way from Mendoza, along the Argentina/Chile border, to fulfill their dream of seeing Ginóbili in the NBA, even if that meant spending $500 a piece for tickets. "Manu told us, 'Let me finish warming up and then I'll be with you,' and he came and signed everything and talked to us," Rubio said in seeming disbelief. "I think I'm going crazy."

"I traded miles, did a few weird things to get here, but here I am," Albamonte explained once he reappeared. "[Manu] is an example of a different type of Argentine. We're known everywhere as cocky, and that stereotype is true. But Manu is not from [Buenos Aires], he's a provincial guy like us. And that's what makes parents like me come all the way from the other side of the world so that we can impress upon our kids Manu's life and professional example."

The difference between a Ginóbili fan from San Antonio and one from Argentina is that the Argentines have been carrying Manu devotion since even before he became the leader of the Generación Dorada (Golden Generation) of Argentine basketball. With the help of former NBA players like Fabricio Oberto (another former NBA ring-winning Spur), Andrés Nocioni, Carlos Delfino and Luis Scola, Ginóbili won an Olympic gold medal in 2004 (with an eight-point victory over the U.S. team, the eventual bronze winner, which included Tim Duncan, LeBron James and Allen Iverson). Besides overachieving, Ginóbili has compensated for any physical and technical limitations with unparalleled heart. On top of that, he's a genuinely nice guy from a country with a long list of flawed sport heroes.

"Argentine sports have a dirty god [1986 MVP/World Champion soccer superstar Diego Maradona, who's scarred by his history with drugs and womanizing], a Catalonia-formatted Superboy [Barcelona's Lionel Messi, who never played professional soccer in Argentina and has yet to win a World Cup as an adult, thus lacking the Maradona-level devotion of Argentine fans] and a collection of stars with feet of clay," wrote sports writer Alejandro Wall in the Argentine magazine *Anfibia*. "None of them convinces us fully. Except Ginóbili, a veteran who shines in the most galactic of leagues, a totem without any contraindications, a hero of political correctness."

Unpretentious San Antonio and the Spurs are a perfect match for Ginóbili — that's why we love him, and that's why his worldwide fans love the Spurs.

"[Ginóbili is] a middle-class man who didn't conquer New York but San Antonio, someone who doesn't lead through shouting but through consensus," Wall wrote. "He's our mundane idol."

Nina 2020
(*San Antonio Current*, March 26, 2020)

I wasn't going to write about Nina Díaz's solo show on March 22 at Limelight and the April 4 one-time-only concert by her former band Girl in a Coma at Taco Fest — both now canceled in the wake of the pandemic. Been there, done that. Many times.

Then my wife, local artist Guillermina Zabala, asked me a question: "Do you still have Nina's phone number? I need to interview her for a school project."

The two connected in early March and, days later, my wife allowed me to hear a brief audio piece she did about their encounter. Just like that, I was hooked on Nina again.

"You can try to run, but you'll never get away," Nina sings on the recording as she performs "Get Away," one of just four songs the former Girl in a Coma frontwoman wrote after she moved from San Antonio to Los Angeles. The track features only Nina's voice and knife-like guitar strums.

The audio switches back and forth between the song and Nina's take on her 16 months in L.A., the difficulties of married life, her daily struggle with her seven years of sobriety and her complex, love me-leave me alone relationship with Girl in a Coma, the band she fronted since she was 13. She just turned 32.

The story of her abrupt move to the City of Angels and her equally abrupt return to San Antonio is one of confusion, liberation, impulsiveness, homesickness and self-discovery.

"I just threw myself into L.A. with nothing planned — just me, my guitar and a couple of pedals," Nina said in an interview.

Her solo album and a self-titled debut by Fea, the group formed by Girl in a Coma's other two members, were both released in 2016. At that point, things were calm in the GIAC camp. But two years later, it all fell apart. Unbeknownst at the time to bassist Jenn Alva and drummer Phanie Díaz — Nina's sister — the band would dissolve after its performance at Taco Fest 2018.

"I knew it was going to be the last time I played with them," Nina said. "That was unfair to them, but I just needed to heal and pay attention to myself instead of having one foot here and one foot there."

To this day, she regrets not telling her bandmates the truth — GIAC was over, as far as Nina was concerned. That's why she'd hoped the now-canceled April 4 GIAC show at Taco Fest 2020 could be a "closure" concert to amend her past mistake. Her former bandmates called it a "one-time only" show on their Facebook page.

"Make no mistake: I take complete responsibility for being the one who ended [GIAC]," Nina said. "I said, 'I no longer want to be in this band.' Even at the meeting I had with them, my hands were shaking, feeling like an explosion was about to happen."

Phanie also vividly remembers the moment Nina broke the bad news.

"Jenn and I were like, 'Oh, shit,'" she said. "Initially, there was panic, GIAC was all we knew, all we'd ever done. We went through every emotion. At first, we were mad, but then we understood and gave each other the space that we needed. And that space made us all grow."

The fact that both Fea and Nina had released their respective debut albums in 2016, two years before the Taco Fest debacle, kept them all busy and helped ease the transition. But the tension remained and, to make matters worse, in the summer of 2018 — less than a year after marrying Jorge González, the drummer of San Antonio band Pop Pistol — Nina filed for divorce and, that October, decided to move to Los Angeles.

"Everything came to a crash at the same time, like Shiva, like Kali — total chaos," Nina said, mentioning Hindu deities associated with destruction. "From the outside, it must've looked as if I was going crazy, but each of those things were a long time coming."

She was no stranger to L.A., having toured the West Coast several times with GIAC. But this was different: no band, no prospects. In the year and four months she spent there, she wrote four songs and had a one-month residency at The Hotel Cafe on Cahuenga Boulevard.

"Coming to L.A. saved my marriage," Nina said of the relocation.

Pop Pistol's González visited her in California, and she visited him in SA and, once they realized they were back on track as a couple, she asked her hubby to be her drummer in her most notable Los Angeles project. She did eight East L.A. performances as guitarist and vocalist for a band in Theresa Chávez's musical play *Evangeline, Queen of Make-Believe*, playing music by Los Lobos. The ensemble included González on drums, and Thee Commons' José Rojas on bass.

"A taut, rocking, psychedelic evocation of an incomparably fertile era, seen through the eyes of a teenage Latina," the *Los Angeles Times* wrote of the play.

Even though her music career featured interesting engagements, it was too sporadic to depend on for survival, so Nina activated Plan B.

She took a job at House of Intuition, a multi-branch "metaphysical store" in L.A. The longest non-music job she ever had surrounded her with candles, crystals and oils, a perfect match for her more esoteric side.

"I was so close to working at a fast food place, so I felt so lucky when this shop called me."

At HOI, Nina thrived.

"She was very fun to work with, cool to have around, and we miss her," Karla Quisquinay, a "gatekeeper" at HOI, told the *Current*. "I'm not at all surprised she was promoted to lead and event coordinator in such a short time. She was skillful, trustworthy, very organized and a team player. She was also very wise and a good listener, and we were thrilled to have her in the family."

The gig increased her interest in spiritual matters. But new songs just weren't happening, so she felt ready to come back home and resume her music career in SA. She submitted her two-week notice and, on January 2, parted ways with HOI and launched Operation Return. But there was still a stone in her shoe.

"All throughout this time, I hadn't talked again with Jenn and Phanie," she said. "In 2018, Thanksgiving came, Christmas came, and nothing. ... When I was ready to talk, I wanted it to be real, not just because it was the 'season to talk.'"

The opportunity to reopen communication came in November 2019, when Nina's and Phanie's mother asked for Girl in a Coma to play at her 60th birthday.

"I couldn't say no to my mom," Nina said, so days later she began talking to Jenn and Phanie "to soften things up a little so the reunion wouldn't be so awkward."

The trio met on January 3, the day before the party, to rehearse "Vino," Ritchie Valens' "C'mon, Let's Go," and "One-Eyed Fool," the songs her mom had requested. As usual, the band sounded great.

"It was all so natural, as if nothing had happened," said Phanie about the rehearsal. "We just went through the songs and we were happy. It felt good, and we didn't have to say anything."

Nina still had to go back to Los Angeles for a February 1 farewell show at Pasadena's Old Towne Pub, but she had to cancel when she lost her voice after a relapse into smoking cigarettes after a year. (Don't worry, she's off the cigs.)

She took the incident as a sign to come back to SA, which she did on February 3.

"I'm now spending my days almost like I did before: taking time to search and create," said Nina, who is recording some of the songs she wrote during her time away. She's staying busy while social distancing. "It's a very uneasy time, but it does force us all to go inward and reflect."

She's considered performing an online solo concert, but she's still "taking it a day at a time."

"We're happy Nina is back," said Jenn. "We're looking forward for all this madness to pass so that, once they reopen the gates, it's on! We'll play all over town!"

As GIAC?

"No!" Jenn said, laughing. "As Fea and as Nina Díaz!"

But don't be so sure.

"We never had any rules, and we're not going to start now," Phanie said. "If we ever feel like playing again [as GIAC], fuck it, we will!"

Rock is dead. Long live *rocanrol*.
(*San Antonio Current*, January 14, 2021)

It only took a promotional poster for the new Netflix rock *en español* documentary series *Break It All* to make rockeros worldwide mad as hell.

"Why isn't [enter your favorite band] mentioned?" some asked. "Why is [enter a band you don't like] in bigger letters than [enter band you like]?"

And the trailer for the six-part series, which began streaming late last month, didn't help much either.

"Where is Caifanes?" Mexican fans inquired. "What are Mon Laferte and Maná doing there?" complained those who don't consider the Chilean songstress and the immensely successful Mexican band to be "rock." "Where are Los Shakers?" asked Uruguayan fans, offended by the fact that the band's greatest hit was named "Rompan Todo" ("Break It All"), (clearly?) the inspiration for the documentary series' title.

For each person praising the series, another is lambasting it — all based on their personal taste or interpretation of history.

Despite those grievances, *Break It All* is the most complete and professional-looking and sounding treatise on Latin American rock *en español* to date. Previous efforts had primarily focused on a single country.

What *Break It All* is *not* meant to be is an encyclopedia of *rocanrol*, as many Latin Americans call the genre.

"There are 100 artists in [the series] and thousands out," said Brooklyn-based Argentine Nico Entel, the series' showrunner and producer. "The other way around would've resulted in a very boring series."

He's right. *Break It All*, which features 127 songs and lots of never-before-seen photos and footage, is anything but dull.

Each of the six episodes covers roughly 10 years of rock *en español*, starting with Ritchie Valens' 1958 song "La Bamba" (the genre's first influential hit) and the Mexican bands of that decade that translated early rock 'n' roll hits into Mexican slang. Among those acts were Los Rebeldes del Rock, Los Teen Tops and Los Locos del Ritmo, who influenced the fathers of Mexican and Argentine rock.

The series finishes by exploring the early fusion of electronica and native sounds including cumbia, banda and norteña created by artists such as Mexico's Nortec Collective and Colombia's Bomba Estéreo in the late '90s and early '00s.

A handful of bands from Spain are also included in the late '80s-early '90s segment, as is the impact of MTV Latino in the genre's internationalization.

The present-day's exclusion comes down to it being too early to assess, according to series director Picky Talarico, also an Argentine: "We need more perspective. Ask me that 30 years from now."

Through it all, *Break It All* shows the friction between rockeros and governments, mainly focusing on major markets such as Mexico and Argentina and secondary ones like Chile, Peru, Colombia and Uruguay.

"The hardest part was to show 60 years of history in six hours," Talarico said. "Rock [*en español*] has so many important parts that every time we had to leave something out it was very painful."

Two Texans had to be cut: the late Baldemar Huerta (a.k.a. Freddy Fender), who recorded a Spanish version of "Don't Be Cruel" in 1957 but failed to have an impact in Latin America, and San Antonian Gloria Ríos (1928-2002), whose 1956 "El Relojito" — a cover of Bill Haley's "Rock Around the Clock" — marked the first time a woman (or anybody) recorded rock 'n' roll in Spanish.

"We couldn't secure the rights to the songs; it's complicated," Talarico explained. "It was a shame, because seeing her dancing and singing that song on TV is a hallucinating experience."

The main problem with *Break It All* is its tagline: "The History of Rock in Latin America." The series doesn't include Brazil at all, which deserves its own series, and it's obviously not the whole story of the genre — only one that's pretty darned comprehensive and error-free.

A key criticism some have leveled against the series, paradoxically, is one of the best things about it: the ample time given to *Rompan Todo*'s Argentine producer Gustavo Santaolalla. (Full disclosure: Santaolalla wrote the Foreword to my first book and I wrote liner notes for albums by Bajofondo, a band he leads and produces.)

It's true that Santaolalla and Café Tacvba, a band he also produced, are the primary talking heads in the series, but is that such a bad thing?

Santaolalla, who won a Golden Globe and two back-to-back Academy Awards for the music of *Babel* and *Brokeback Mountain* — something only achieved by two others in history — is one of the most influential artists and producers in rock *en español*'s history. What's more, Café Tacvba is the most critically acclaimed Mexican rock band ever. In 2012, *Rolling Stone* chose 1994's *Re*, the group's sophomore album, as the best Latin rock album in history.

But to dismiss *Break It All* as the "Santaolalla Fest," as too many have claimed, is not supported by facts: out of 226 artists featured or mentioned in the series, he only produced 13, and many of those are featured in the series with accompanying music he had nothing to do with. So, screw that.

The film itself has remained in the Netflix Top 10 in virtually all of Latin America since its December 16 release, according to data from FixPatrol.com, and it's continuing to inspire ferocious debates on social media.

If anything, *Break It All* is a terrific introduction to a genre that not only refuses to die but is seeing new success thanks to streaming. Especially among female audiences. A paradox, considering that, among the many complaints about the series, is the fact that only one episode superficially deals with female *rockeras*.

"The other day I read a statistic [indicating] that the sale of electric guitars had dropped a lot, but the number of women buyers had gone up," said Uruguayan Juan Campodónico, from Peyote Asesino, Bajofondo and Campo fame. He agrees with Santaolalla, who (prophetically?) said:

"Rock is in quarantine, the vaccine is Latin American and has a woman's perfume."

About the Author

Enrique Lopetegui (Montevideo, Uruguay, 1964) is the author of *Ruta Alterna: Rock en español en Los Ángeles (1993-95)* and *Nobody Told Me Nada: Latin pop, llama poop & other unexpected writings (1992-2021)*.

After publishing in Uruguay (*La Voz de Paso Molino, Belvedere y Capurro, Ecos, El Debate, Sábado Show* and *Somos Idea*), in 1984 moved to the United States to sell ice cream, wash dishes and chant Hare Krishna in Texas before moving to Los Angeles in 1985, where he lived until 2004.

His bylines include *La Opinión, LA Weekly, Los Angeles Times, Billboard, The Guardian UK, Grammy.com, Dallas Observer, Phoenix New Times, Miami New Times, Dallas Observer, Rumbo* (music editor 2004-2008), *San Antonio Current* (news, music and film writer 2008-2014), and *Rolling Stone* Argentina, among others.

He wrote, edited, and translated the first three official program books for the Latin Grammy Awards and is a two-time finalist of the AAN Awards (Association of Alternative Newsmedia; Third Prize in 2010 and Second Prize in 2011 in the alt-weeklies under 50,000 circ. category).

Under "Lopetegui," in 2015 he released *Defectos Especiales: Demos (2004-2009)*, a collection of mostly original songs.

He might've done other things but can't remember them due to his advanced age.

He lives in San Antonio with his artist/teacher wife Guillermina Zabala, daughter Shanti Radhe, and dog Bagel (she/her).

ENRIQUE LOPETEGUI

El último tren pasaba
un martes de madrugada
y yo la pasé durmiendo
pues nadie me dijo nada
(Jaime Roos, "Nadie me dijo nada")

Ya no quiero vivir así
repitiendo las agonías del pasado
(Charly García, "Canción de dos por tres")

www.ingramcontent.com/pod-product-compliance
Lightning Source LLC
Chambersburg PA
CBHW081353070526
44583CB00020B/2541